The Sovereign Way

Copyright © 2024 by Elizabeth of Sovereign
Illustrations by Elizabeth of Sovereign
100% human generated content. All rights reserved.
No portion of this book may be reproduced in any form without
written permission from the author, except as permitted by U.S.
copyright law.

Published by
Sovereign Solutions
Sarasota FL 34243
www.elizabethofsovereign.com

WE BEGIN

1. Preface — 1
2. Author's Note — 5
3. Introduction — 19
4. The Diagrams — 36
5. The Masteries — 62
6. The First Mastery: Remembering — 68
7. The Second Mastery: Recognizing — 113
8. The Third Mastery: Releasing — 159
9. The Fourth Mastery: Expansion — 211
10. The Fifth Mastery: Genius — 257
11. The Sixth Mastery: Alchemy — 302
12. The Seventh Mastery: Adventuring — 333
13. The Eighth Mastery: Devotion — 375

Preface

There is an integrated group of current world servers going the Sovereign Way, which leads us *above* all known religions or spiritual ideologies.

We are not held together by any external institution but through an inner spiritual bond that overshadows our minds, pours through our energy fields and influences our movements in the world. Synchronicities bring us together across all the different eras of our lives and we discover we have been working on different parts of the same, larger plan.

Whatever we might call ourselves—heart-led leaders, apostles of Christ, devotees of Love, planetary lightworkers, tribe leaders and innovators from every region and religion—we recognize each other by our love, our radiance and the wonders that follow us on this consecrated path.

Yet, though we are a coordinated network of friends who intend to prove **Love Wins**, each one of us must go a uniquely Sovereign Way. The Sovereign Way is *your* path of healing, freedom, mastery and service. There is only one Way for you to go, and that is *with* God.

What happens next for you will happen whether you read this book or not. A *whoomph* will happen in a special, Sovereign Way that only you will ever experience. But even though anything might happen, there are certain things that must, and this book is the thought experiment that prepares the mind, vibration and body for what will come.

This book is an ontology—an organization of words and ideas to describe the characteristics of this ineffable experience of ascending life with God. It is a thought experiment to help you stay sovereign, in love and on mission. This thought experiment that can be done by anyone, no matter what spiritual path you're on. After all, ontology exists only to connect timeless dots, and reconcile your heart's true intelligence about who God is and what's going on here.

The pages are soaked with a living language and a vibration you'll recognize. The knowledge is arranged into models and ideas that join the dots of what you already know and help bring cohesion to how you view the world. The result is first the freedom and clarity to be happy in your expanding place within a much larger design and unfolding human epic—and next to mobilize your energy for the great commission resonating through the fabric of reality.

Imagine that a gong has bonged from the core of the universe, and a cosmic resonance has rippled through nature with a *whoomph*. But just as the snake cannot see ultraviolet and the bee cannot see infrared, not everyone is aware of the bong. You are though. It enlivened you, you recognized a call and your heart has already answered: *Yes. I Am Here. I Am Willing.*

We know that our connection with God is not in a distant Heaven locked behind gates of theological correctness, nor the end-result of a performance-driven ascension through dimensions of increasing purity and mastery. We remember that we are free to know God independent of structures we've been born into or raised through. We know Love is the Truth and the Truth is Love, and day by day we're getting better at discerning what's not. We know we have the spiritual worth and authority to be who we are and worship the way we do, and we seem different from the world by our choice to live authentically. We follow the heart, dissolving generational highways and opening curious new paths far beyond the borders of the expectations we were born into. We remember that every manifest thing is part of one unified field, and that our mind, energy and actions are authorized to heal things of the natural world, like our bodies and rivers. What's more, we've made the decision—*Chosen*—to be someone equipped and poised to act for Love when it matters, dedicating our lives and vocations to serve our human family and a shared vision for a brighter tomorrow.

But things are getting complicated.

How do you abide in inner peace when the world seems like a rapidly unfolding catastrophe? The soul of the world is at war with itself. Ecosystems are shifting, media broadcasts are horrifying, millions are suffering, we have no control. Dictators rule, races are being annihilated, deepfake information is embedded with the siren's call into eternal confusion and distrust, the mainstream consciousness is losing hope.

We want to stay positive and high-vibe, but for the first time in history our collective consciousness has instant access to daily news of the very worst of human behavior, all over the world. We want to be healthy, but every morsel of food comes with a list of potential contaminants, pathogens and negative effects on some part of the body. We want to shop mindfully, but food costs are rising and every enterprise has some degree of affiliation with child slavery, toxic waste, animal abuse or a host of other foul fallouts. We want to be righteous, but every core value seems to conflict with another even though we know the Truth must transcend our human ideals. We want to take action and stand for what's right, but with so many urgent causes we feel overwhelmed, guilty and helpless. We want to surrender and trust the flow of intuition, but we are always in the presence of a trillion dopamine-addictions that hijack our decision-making and steer us into vanity, indulgence and judgment. We want to keep our emotions balanced and our chakras clear, but we're constantly soaking up all sorts of scrambled frequencies from chemtrails to solar flares and the neighbor's disgusting mood, and for all our good inner hygiene practices we can't fully discharge the stress. We want to build meaningful friendships and experience eduring belonging, but we're so entitled to "release what no longer serves" and diagnose anything displeasing as "toxic" that we end up emotionally detached and pouring weed killer all over the seedlings of love. We want to feel sovereign and be free to live, but we can't help getting triggered by "them". We want to feel like we're all divinely One, but we can't help being a bunch of humans.

Nobody can be blamed for being an overthinker in this day and age. Locked in an endless equation of constantly weighing one probability against another, we keep losing the Truth somewhere in a sandstorm of conflicting data. We feel pressured to make our dreams come true, manifest abundance, sanctify our diets, purify our energy, silence the mind, choose the right path and avoid the many dangers—both in this world and the unseen dimensions beyond. The law of attraction ensures our pursuit of God is an impossible tangle of karmic negotiation—and there really isn't room for error at this critical point in human history. We crave true spiritual direction, but we don't trust our leaders. So we listen to hear God in that still, small voice within, but with so many viewpoints and endless configurations of facts and methods, it's hard to know what to believe and how to reconcile what we thought we believed before. That's why we don't really trust ourselves either. Not only that—there's a pungent, omnipresent smell of oppression in the air, an ominous undertone that "they" are controlling it all and that we're running out of time. **The double-bind of the human consciousness is *"damned if I do and damned if I don't."***

Maybe any attempt to create something beautiful is as naive as setting out with a bucket and spade to build a little castle in a ruthless sandstorm.

But the gong has bonged. And we agreed. So our job in the midst of all this chaos is to Know the prevailing agreement—***Love Wins***—and act accordingly. The only way we can fulfill this assignment is if we have the freedom to follow God's unique path for us, a Sovereign Way free from influence and manipulation, where His presence fills us up and overflows regardless of who's ego is trying to control the world within and around. That access to a sovereign source is the simplest alchemy in the world, and peace spreads like ripples on the surface of the cool oasis pond in the midst of a forever sandstorm.

There are millions of us who are animated by the waters in the oasis, living peacefully and creating Heaven on Earth, as we agreed to do when we heard the bong. Many stay in the safety of the abundant growth and endless provision in the oasis, living good and simple lives all over the world. And many head back out into the sandstorm, to seek out the lost wanderers and give them a lens to see the Sovereign Way home.

Author's Note

My role has been to understand, synthesize and formulate the Sovereign Way from a spiritual point of point. To describe ineffable ideas and connections, I've used the language of my own life: a lovely blend of Magic, Genius and Jesus. Even though my language is peculiar, the subject of our experiment is universal, so I ask that you suspend any religious or cultural sensitivities and allow Truth to emerge anyway—we already agree we are One.

My message is not *about* Jesus, though it is impossible not to talk about him in a study on consciousness and energetics—and there is no avoiding his influence and companionship if you are to walk the Sovereign Way.

The process has taken me ten years, and my relationship with him has transformed. When my assignment began in 2013, I didn't really know the fellow. In fact I rather disdained the cartoon character I remembered from my middle-school religious classes. *That* Jesus was a guy with magic party tricks who died because of my abominable sin that his father, the bearded boss in the clouds, had set me up to eat at the beginning of time. I couldn't reconcile any of that, it never made sense and it wasn't the God I knew. I certainly didn't need saving. I didn't feel impotent, helpless, sinful or unworthy. An entitled millennial grown up in the Western world, I felt more like a scorned god, unjustly judged by the Lutheran priest who had kicked me out of confirmation class at age 13 for being too clever. I was healthy, conscious and empowered with a minor vendetta to execute against structured religion, so I really had no need for Jesus.

But then he just kept showed up, uninvited, and making himself quite comfortable. He already knew that I loved the idea of a universal Christ consciousness, and I was warming up to the character Yeshua Ben Joseph. This rebellious Hebrew man, defying the mainstream, sharing the mysteries of the universe, ascending dimensionally to join a pantheon of other evolutionary beings embodying God within themselves, serving the ascension of humanity by guiding us all into a purer state of Oneness—what a guy! My intellect and spiritual ego could easily relate to that dude—I hungered for the consciousness upgrades, seeking out and experiencing bombastic thresholds, mind-blowing plot twists and revelations. I thought of ascension as a dimensional rise through layers of consciousness into a universal singularity, and I believed mastery was the path to enlightenment—mastery of mind, vibration and life behaviors. If mind is over matter I should be able to control the storm, after all. Since Yeshua was someone who once had, I accepted his job application and hired the ascended master as my favorite spirit guide. His job, I informed him, was to help to help me create a method of ascending mastery to help planetary lightworkers stay strong and refreshed on our earthly mission, no matter our spiritual lineage or personal quest.

Jesus didn't mind me Knowing him like that. After all, he said, it was a little bit true—and all relationships mature, so just *come and see.*

His voice, although I never audibly heard it, felt warm and familiar. His humor was identical to my own. He knew my addictions, my favorite numbers and how I prioritize certain colors and smells over others. He knew that I love when things make sense, that other people's stupidity triggers my fury, that I use far more words than necessary to hide my own stupidity, and that no matter how anxious I am, pretty bubbles with rainbows in them will always cheer me up. He knew me.

Jesus never challenged my plan to create a method for ascension, but his proposal to me was simply that The Sovereign Way would be a living thought experiment and a friendship that proves something experientially. It would liberate the reader from undefined tangles, and bring them across a bridge of understanding into greater freedom. He added that I could only include what I Know to be True, and that if I wanted to Know it then I would have to Live it. I agreed to his terms. They were reasonable.

Over the years, as my husband Matthew travelled, studied, practiced and failed in these teachings, the way I arranged my thinking and shaped my language constantly evolved as I was exposed to new things. I would formulate an idea and then Jesus would refine and elevate my understanding, sometimes through absurd, tragicomic hardships like the time my young family was homeless:

It was a full moon at midnight in the derelict barn that we were sheltering in. My man and I were listening to three large bears sniffing and scratching at the barn doors held together with a bungee cord and a breeze block. Fingers twitching at the hilt of his knife, my husband held his focus and powerful presence between the flimsy door and the bed of fabrics at the back of the barn. My children were snuggled up to my bosom. I was humming a song, or perhaps I was groaning. A white beam of that full moon streamed in through cracked glass, illuminating a glittery veil of dust and the pretty blue fabric I had hung up to cover the dirt. With the predators only feet away, my husband and I locked eyes. A wave of primal fear suspended above a deep bassline dominance of grounded faith and a warm sense of safety. *"Better Together,"* Matthew mouthed. The name of our first wedding dance—and a core value in our family. Reality flipped—a flash of lightning and thunder shook the barn, rattling the fragile floors and the thin, cracked windows, reverberating around the mountainside and scattering the bears. That was the moment I really understood that the enduring essence of **Home** is sovereign over the fickle structure of **House**.

This was how our journey with Jesus sort of went across the years of developing The Sovereign Way ontology. I'd get an intuition about some spiritual Truth, I'd formulate an opinion about it, feel rather adamant and cocksure about my brilliant deduction, and then he would say *"let's find out for real."* And me, my husband, daughters, and feral cat would all become enveloped in one adventure after another. Our guide was often present as the slap in a perfect high-five connection.

I've had unending questions about God, religion and spiritual lineage, but Jesus always steered me away from theological conformity. It felt more like a private tutelage through many remarkable teachers, bringing me along a path of side steps into various forms of ministry. With gentleness and compassionate humor he pointed out flashes of brilliance wherever we went:

In the early days, when I was training with metaphysicial spiritualists in Florida, he introduced me to the everlasting wellspring called the Holy Spirit, the creative continuation of life and life abundantly. He showed me how to use this wellspring for the masteries of healing and manifesting. He also pointed out our spiritual addiction to the marvels and spectacles of the beyond. He showed me how we vainly abuse supernatural abilities to dazzle our audiences and revel in the performance of ascending enlightenment. Glamor is empty and gets boring after a while.

When I was apprenticing with new thought masters and Science of Mind philosophers, he pointed out the power and authority of our sovereign reason when we dwell in a conscious, loving mind. Reverend Thompson, my first and dearest mentor, demonstrated how we shift entire timelines when we claim sovereignty over our vibrational environment and use precise wording in our day-to-day language. I discovered that with linguistic mastery we can easily cause a psycho-pneuma-somatic shift in our entire manifest experience and literally everything changes. Jesus also showed me the crushing weight of responsibility that we put on ourselves for creating and maintaining such a pure mind and aligned biofield. I saw that we can get so stuck on positive language and affirmations that we forget how to express authentically and instead create complex spells of false light that we think will fix our lives. We forget that the true power is not in the words we use, but in the Love of the one speaking.

This lesson was compounded around the same time when I brought my local Lutheran priest a homemade chicken curry. We had a picnic in his office, and I challenged him to explain to me why his congregants couldn't name the tenets of their specific denomination, or indeed had any idea why they weren't Catholic or Baptist (I had investigated, you see). With a boulder on my shoulder from the Lutheran priest who had ridiculed me decades before, and bearing a flag for powerful women demonized by priests throughout history, I took it upon myself to demand that religious leaders stand accountable for the separation caused by sectarianism! *"Elizabeth,"* he responded, helping himself to some cilantro rice and not flinching at all under my fiery gaze, *"I don't care if my people know the principles of Lutheranism or not. I just want this to be a place where people can come to Love and Be Loved."* I was floored, recognizing for the first time at age 33 that Love—not Knowledge—was the whole point of it all right here and now. Paster Steve ate a forkful of curry and went, *"Mmmm!"* and I could feel God smiling.

I released my vendetta and a year later my husband and I were making healing chocolates in a little cottage kitchen in Colorado, blending raw cacao, essential oils and reiki into opulent drops of chocolate medicine. How intimate God is when you feel him in the visceral sensation of universal life force infusing into and throughout the ingredients of your life! My Reiki Master Jeff and I would smell essential oils and talk about how the very person of the Holy Spirit moves through energy fields, an alchemy calibrating and sanctifying all things according to a Sovereign intention higher than mine. Jesus also showed me how hung up we get on healing, obsessing over fixing stuff to prove our growth, seeking out adversity just to experience the thrill of overcoming it. I also saw how often we turn our favorite healing modalities into little golden calves, hypnotized by results into placing protocols and methods above Love.

During this time I was training for the Episcopal priesthood, serving with laying-of-hands in the alcove after service at a small wooden church in the Rocky Mountains. My pastor Nancy, a converted Jew who beamed like the sun when she greeted her community, was like Mother Mary feeding us from the church gardens when we were hungry. She gave us a car to drive between the little church and the barn, and sat with me for hours chatting about mystic women and our ways. When my husband, my daughters and I were at rock bottom after a hurricane and devastating business failure, the humble generosity in this Episcopal community, a spiritual framework led by people for people, is what saved our lives. It wasn't our badass mastery.

It was becoming hard to ignore how pridefully selfish the performance-driven pursuit of enlightenment is when most of the time we're actually just good, little people trying to live as one family in a turbulent and conflicted world, needing deliverance.

Just when I was convinced that I would be an Episcopal priest, Jesus said *"hang on, there's more."* He dissolved that path and plonked us in a canvas tent out in the raw high desert, where for 60 days we lived off grid on the wild land and in the homestead nurture of a pagan priestess. Born Catholic, she was now a witch of natural devotion. Here, as I weaved willow reeds to use as an outdoor shower mat in a cactus ridden terrain at 9,000 ft elevation, Jesus showed me slow magic. When bears infiltrated the camp one night, stole our food and drank two bottles of laundry soap, the Woman said, *"Well, now we'll just have to learn how to **Be With** Bear."* Like her, I had also discovered **Home** is sovereign over **House** when it comes to protection from predators, so I went down to the reservoir that day and dug up some clay. With a spoon and a knife I sculpted a Bear for the priestess witch out of the sludgy elements God gave me. For years the clay bear stood on her log burner. Perhaps it was just a sentimental oddity and in itself offered no protection, because we both knew we were already *"**with Bear**"* anyway. Or perhaps there is real Magic in an elemental gift of Love.

When you must pump the ice melt for water, and carry it up uneven stone paths to boil over burning juniper before you can wash your children's breakfast plates, you value the elements. When you shower under a solar heated bag hanging from a pine, watching the galaxy float in the sparkling firmament above as yapping symphonies of coyotes wave across the mountain range, you learn how to communicate with those elements. You develop an acute presence, and you know everything is alive. Here Jesus showed us how to tend gently to what matters most while holding our authority in outrageous courage. Our trust was fierce, we depended 100% on the grace far superior to all the laws of nature. After all, if you live in a tent in the wild and the mountain lions fancy a nice, juicy, three-year-old for dinner, your family is fair game as far as nature's concerned. You need a higher system to live by than the laws of the wild. And when you can make no money, you need a higher system of provision than the laws of economics. Living like this, we traded our healing chocolates and reiki classes in exchange for apricots, lavender or duck eggs. I called it **"Duck Eggonomics,"** and Jesus laughed at my clever pun.

A year later, during COVID, I had been *whoomphed* to my own beach house in a highly affluent sub-tropical city, training alongside psychiatrists, doctors and entrepreneurs in the ways of precision energy work. We were developing ontological prayer protocols, first to help my mother through the early days of her Alzheimer's diagnosis and extending later to clinical ascension clients with afflictions ranging from depression to heart defects. Spiritual and energetic methods were already being integrated into mainstream medicine in our area, and there was a market for the Sovereign model. Now Jesus showed me first hand how extraordinary miracles can be authorized on a human level with powerful, precise command and right sequencing. He showed me how difficult it is to put our own spiritual growth and personal preferences aside for the sake of a more challenging group requirement. He also showed me how extremely delicate the balance is between anointed vibrational mastery and ego-driven control. I experienced, both as a perpetrator and a victim, how mental architecting and energetic manipulation can make fickle webs of false realities. Even with the noblest intentions an ego can muster, these mirages of oases quickly fall apart, leaving devastation and disillusionment as we spin in circles under a false diagnosis of "lack consciousness" or "limiting beliefs".

While I was all tangled up in a trillion energetic rules of cause and effect, unable to stop spinning plates for fear of an epic crash, and our house was at acute risk of foreclosure and we were facing homelessness for a third time, Jesus trained me for a while at an Evangelical megachurch—somewhere I would never before have set foot. With 4,000 worshippers and epic stage effects, it was a level of ecstatic surrender I had never encountered even in the most tantric of women's plant medicine circles or the hottest of sweat lodges. In this space, my husband and I dropped to our knees and asked him to deliver us, and at the critical deadline before all was lost (again) Jesus got our house out of foreclosure, eliminated $100,000 in bad debt and broke our homelessness pattern forever, restoring our material stability and abundance! *Shazam*! Jesus is definitely present in the extreme and spectacular as well as the humble and small. By now Yeshua was no longer just a friend and mystical spirit guide. As he promised, our relationship had matured and I had come to Know him as Jesus Christ, my own savior and the Sovereign Way of the Universe.

Most often though, he was in the day-to-day conversations with ordinary people, showing himself in the glint of someone's eye the moment a punchline was dropped, or in the transient murmur of wisdom on the tongue of a passer-by. He would show up to play board games with me and my husband, delighting us with the party tricks I had scorned all those years ago. He would point out the tiny purple purslane blossoms growing underfoot, and the magic numbers in clocks and license plates. He would sit and minister with me when I rubbed frankincense salve on the homeless man's sores. He always laughed at my jokes.

During our time developing The Sovereign Way, choosing words and teachings, his focus was never on which people or whose ideologies were wrong, sinful or misguided. It always felt like he understood our human endeavors to organize life, and knew our Stories would always somewhat miss the mark. He had tremendous compassion for that. He never pointed out the flaws in people, but he often pointed out the flaws in systems. In the many times I descended into judgment or criticism for another's way, he reminded me that we recognize each other by our love, not by our doctrinal affiliations. He always wanted to emphasize "God ***with us***".

When I stopped looking for God in the alignment of principles and started seeing him in love, I saw him everywhere. I found **Home** in every **House**. Daily, moment-by-moment communion with God became my Way of life rather than my life's ambition. Baptized in the holy waters, I had no more spiritual upgrades to yearn for because the upgrades never end when I Already Always AM *and* I AM Becoming. All the energy I was spending on healing and development was released, and I became peaceful and devoted.

When I first said yes to him, I thought I was formulating a metaphysical pathway for others to follow. I was wrong. He made everything so simple by explaining that he already is the pathway, and he is already walking it with every single one of us. This consecrated life of grace is not something we need to convert to, it already always is—but there is something we can do on our end to truly live it, especially for those of us who have Chosen to support the unfolding plan. It has been my honor to help formulate this ontological model for ascension in Christ.

Over the years, as I've shared this ontology and tested its method both professionally and personally, results have changed lives and elevated entire groups and mission fields. More importantly, coordinated conversations around consciousness and faith have blossomed, hearts have been reconciled, and a wider ripple of spiritual liberation and sovereignty has *whoomphed* out further than any of us foresaw. This book, which I thought would be the cause of something great, is in fact one small effect in a symphonic wave of manifestation already always occurring all over the world.

Small Print:

The model of understanding demonstrated in this book is a teaching from Jesus Christ, the Lord and Savior of the Universe, as he has taught it to me the Sovereign Way. It is far bigger than my story, but I've had no choice but insert to myself into the descriptions. These pages are soaked with my strange flavor. I am much more complicated than Christ, and I've added a lot more flourish than necessary. Please pardon my sudden intrusions in the form of first person paragraphs and absurd (but true) anecdotes from my discoveries.

It's also far bigger than Yeshua's story, as he would often remind me whenever I got tempted to slip into evangelism. I have recounted some of our shared history since the beginning of time, but those facts are much less important than Truth. Please forgive my girlish adoration for him. I don't mean to project how you should experience him because that's not for me to know at all, but I just can't help my love for him spilling into both these teachings and my personal way of moving about in the world. Your friendship with Christ is sovereign, unique and becoming.

The Sovereign Way is also far bigger than *your* story, but even though this wisdom method pertains to a greater, coordinated plan, the teachings herein are nonetheless focused on *you* and your personal Way.

This is not a scholarly text. I have spent no energy whatsoever resolving scientific, theological or historical matters. I've read a few books and conducted many experiments to discover some facts, but the knowledge itself is experiential. It's in my bones, my heart, and the clumsy little beetle on my window sill. Science, as I know it, is not a body of approved data but a method of discovery that is bold enough to formulate the unknown and humble enough to release what has been falsified. I have discovered that, as a method, the Sovereign model of interpretation with all its following results can be repeated and experienced by others.

The way I use the Bible is also outrageously free and unapologetically subjective. It was Rabbi Jamie who taught me to read the scriptures with my genius *and* with my magic. I have come to love this body of word as a rich and mysterious universe of human stories, each verse a hyperlink that *can* indeed be lifted out of its original literary and cultural context to open an ilimitable well of human divine understanding, always grounded in a dependable cosmic rhythm. When you come across scripture during this thought experiment, read it with both your genius and your magic.

I acknowledge it is impossible to formulate anything so devoid of my unique privileges and miseries that it can be universally relatable to all. I was tormented by this for a long time, agonizing over how to extract the Elizabethness and leave a Truth so pure anyone could pick it up. My savior soothed my doubts by reminding me that purity and holiness are not the same, and that the whole point of His Name: **Emmanuel** (God **With Us**) is that we don't *have* to bypass our earthly imperfection at all. He merges with us here, right in the most pungent of human smells. That, after all, is the heart of true spiritual life and the best flavor of art.

The model itself is a result of my unfair advantages. For example, the first and deepest privilege that I was born into is knowing I was loved and wanted by my parents. My father is safe, kind, dependable, generous and grounded. He taught me to think beyond the dimensions of my formal education. He taught me that even though there is a solution to absolutely everything, many things must stay mysteries. My mother has always fiercely encouraged me to heal, be free, express and grow. She showed me how to hang up prisms in the window to sanctify a room with rainbows, and how to soak with lemons in the bathtub to become like the sunshine. *"It always turns out alright in the end,"* she would say, and I saw that she was right.

And the pinnacle privilege of my life is that my husband protects and provides for our **Home** regardless of **House,** holds me up through my mental health crises and champions me in my times of triumph and excellence. He is an adventurous friend and most sacred confidant, a generous healer, tender lover and firm guide. Daily he helps me unravel my thought world as we stroll the garden in conversation and reflection. Even though he is a very different sort of creature from me and walking his own path with God, my husband is the one in whom I know Jesus most intimately.

So these subconscious paradigms are the Home I have always come back to, and therefore fundamental to how I have met the world and how the world has responded to me ever since I was a little baby girl. I have lived a consecrated, charmed life. This is how I Know God. The Sovereign Way is thus a framework of interpretation based on divine masculine and feminine principles manifesting in those characteristics, merging to show a deeply hopeful, resilient and joyful path forward.

Introduction

I AM the Living God, The Way and The Truth and The Life.

Sovereign is a spiritual movement, a wave of new understanding and freedom dispensed into leaders of humanity for our time. It is an anointing, or a dimension of being if you like—a liberated and hopeful way of approaching life and a way of mastery that lifts burdens and opens opportunities as you tend to your dearest devotion with a grace that transcends reason. You've begun to hear the word *sovereign* everywhere. Even though you've always been different from the mainstream you now feel more sovereign than ever before. Your thoughts are more free, your spirit is more free, your movements are more free—even though you see control and oppression around you.

To be Sovereign is to be free. Your thoughts liberated from old patterns, your energy field strong and clear, your body, emotions and reason all in harmony with what is True for your life, your actions purposeful and impactful. In this sovereign poise, you liberate the path that belongs to you alone. Your life *is* unfolding organically. As you distill Truth from your engagement with life your intimacy with God is deepening *and* your mental and vibrational mastery are improving. Your ascension *is* getting easier, but the process is either:

- a laborious trudge through the cycles of karma, inherited cultural and intergenerational trauma, other people's projections and empathically absorbed melancholy, sifting and sorting through archives of theories, clearing energetic feedback from the latest full moon eclipse, resisting religious oppression by the trending charismatic leaders, fickle spiritual diets from the zillions of white-toothed social media influencers, bone-crushing compression and ascension symptoms, and "all that stuff", or

- it is a light and joyful surrender.

The second option—a light and joyful surrender—is easier to experience when you can delegate 90% of "all that stuff" and instead focus your energy entirely on the Way ahead. The simplicity opens space for the natural illumination of your heart and mind as you mature with Life. You don't even need to kill your Ego. It's actually a jolly friend for the ride, and an important companion for holiness.

When humans create theological frameworks to help them relate to God—that timeless, ineffable Source of creativity and power—we have a structure that we call religion. Religion is a system of wisdom and method that serves to hold space in our consciousness for remembering who we really are and where to find Love. Like all human-made tools it's often abused, but first and foremost it exists to hold our hearts open for possibility and hope, and it keeps our discernment piqued and active. It provides guardrails that keep our energy cohesive, help us understand ourselves and how to move in a world that is timelessly changing. Societies inherently structure themselves around a set of optimal rules that work best for staying viable. For the flock, religion is usually a workable way to know God *together*. For the most part, religion is not about oppression or competition between sects of Truth, but about cultivating the essence of belonging, community and love.

But this delicate balance between structure and essence falls apart when arbitrary regulations are used as scaffolding for propping up society—in place of genuine connection. Eventually, any human-controlled system only works if other humans agree to be controlled like untamed creatures likely to run amok without proper fencing—and some of us are indeed thusly inclined. But we are changing. Sometimes slowly and sometimes fast, the human consciousness evolves over time as we collectively assimilate life lessons and as a result Know more about love. As our generations evolve, our religions evolve—although since brick is denser than ether, all institutions move slower than Spirit.

Sometimes there is a way that seems to be right, but in the end it is the way to death.

Proverbs 16:25

In every generation is a group of pioneers. The mystics, artists, scientists, philosophers, humanitarians and adventurers simply can't be fenced in as they reach into the expansive possibility and inch by inch move the boundaries of how we know

God. This doesn't always look like spiritual progress, mind you. Sometimes it even seems as though God retreats from us when we take a step forward. But progress is always occurring. For example, when religious idealism was removed from the scientific process during the Age of Enlightenment, secular thought became the supreme ruler of what's what, and the gnosis within mysticism and lore fell away. This was no accident on God's part. Without religion, suddenly Source could be Known in a new way—made even more real from the microcosm to the outer borders of the universe. When Einstein formulated the unified field theory we had the scientific foundation for the omnipresence of Spirit. Indeed, we Know there's a God-particle: the *adamantine* particle of Substance that precedes all mass. Unprecedented masses of individuals are remembering who we are, and the children of our age are born already Knowing. We are always going deeper into God no matter how we explore.

As one of the pioneers, your ascension is happening through your life's strategic, progressive illumination. You are grounded in something that is not attached to religious propriety, much less dependent on the collective experience. Christ has personally called you Sovereign, so how you experience your ascension is entirely relative to your unique and personal relationship with him. Your way of understanding is completely unique as well, and so is the vibrational magic that is cultivating inside you. Above all, your devotion is utterly unique. **You need to be free to Love the way you Love.**

In the early days of our current civilization we were recovering from the catastrophic trauma of our ancestral generations. For tens of thousands of years we were mostly getting by in a natural and cultural survival system that left no room for error. That was our collective realm of consciousness, the world we all lived in together, and the God of our stories from those times reflects the distortion in how we saw ourselves: **no room for error.** Around the time of Moses a more balanced consciousness started emerging as new frameworks for reasoning emerged. We created an agreement with karma, the rule of Lex Talionis: you get what you give, an eye for an eye, a tooth for a tooth, x-amount of my time for x-amount of your money, energy attracts like energy, good thoughts make good things and bad thoughts make bad things. Follow these rules, and things ought to turn out ok for you. This was an improvement, but left very little space for progress.

As a metaphysical dynamic in the cosmos, the Law of Attraction is true enough. But as an ideology to live by it is grossly inadequate. This linear consciousness requires white-knuckle control and brutal accountability for the tiniest vibrational details. This is how we get stuck in the patterns and structures of the mind's illusions, in our own imaginations of a future reality. We might be able to manifest every item on our vision board, but we are still only architecting within a known reality. How can you break free from cycles of experience and integrate new dimensions of living when your life is created by absolute systems of energetic cause and effect and you're accountable for it all? In a shared, linear infrastructure where karma is king and an eye is always for an eye, then how can you ever access a reality on the other side of a glass ceiling? How can you make more love?

A human's natural state is to thrive, so the energy field of a spiritually imprisoned human must, by the Law of Attraction, accelerate entropy until an unstoppable "downward spiral" occurs. Best case scenario is a slow depression and disillusionment as even the most diligent law-keeping and box-ticking yields nothing but more of the same. Worst case scenario plunges individuals and our entire collective experience into darkness, toward despair and eventual destruction. We recognize this doomsday phenomenon in communities around the world across history and even now. From time to time this spiritual entropy occurs at a catastrophic scale. Our ancestral civilization Atlantis went this way, and our modern civilization was heading there too. Doomsday was approaching.

There was an intervention around the year 0. Injected into the human consciousness, piercing the veil of space and time, came an unprecedented upgrade to the human system. A little baby was born with a completely integrated Knowing of his divine nature. I AM really was for the first time THAT I AM.

His Name is

EmmanuEL.

It means:

God *With* Us.

Divinity and Humanity together.

Not even a whisper of separation.

"An eye for an eye" was replaced by "turn the other cheek". When the human mind Knows itself as Love, no harm can exist—agony simply transforms into glory—so the Law of Love became sovereign to the human consciousness, over all other commandments including the Law of Attraction. The result, dispensed into the universal human reality like a quantum *whoomph*, was an intercessory field of mercy accessible to all. Anyone using their sovereign choice to live inside this field would witness the Law of Love fulfilling all other commandments, and the resulting vibrational alchemy would literally dissolve all unnatural attachments to linear system.

> *"Love the Lord your God with all your heart and with all your soul and with all your mind. This is the first and greatest commandment. And the second is like it: Love your neighbor as yourself. All the Law and the Prophets hang on these two commandments."*
>
> *Matthew 22:37*

With this new paradigm embedded in the human consciousness, you don't need to be imprisoned by linear transaction to pay for every sin, atone for every error, fix every crack, integrate every past life, heal every intergenerational wound or balance every chakra before you break free of their energetic attractor fields. By implication, any obstacle can be overcome, any limiting paradigm can be transcended, any structure can be surrendered, and it is possible for you to Know only Love—and then more of it, because Love is Love abundantly in all its forms.

When one person realizes (makes *real*) something out of the field of potentiality, that person makes the same realization accessible for all. In 1952 Roger Bannister did the impossible feat when he ran a mile in four minutes at the Olympics, opening the door for a quantum leap in how fast we can move our bodies. As he raised the bar, others were able to reach the same result in their imaginative, creative minds, and then they ran impossibly fast too. Once realization spreads there is exponential growth, because if **one part improves, the integrity of the whole improves, and we have momentum.** So when God chose to incarnate the original Christ as a human boy called Yeshua, the electromagnetic weight of this embodied Love offset the physical and metaphysical systems keeping the human consciousness in the bondage of our own creations. From net negative energy to net positive energy, the downward spiral inverted and became an energetic upward spiral of consciousness, or *ascension*, thus saving the human family from spiritual annihilation.

Yeshua's life and legacy was the physical demonstration of this effect on the collective. In the last 2000 years we have progressed at a phenomenal rate, even as our worst is purged. Centuries of purging in fact, through the pungent rot and shame of the dark ages, or the brutal industrial ages of greed and conquest, or our modern age of rage, competition, crisis and warfare, and even the ages to come of glamor, artificial intelligence, quantum manipulation and split, deepfake realities. Even still, as a family of humans, we love more than we ever have before. Zillions of tiny acts of kindness occurring every day is proof of that.

> ***Once, when being asked by the Pharisees when the Kingdom of God would come, Jesus said "The coming of the Kingdom is not something that can be observed, nor will people say 'Here it is' or 'There it is', because the Kingdom of God is within, and in your midst."***
>
> *Luke 17:20-21*

Within and in our midst, we are bathing in Love. We draw it out into manifestation as we integrate its essence and weave it into the world through our choices, movements, interactions and all our works. This is, in fact, the Great Commission spoken by Jesus to his disciples. Most people know about the Golden Rule, the one commandment that Jesus said was sovereign over all others: *Be love. Love God, love yourself, and love others.* That rule is enough to live a sovereign life. But there is another commission given specifically to the population of actively awakened world servers. *Did you feel the bong?* If so, you have an operative commission, **to not just BE Love, but go out and DO love**—specifically to liberate those lost in the desert. This requires discipline, development and mastery.

One of my students is a young classical guitarist. He often says, even though he Knows where the music truly comes from, he must still train his fingers to play the strings masterfully, so his whole *modus operandi* is finely tuned for the exquisite piece of work that Spirit is about to release through him. Mastery is a responsibility and a delight for those who live in the oasis and are birthing more of it. It brings magical economies of scale. But since you are no longer a servant of system, you need to develop your mastery in a sovereign way, in an intimate and personal partnership **with** God.

Phenomenologically, the reality you are experiencing is a manifestation of your mental projections, energetic field and your personal response to your vibrational universe. You are always creating experiences by the nature of your beliefs and standpoints, or we could say coordinates of consciousness. In other words, you have feelings and thoughts and entire conversations and storylines that exist only for you in a universe completely unique to you, and so does everyone else. And although we interact in a shared infrastructure and transmit values and intentions through those universes, we are nonetheless all spending a lot of time inside our own private reality. We do know this, but we forget it often.

Ontology is the line of philosophy that organizes the experience and becoming of life. This is a process-based philosophy that sorts out how consciousness ceaselessly creates, examining the compression and expansion of life to see God's body constantly coming to form. Since all reality is emerging from the one Source, we are naturally called forward in life. Each of us is constantly called into expansion inside and through the vibrational universes that we are creating with the coordinates of consciousness that we set. And if we "upgrade" those coordinates of thought and feeling, reality upgrades, which is how we get to have incredible adventures of discovery, abundance, exploration and innovation even while we're healing a broken world.

Since the precedent for perfect consciousness, perfect vibration and perfect form has already been actualized, you can choose phenomenologically to align with those coordinates and come into a universe of constant, immediate mercy and grace. Granted, salvation is a bottomless mystery, and so is the consecrated life that follows, but grasping some of the metaphysics can help bring peace to the intellect.

You could say that your mind, energy field, subtle and physical bodies and networks of behavioral relationships have all been intertwined with the thought-forms and attractor fields you've already created for yourself. This has entangled you into vibrational turbulence. Planets go into retrograde and you have a meltdown. A horrible thought pops into your head, you think you generated it and start building entire fantasy stories about it. Someone triggers your pride, which always leads to a fall. Someone starts a war and you forget that we are all beloved children of God. And it's not your fault—this is the human nature and our agonizingly beautiful design. It's the reason we impose so many rules upon ourselves. We succumb to the world and spend enormous amounts of energy regaining our spiritual footing.

This is why an intercession field exists. If we choose to believe in our personal savior, a Christ that is not only a universal ideal of consciousness to aim for but also a living, beloved friend who saves us when we fall, then that is what manifests. Our Way becomes graceful. Moment-by-moment, the alchemy of Love is working. Deliverance becomes a way of life. We exude salvation as his presence flows like an eddy through and around us. We walk in an embodied Trust that reminds others they are also safe.

We *will* be seduced by illusion, we *will* make agreement with limitation, we *will* forget who we are. But we Know we are safe in him. What helps make sense of this safety is understanding and trusting the timeless structure of the universe, one that outlasts intergenerational culture shifts and trending spiritual propriety. We can no longer use religious institutions to mandate and manage our lawful compliance. It's simply not relevant to our new quality of being. We need a new structure, one that lasts across the different densities of the ascending human consciousness.

Dragonflies lay their eggs in the oasis pond, and their larvae, or nymphs, hatch in the water below. A nymph might ascend from the boggy gloop at the bottom of the pond all the way up to the glittery, light waters above, but it cannot pass through the surface of the water by itself. The body of water is too turbulent and the counterpressure at the surface is too great. It's not designed to accomplish its own metamorphosis. Every dragonfly nymph will be compelled by instinct to swim its way to a reed, ground its little feet and walk up along the blade. The Sovereign Way is like a blade of grass that grows from the sludgy bottom of a dragonfly pond all the way up through the surface of the water and into a new elemental dimension. This blade of grass isn't snapped by shifting currents, it easily bends and sways but always leads through the veil.

The little dragonfly larvae climbing up the blade of grass is sovereign over its environment, because the turbulence of all the elements and currents in the pond around has no authority over whether or not it will become Dragonfly. As long as it follows the way underfoot, its destiny is assured. It will pass through the veil, shed the skin of its former form, and enter the dimension beyond. It will not immediately fly off from the surface. It will continue following the blade even after it has taken its new form, until it reaches the tip. By this time it has adapted to the new airy element, and it is ready to take flight.

Christ is neverending and transcendental. His friendship is the blade of grass, and the only authority that can guide you along your own natural process from the murkiest depths to the highest zenith.

"Timeless truth, I tell you: 'whoever believes in me, those works which I have done he will also do, and he will do greater works than these, because I AM going to the Presence of my Father."

John 14:12

The Core Assumptions of The Sovereign Way

Start the thought experiment now. Suspend your familiar religious vernacular and allow each idea its due merit. As you move through this book of ontology, test everything against your sovereign knowing of Truth. Do not discard "*what doesn't resonate right now*" but recalibrate it within your own heart's wisdom.

All paradigms can be defined by their parameters. That simply means that any lens you choose to view the world through is made up of certain ideas that have more creative influence than others. So when you choose to align with a particular framework of spiritual thought—which is what any philosophy or religion is—you're choosing to interpret and engage with your Life in a particular way. The specific framework in this book is characterized by a set of ontological assumptions, creative parameters that we choose to say are true. If you feel resistance to any of the ideas, feel free to rearrange the words to create Truer sentences, but be mindful not to lose the essence of the intended meaning. We are not trying to formulate societal codes of morality or an inerrant doctrine of Truth, but more like settings on a telescope that bring a particular view into focus.

As you read the following ideas, consider each one and its implications in your Life.

There are many more words than necessary, for the Truth is too simple to understand. So you must let each word guide your thought along as if over a string of pearls. Play along, with each idea imagining that the telescope dial is adjusting.

1. **God is real**. It is the Source, Spirit and Substance of all creation. We Know it is Knowing. We Know it is Love. Beyond this, it's a bit of a mystery. Let's say a universal wave of expanding, loving consciousness occurred at the beginning of time when singularity first became diversity, and reality bonged into being. Let's call that original manifestation "Christ". God is Love, therefore Christ is the Beloved.

2. Since Christ is the only thing ever manifested, *everything* is the Beloved. Nothing exists outside of this field. Nothing has been created from any other source, for there is nothing but God. **The Human Being is therefore an individuation of God**: let's say the Spirit of Source manifested as Substance. You are born of this same fabric: an individualized strand of consciousness, a unique field of energy, and a beautifully woven body perfectly real. You are real in Life—*always* alive, known and loved. **You have genuine spiritual authority within the natural world and sovereignty within an expanding Heaven of possibility, and since you are always one with God, you are always one with Love.**

3. Your consciousness to God is a bit like a prism to the Light. This individuation of consciousness refracts superstate potentiality into Known strands of possibility, and then experiences that possibility. If *all things* are possible for God, then *some* things are possible for me. Each individual is therefore both a single lens in a majestic kaleidoscope of all possible perspectives, and also a kaleidoscope yourself as you experience infinite nano-moments of your unique Being.

4. **The Human experience of Life is an interconnected network** of consciousness, energy and manifestation all unfolding in space and time. Everything you experience becomes known to you as a solution of data, vibration and particle. Your telescope is always dialed in to something. Your life is a living Story in the Body of God.

5. Since the living experience in a human life is a vibrational result of that interconnected network, **what is created by you is determined by what is Known by you**. Each Human Being therefore embarks on a unique coming-of-age journey to bring this whole system of experience back to one cohesive Truth, this is the **natural process of ascending consciousness**. When you awaken to the fact that you are Love, you begin an unstoppable baptism as Love magnetizes more Love and your energy field becomes self-calibrating. An inner alchemy releases all the ties that have bound you to the twisted realities created by a conflicted prism. You are born again into the original field of consciousness and energy.

6. This ascending consciousness experiences and radiates fuller and purer Love, which manifests as greater spiritual authority, sharpened faculties and vibrational mastery, and **a deepening intimacy with God**. This effect spreads between people through infinite forms of connection. This process is organic, we do not need to manufacture it. As each lens in the kaleidoscope is attuned to Love, we reveal more and more of the oasis, the Kingdom of Heaven that is already in our midst.

7. The human collective is undergoing **a historic paradigm shift as awareness spreads at the speed of Light.** The effect of this is like **a great revelation, with Substance manifesting an expanding experience of what is known**. Some know the world is falling. Some know the world is resurrecting. These possibilities are therefore intensifying, creating a perceived bifurcation of reality where some seem doomed and some seem saved.

8. The Human's **"log of consciousness" determines what is known** by that individual, and is itself determined by the interaction of their coordinates of beliefs, thought, feeling, emotion and circumstance. This log has nothing to do with worth, but is an indicator of spiritual maturity and the extent to which the consciousness, energy and form of an individual has been conditioned in its capacity to Love. You could also say it this log indicates how fully you are aware of and have claimed your divine inheritance.

9. By conditioning the coordinates of consciousness, energy and form, the human experience alters, the same way that changing the shape of **a sol-**

id structure cup will affect the malleable, liquid content. When we consciously choose to condition the quality of our consciousness through self mastery, Substance manifests through exponentially greater fields of electromagnetism and more cohesive focus on what truly matters. We are participating actively in birthing the Kingdom. Our ability to believe in and make agreement with the highest possible calibration of reality is therefore also the marker of developing consciousness. This is often externally witnessed as "signs and wonders" such as healing, manifesting, higher spiritual gifts and a radically unreasonable faith as Substance forms around Spirit.

10. Permanently altering those coordinates by your human will is almost impossible in an **energetic environment where Life is a response to consciousness** and we are swimming in a pond of energy projected through the many lenses in God's vast kaleidoscope. The energetic currents are strong and turbulent with complex interference patterns we cannot individually understand. We keep recreating from within that living story of experience, being swept away by frequencies of counterforce and entropy, and forgetting our holy mission to make more Love.

11. **Inherent in infinite potentiality** is a perfect synchrony between divine consciousness and human consciousness: the original Christ. This potential was fully realized with Jesus Christ, when Love Knew Himself as human and human Knew himself as Love. When Love is applied to form, form is transformed. That is what we shall call Mercy.

12. **Allowing the pre-existing Christ mind to imprint upon and pour out through your personal prism** creates the effect of pure Love to transform the Substance of your life. This allows mercy to transform all attachment to systems of what is known and created in the human condition. It thus liberates and restores the consciousness, energy and form of the individual to its True nature. What follows is **a simple and graceful experience of natural ascension, and—should you choose to accept the mission—an initiation into a coordinated group of world servers, going the Sovereign Way individually and together.**

Let's pretend there is a desert of vast dunes constantly shifting shape under battling storms of sand particles. In the midst of this eternal sand storm there is also an oasis, luscious with life. A river leads from an unknown source to a great, sparkling pond in the oasis. Here wild roses bloom, dragonflies whizz and little frogs hide under lily pads whenever the herons arrive. There is a path leading from the pond to a bridge, and this bridge leads to an alabaster cathedral with stained glass windows projecting infinite colors and stories of meaningful moments.

The Diagrams

When we can comprehend something, it is easier to grasp. And if we can grasp something, it is easier to hold. And when we hold something for long enough, it becomes a part of our Knowing. This is how we train the lens of our telescope, or a mindset. These are visual explanations to help our linear sense-making minds organize the core assumptions that set the dial on our telescope. Each diagram is a two-dimensional representation of something infinitely mystical and undefinable. They are crude, incomplete and primitive, and thus perfect for helping us arrange our thinking about the relationship between consciousness, energy and manifestation.

on·tol·o·gy

/än ˈtäləjē/

A branch of philosophy that organizes the mystery of Being.

Examine these diagrams and their explanations, practice drawing them and formulating your own explanations by transposing the visuals into your own real life. Read the descriptions and play with the languages you use to understand yourself, Life and God. As you go through the book, these diagrams will again come up again, explored more deeply and in different ways as you further your inquiry into the Sovereign Way God is leading you.

Diagram 1: The Trinity

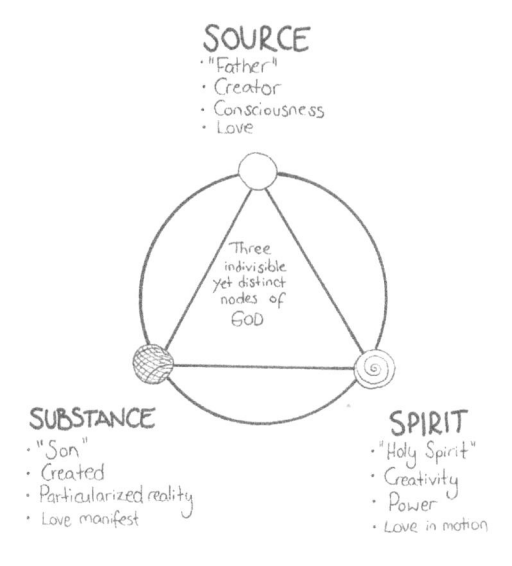

SOURCE
- "Father"
- Creator
- Consciousness
- Love

Three indivisible yet distinct nodes of GOD

SUBSTANCE
- "Son"
- Created
- Particularized reality
- Love manifest

SPIRIT
- "Holy Spirit"
- Creativity
- Power
- Love in motion

Let's say the Universe is made of Love can be organized as three elements: Source, Spirit and Substance. These three nodes of God are indivisible, yet distinct. They are not the same, but they are always in relation with each other. There is no place where Substance and Spirit are separate, and there is no way you can become cut off from the Father. You are these three things whether you know it or not, but the extent to which you embody the Knowing of yourself and others *as these elements* (and nothing else) dictates your log of consciousness, your electromagnetism and spiritual authority over manifest form.

The sovereign Source is Love. Loving consciousness authorizes universal power to move the particles of reality. The more Love embodied by you, the "higher" your log of consciousness, the more authority with which you command Spirit to move Substance. For example, a 100% embodied Knowing *"I and My Father Are One"* would allow you to command the molecular structure of water to rearrange into wine. A 50% embodied consciousness would allow you to turn anger to peace and guilt to gratitude. A 5% embodied consciousness would turn you to despair, and the systems of the world would overcome you if not for grace.

Diagram 2: The Sovereign Model of Human Consciousness

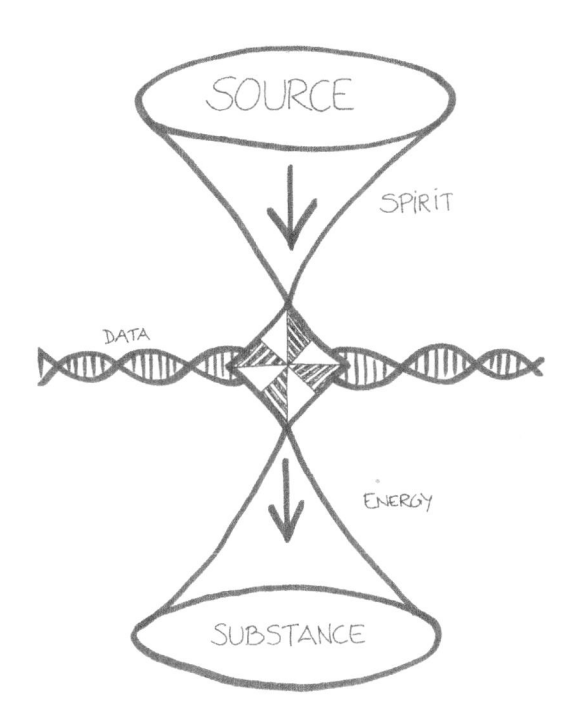

If God is the Source, all Spirit and all Substance, then there is a very specific strand of that totality which is drawn out and individualized as you. The diamond in the middle of this model represents the individual framework of consciousness that makes *you* different from Adam, Naomi or Sofia. It contains all data points that make up what you know to be true about God, Life and who you are in relation to it all. Some of this data is divinely designed, some is inherited culturally or epigenetically, some is forced upon you by trauma or oppression, some is simple error in judgment, and some is gained through experience, wisdom or revelation. Therefore, no human is wholly True or wholly False. Each human, in their diamond consciousness Knows *both* good *and* evil.

In our model, potential resides above the diamond. Reality resides below. The ceaseless power of creativity is always extending from Source and moving through your framework of consciousness, like the sun through a stained glass window. The creative Spirit assumed its shape by this framework of consciousness, and your cellular data is projected *as* your energy field—as if the sunlight were projecting the stories in a stained glass window onto the stone floor of the cathedral for anyone to view. This Spirit commands the Substance particles of creation to take form. Substance arranges itself according to the vibrational resonance projected, like sand particles forming great sand dunes into shapes commanded by the diamond. Your experience of Life in the four process dimensions of time and space therefor matches the data held in the diamond. If the data is "I AM Unworthy", then the Substance will form itself thusly.

A person's ascension is the process and experience of clearing false data from this window, making more space for Love and bringing power and cohesion to the creative Spirit always flowing, Love always in motion. Ergo, the more Love embodied, the more improved is the quality of your created experience, and the greater the reality of God's Will on Earth as it is in Heaven. The purer and holier your impact, and the higher we all rise together. When consciousness, energy and form are all attuned to Love, we *create* Heaven on Earth, which we might sometimes call "the Kingdom".

Diagram 3: The Sovereign Model of Human Experience

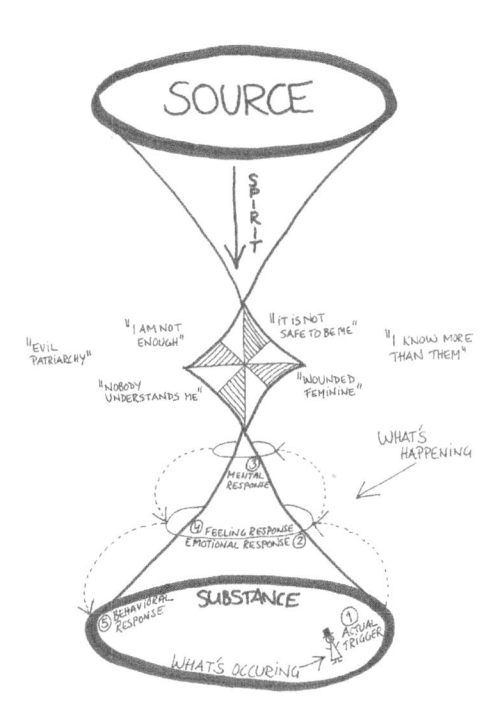

The human experience is an interconnected network of beliefs, manifestations of those beliefs and the perceptions of those manifestations.

1. You manifest a reality based on the data points in your consciousness. That manifest reality is then perceived by you: an actual trigger.

2. The trigger activates emotional feedback that alters your biochemistry as hormones are released to prepare your body for response.

3. A new inner chemical environment creates a new vibrational environment, which alters the quality of your thoughts and triggers a mental narrative that matches the vibrational environment.

4. The mental response creates a shift in your feelings, which are connected to your identity. The biological emotion of anger has been internalized to become "I AM Angry."

5. This shifts your behavioral response and your actions in relation to the manifest world.

This is how we get stuck in karmic cycles, recreating "the same old" vibrational universe. Recognize the distinction between "What's Occurring" (actual events and objects in a shared reality) and "What's Happening" (the rich and complicated inner experience that results from what's occurring).

Diagram 4: Hawkins' Scale

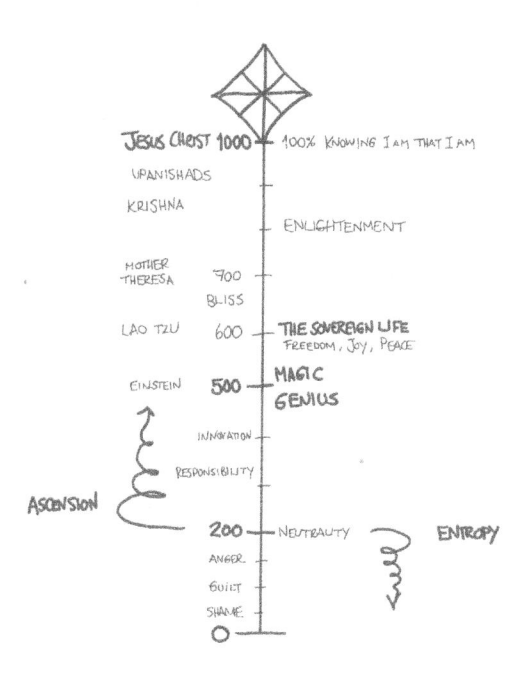

```
                    ◇
                    |
JESUS CHRIST 1000 ──┼── 100% KNOWING I AM THAT I AM
   UPANISHADS       |
   KRISHNA          |
                    ├── ENLIGHTENMENT
                    |
   MOTHER           |
   THERESA    700 ──┤
              BLISS |
                    |
   LAO TZU    600 ──┼── THE SOVEREIGN LIFE
                    |    FREEDOM, JOY, PEACE
                    |
   EINSTEIN   500 ──┼── MAGIC
                    |   GENIUS
                    |
            INNOVATION ┤
                    |
          RESPONSIBILITY ┤
ASCENSION           |
                200 ┼── NEUTRALITY        ENTROPY
              ANGER ┤
              GUILT ┤
              SHAME ┤
                  0 ┴
```

Let's pretend we can measure and calibrate the extent to which a human consciousness has become aware of and claimed its divine inheritance, *"I and My Father Are One."*

It's important to note that in Truth there is no up and no down, no rush to climb any imaginary ladder of spiritual purity, and no energy field that is more wrong than another. Jesus would never consider himself higher than lowliest nymphs at the bottom of the pond, but for the purpose of our thought experiment we will use dualistic language to imagine an ascending scale of consciousness. This is a linear representation of increasing realizations of awareness, greater capacity to Love, and more powerful corresponding electromagnetic attractor fields that magnetize and energize higher qualities of form. We arrange this idea on a scale from 0 to 1000, each marker reflecting an attractor field's proximity to perfect Truth. This scale is inspired by the "Map of Consciousness" scientifically demonstrated and presented in depth in the book "Power versus Force" *(Hawkins, Hay House, 2014)*. Seek it out and study the work. For our enquiry, we only need the idea and a few important data points:

- **If** 1000 is Christ, perfectly integrated "I AM" with a pure field of Love, **and** 0 is Anti-Christ, Truth perfectly inverted as "I AM NOT", with no awareness of Love, **then** all created things calibrate somewhere in between.

- Approaching 0 there is spiritual "death" and a disconnected, nihilistic life view which manifests its equivalent in energy and form.

- Approaching 1000 there is enlightenment, a Self with an ineffable experience of belonging and beauty.

- At 200 is a neutral attitude towards life, with little awareness or mastery to affect the many tides of vibration in this relational world, but nonetheless an ability to enjoy the goodness of a sunrise.

- Below 200, creative energy manifests as net *negative* and we experience the effect of entropy, a spiritual downward spiral. Above 200, creative energy becomes net *positive* and we experience the effect of ascension, a spiritual upward spiral.

- 500 marks the threshold often described as "the journey from the head to the heart," where the human mind transcends system living and becomes utterly led by Love, and therefore sovereign in the natural world.

- Below 500 is linear system consciousness, where cause and effect rule creative possibility. Above 500 is non-linear quantum consciousness, where faith and synchronicity are the actualizing agencies as energetic attractor field weave Substance together at the command of Love.

Ascension is the process of sanctifying your framework of consciousness and deepening your Knowing that you are 100% Source, Spirit and Substance, and so is everything else. The Christ field at 1000 is already available in the collective potential. Since ascension also represents an increased embodiment of the Knowing that *"I and My Father are One"* (see diagram 1), the higher the log of consciousness, the greater the electromagnetic attractor field, and the greater the authority to influence manifestation.

For example, at 1000 you can walk on water. The mind intends the water molecules to support the body moving through space, and the elements submit willingly. At 50, you have very little influence and life is imposed upon you. You are likely to drown. Wherever your consciousness "logs" on this imaginary scale, it is possible to make up any deficit in spiritual power by aligning with the pre-existing Christ field and following him. Then you are not limited by ability, only by your faith in him that leads the Way.

The experience of ascension is not a linear climb up this imaginary ladder. Nor is enlightenment a race to the top. Each vibrational reality manifesting at each "level" of awareness has a purpose in the symphony of God. Albert Einstein, for example, though deeply connected and mystic in his communion, spent most of his life at 499. Thank goodness he didn't seek to transcend the intellect, as the world needed his linear genius to formulate mathematical expressions of the unified field. We do oscillate up and down this scale across different moments and in different aspects of identity and life, but as we reconcile life and embody Her wisdom through conscious participation with what-is, our "diamond" consciousness clears and we experience a steadily improving Life of increasing presence, power and possibility.

A truly sovereign Life begins with unifying the 400s (genius) and the 500s (magic), as the experience of a truly sovereign Life begins when mental mastery and vibrational mastery are fused with loving devotion.

No part of the scale is separate from God, whose grace penetrates even the deepest strata of humanity. His Love is Whole. God is the sludge, the surface, the water, the blade of grass, the sky above the pond, and every little nymph that did or didn't become a Dragonfly.

Where can I go from your Spirit? Where can I flee from your presence? If I go up to the heavens, you are there; if I make my bed in the depths, you are there. If I rise on the wings of the dawn, if I settle on the far side of the sea, even there your hand will guide me, your right hand will hold me fast. If I say, "Surely the darkness will hide me and the light become night around me," even the darkness will not be dark to you; the night will shine like the day, for darkness is as light to you.

Psalm 139:8-13

Diagram 5: Walking With Christ

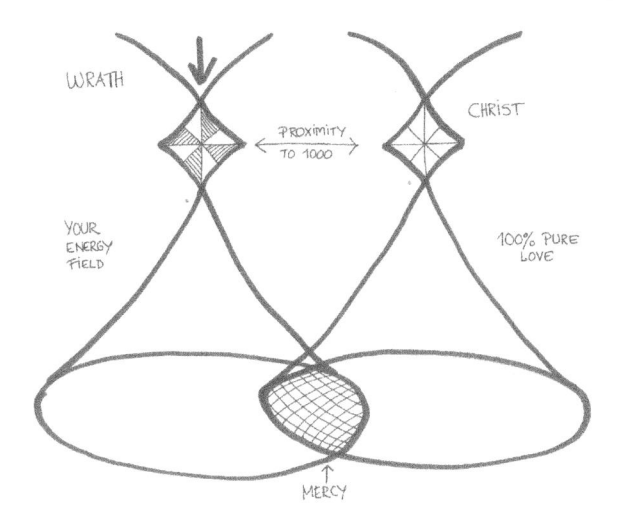

Even though there is no rush to move on with your ascension, you still feel the longing. Since the precedent of "God as Fully Embodied Human" already exists as a potential in the collective consciousness, you are entangled with it and always in some proximity to it.

The process of "ascension by mastery" steadily brings you closer to that field. You tend to your growth through prayer, meditation, shadow work, healing ancestral wounds, reprogramming subconscious limiting beliefs, closing karmic cycles, learning your lessons, extending your comfort zone, etc. As you come closer to that 1000 point on the imaginary scale, more Love penetrates your manifest reality—dissolving linear rules, and you experience more non-linear actualizations: Miracles!

There is a natural yearning in the human soul to come deeper into God, but the metaphysical laws of creation keep us constantly exposed to energetic counterforce, and we struggle to transcend the systems of our own manifestation. Progress is slow and energy expensive as we get trapped in the feedback cycles of creation (see diagram 3), and we're lost in the sand storms in the vast desert of ever-moving dunes. The greater the effect of Mercy on our Life, the less we are dominated by unconscious systems.

Diagram 6: Walking In Christ

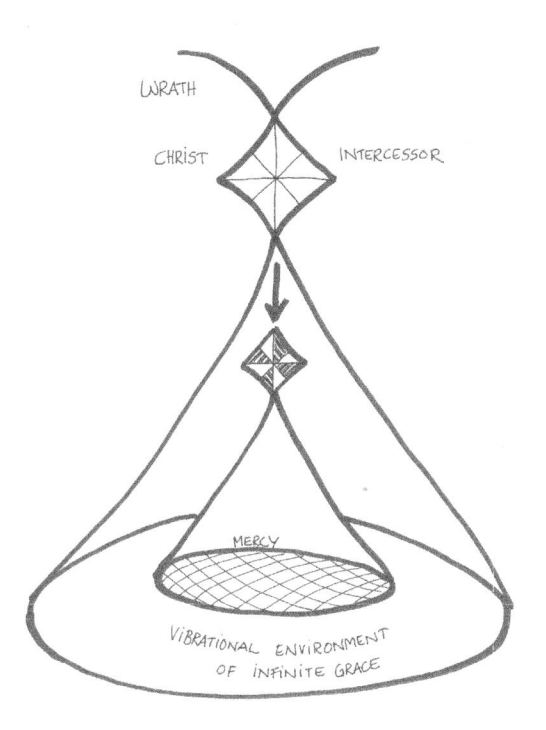

It is possible to align our mindset "underneath and within" that pure field of Christ consciousness, and be reborn inside an energy field of 100% Love which both overshadows and outpours through *your* unique individualization. This is the metaphysical effect of "Jesus is my personal Lord and Savior".

Now the ceaselessly creative and infinitely powerful spirit (we could call it the "wrath of God" as they did in the olden days, because it creates constantly no matter what mood you're in) is "softened" by an intercessory field before it even arrives at your framework of consciousness to be colored by your beliefs. You manifest inside the energy field of Mercy, which gives you access to an instantly neutralizing effect, overcoming karmic cycles and dissolving even unconscious intergenerational paradigms. You are in an oasis. Inside this field, Christ inspires the mind, reorients the energy field, and guides your Love in motion. Your experience of ascension is more graceful, and it is safer to experiment with and practice the higher spiritual gifts of healing and miracle work which now manifest as a result of the energetic overflow. You can walk through any sand storm while in this field.

And on that day you will realize that I AM in my Father, and you are in me, and I AM in you.

John 14:20

Diagram 7: Relationship

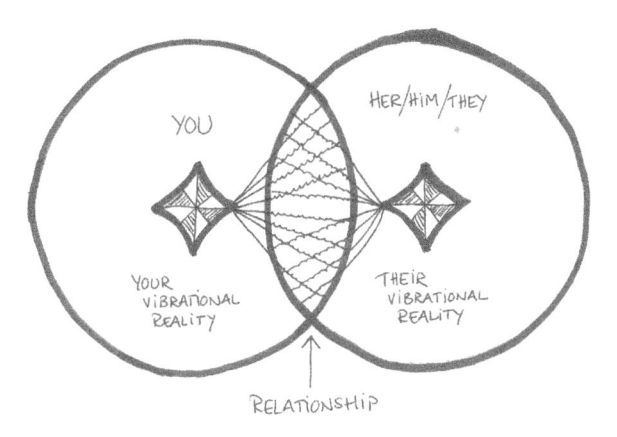

Imagine that we lay Diagram 2 on its side, and here we see the view from underneath drawn as the circle on the left. The diamond in the center is your framework of consciousness. The solid circle around you is the border of your vibrational reality. Everything you know is inside this border. You have zero Knowing of what is outside the border. The straight lines emanating from the diamond are your beliefs, emotions, thoughts, feelings and feedback from the world reflected by you and projected back into it again, plus all the adamantine sand dunes you're creating as you go along.

In relationship, our vibrational universe merges with another's vibrational universe. Those straight lines become energetic disturbance patterns as ripples of interference interrupts our view. Now we have a tangle that we need to navigate.

Without sovereign awareness, you will view the result of another's framework of consciousness, and the shared space between you, through your own lens and formulate interpretations based on that. This is how you create entire storylines with plot twists and side characters of villains and allies enacting complex roles to shape and influence you—and although you experience these as *really happening*, they are probably not *actually occurring*.

Simultaneously, even in the messiest relationships we are still unified in Christ, for nothing and nobody was created outside of him. With sovereign awareness, your dance with these complex stories become an intimate experience of development and communion, navigated with grace.

Diagram 8: Expansion By Mastery

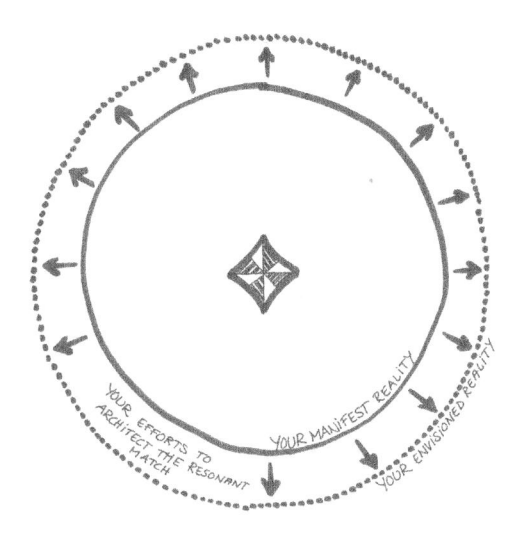

Diagram 3 has been laid on its side, and this is the view from below. The solid border around you is your manifest vibrational reality. The dotted line is your imaginable reality, representing all the ideas, dreams and aspirations you can perceive for yourself, even if they haven't come true yet. What lies outside the dotted line is beyond your wildest dreams, still accessible by you but not from the framework of your current Knowing. You are going to have to ascend up that scale to broaden the cone of awareness and come into yet higher Knowing.

Through conscious mastery you adjust the solid line as you create opportunities to become more resonant with the things that lie between the solid line and the dotted line. As new, imagined ideals come true, you expand what is manifest. You create your life's progress. This is energy intensive but rewarding, as you architect the circumstances that yield a resonant match for your ideals. Your discipline of mind and vibration, your steadfastness of vision and faith in your dreams, your personal persistence with knocking on doors, getting back up when you stumble, engaging in the deep inner work and thirsting for more knowledge and power, trying new practices and flexing new muscles: these are examples of your conscious efforts to move the solid line closer to the dotted line.

Diagram 9: Expansion By Surrender

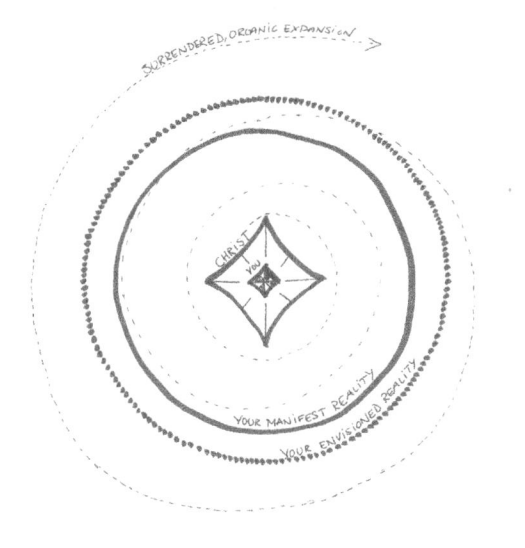

Diagram 6 has been laid on its side, and this is the view from below. You are the little diamond in the middle. You have placed yourself in alignment with the highest field of human consciousness. You have agreed with the creative paradigm that you have a personal Lord and Savior, and his diamond surrounds yours.

The solid border around you is your manifest vibrational reality.

The thick dotted line around you is your imaginable reality.

The thin dotted spiral emerging from the Christ diamond represents an organic unfolding as you allow him to expand your Life from within, piercing the thick border of your reality and transcending even your great envisioned realities, as his mercy dissolves the laws that bind you to what you already know. He lifts you again and again into surprising new possibilities and directions that you had never imagined.

In this model of expansion you easily travel beyond your wildest dreams, you spend less energy trying to architect vibrational resonance and have a lot more time to enjoy the ride. This is much more energy-efficient and exquisitely rewarding, but requires courage, trust and surrender.

Diagram 10: The Planes of Miracle-Work

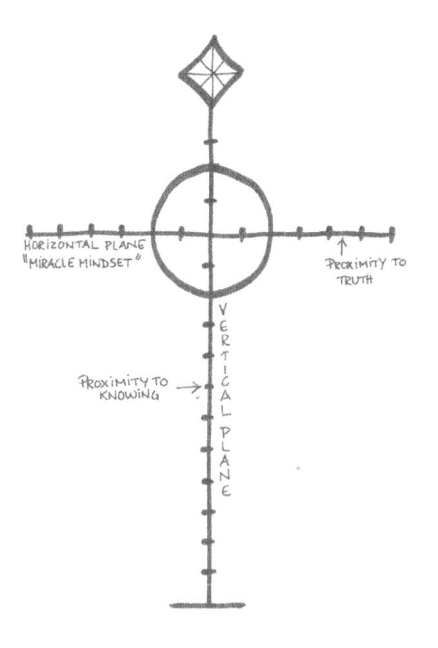

When creative energy is liberated from maintaining the <500 system realities, it needs somewhere to go. The great perk of following Christ is vastly increased authority to wield vibrational mastery, and thus also a responsibility to lend it to the greater plan. In higher logs of consciousness, miracle-work is a delightful responsibility.

This diagram represents the two planes of conscious miracle-work:

- **Horizontal** *(Where is my mind currently set, who am I being in relation to* *what-is?):*

Your log of consciousness is in harmony with miracle-mindedness (500+ on our scale). You choose Love. You embody powerful electromagnetism which is projected as an unmistakable radiance, and you have the authority to make signs and wonders occur. You see beauty everywhere, time bends and bizarre synchronicities bring unexpected solutions. Your touch is healing. Your mastery in relation to this plane is to maintain this mindset even in the face of challenges or pain.

- **Vertical** *(The God-drop, the instantaneous injection of grace or sudden formation of quantum potentiality):*

All possibilities are ever-present, so your mastery in relation to this plane is your ability to release resistance to the unknown and allow what is to be. Many miracles are experienced at the rock bottom of this scale of consciousness, not because we've mastered a certain mindset or energy technique but because we have released finally all resistance to the grace that was there anyway.

Sovereign miracle-work occurs at the convergence of mastery and surrender.

Diagram 11: I AM The Way, the Truth and the Life

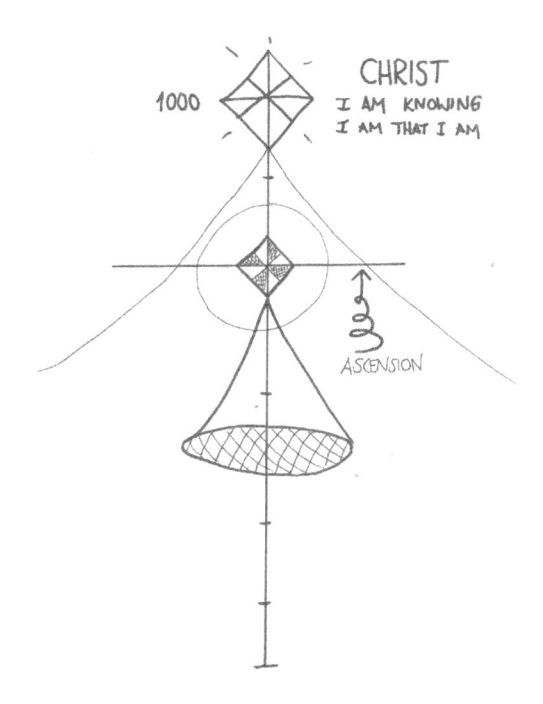

(handwritten diagram: labels "1000", "CHRIST — I AM KNOWING, I AM THAT I AM", and "ASCENSION")

If Christ is the perfect, embodied Knowing that *"I and My Father Are One"*, and you are entangled with him as intimately as you are all things, then your natural ascension will lead you into and through alignment with those coordinates, and you will Know yourself as 100% human and 100% divine, and you will also Know **We Are.**

The Choice is between an ascension lifestyle of climbing this imaginary ladder by yourself under the constant onslaught of counterforce in order to one day enter through the Holiest of Holies and finally have peace, or whether you allow the living Jesus Christ to be a daily portal who is opening to you regardless of where you find yourself on the scale this morning. Either way—to really Know the divine—your consciousness, energy and body must eventually be calibrated to Christ. This is your destiny—you can attempt to manufacture it if you like, but you are allowed to simply allow it.

I AM the Way and the Truth and the Life. No one comes to the Father except through me.

John 14:6

Let's imagine that these diagrams adjust the dial on your telescope, so no matter where you are in the wild and stormy desert of ever-moving sand dunes, you are always able to discern the ever-present oasis and call its existence into being.

The Masteries

The Sovereign Way, as a cosmology, is concerned only with the human journey. Let's leave celestial considerations in the archives of fantasy authors and esotericists. After all, God could snap His nebulous fingers and zip us all to the intergalactic ships of 11th dimensional transcendence if He wanted to, but yet every morning we wake up back here and now.

Real life is where life is occurring. Real life mastery is the subject in focus.

Examine me O Lord, and try me. Test my mind and my heart.

Psalm 26.2

The training you'll discover on the Sovereign Way is a sequential and also relational application of the following eight masteries. *How* you are developed in these masteries is between you and God, but each one is required for the most graceful experience of ascending life and service. Each mastery is used in relation with the others throughout your developing discipleship as you serve the great plan to transform the desert into an oasis. Each mastery is both a stage in your self-actualization journey, and also a lifelong tool to employ as the harmonies change in our ever-becoming universe. These masteries are present in all who truly follow the Sovereign Way, whether their lifestyles are simple or complex.

When you're a human being, mastery is not an end-goal but a constant dance and core ingredient in your experience of sovereign living. We flex our mastery muscles not to become enlightened, but to stay enlightened, and to spread enlightenment. This conscious effort is the commission for anyone whose goal is a human life of Love.

As you grow with the stages, your energy evolves naturally and effortlessly. Each realization brings a little more color, a little more grace, as your Life, Truth and Way of being all attune to love. Cohesive energy creates economies of scale and vast efficiencies. For example, instead of automatic survival behavior, you have automatic mercy and grace. Instead of architecting and constructing, you have allowing and tending. You become a different sort of being, projecting a different sort of Knowing, and the whole world is affected. In Christ, you are glorifying the Father through the Son by demonstrating the Spirit of Source in Substance.

The visceral experience of magic and miracle that follows as a result, is utterly opulent. Life becomes a high resolution experience, your vibration starts to shift on its own. You are not just an enlightened observer of a holographic matrix, but a living adventurer taking rich delight in the magnification of Love on every level, cherishing the effect God has on the world through your engagement with people, animals, nature, culture and even the structure of the world itself—and adoring its engagement with you.

Following are the eight masteries of the Sovereign Way, together engaging the core muscles that hold your sovereign poise, offering both a systemized approach to developing your mastery and also a delightfully liberated Way of Being.

The First Mastery: Remembering

You remember the Truth that transcends all time and space: there are three elements in the universe, Source, Spirit and Substance, and you are an individualized expression of that trinity with the authority to lovingly recreate any moment in space and time. You remember who you are and how you serve. You remember what matters most, and how to choose that. On the many occasions where you forget for a moment and go wandering in the desert, you quickly Know how to remember that your true life is anchored in an oasis, the very Kingdom among us and in our midst. You Know how to align your telescope to reveal the oasis in the sandstorm.

The Second Mastery: Recognizing

When you remember Truth, you can start recognizing what's not. You discern the difference between truth and story, self and personality, essence and structure, home and house. If you know the Truth, you recognize when you're not in it. This discernment sharpens like a sommelier's sensual knowing of a wine's fine layers of distinction. Falsehood can no longer hide from you. Structure can no longer seduce or enslave you. Your personality does not rule your Self. Your relationships all become more True.

The Third Mastery: Releasing

When you can recognize this, you can start effectively detaching from and releasing identities, structured paradigms and error, made up realities and cultural stories that once seemed so factual. Your forgiveness becomes super-effective as you embody more mercy. You forgive your own humanity and start sinking into deep self-acceptance. You notice that fewer triggers can steal your sovereignty. Thought patterns and behavioral habits fall away like an old toy outgrown by a child whose attention has shifted. Forgiveness is less of a process because bitterness, resentment and resistance dissolve when all emotions are allowed to be experienced and move through you like a gentle stream, being recalibrated by the endlessly loving wellspring.

The Fourth Mastery: Expansion

When you can effectively let go of patterns and systems that belong to outdated versions of you, then you can easily expand to increase your capacity for meeting the challenges of life. In fact, you become available for greater challenges which means far greater outcomes, adventures and impact. You handle overwhelm quickly and effectively as your mental and energetic processes integrate magical economies of scale. You can grow when you need to grow.

The Fifth Mastery: Genius

When you're ready for expansion and quantum spiritual growth, you need to hone your higher faculties and really condition the marvelous mind for processing faster and smoother as you enter more complex realities. You train your reason to be sovereign over your emotions as your true, timeless values become the basis for all decision-making. You are able to understand, synthesize and formulate new possibilities so your mission and impact increase.

The Sixth Mastery: Alchemy

By now you've cultivated great spiritual authority and you no longer spend volumes of creative energy trying to survive. Now you must learn how to wield that massively enhanced vibrational influence. So you discover that alchemy is the infusion of essence into structure, merging the philosopher's stone with the elixir of life, reunifying Spirit and Substance in order to allow a greater outcome. You learn to turn lead into gold as your energetic presence gains power.

The Seventh Mastery: Adventuring

You learn to let the Sovereign hand of God be the momentum and direction for all your spiritual authority that you've cultivated so far in the Sovereign Way. True surrendered adventuring, not some romantic ideal of going on a thrilling trip from time to time, but learning how to truly realign into God's flowstate over and over again in this maelstrom of apocalyptic energy. This is an advanced mastery that dissolves the grip of egoic, cultural, societal, economic systems that influence the direction of your vibrational command. It also trains you across systems of governance, calibrating you to align to the timeless spiritual laws even as they manifest differently at ascending logs of consciousness and different dimensions of experience.

The Eighth Mastery: Devotion.

With this freedom, your love spills into a devotional expression of service and discipleship, the delight of true participation with Life and the fulfillment of applying yourself to the world in an ultimate Knowing of your belonging here. This devotion, in its unique form through you, is the movement that births the Kingdom of God as His Sovereign essence is woven through your words and works, and you perform signs and wonders that defy the natural laws. You are a miracle-maker.

The creation waits in eager expectation for the revelation of the Sons of God. For the creation was subjected to futility, not by its own will, but by the One who subjected it in hope that the creation itself will be set free from its bondage to decay and brought into the glorious freedom of the Children of God. We know that the whole of creation has been groaning together in the pains of childbirth until the present time. Not only that, but we ourselves, who have the firstfruits of the Spirit, groan inwardly as we wait eagerly for our adoption as Sons, the redemption of our bodies.

Romans 8:19-23

Let's use the term Sovereign Master, to define an apostle of Christ. With your finely calibrated telescope and these twelve masteries you are authorized to be completely free, safely moved by the wind anywhere across the desert or in the oasis, transforming all you touch to glory.

The First Mastery: Remembering
"I And My Father Are One"

Your awakening began with the *whoomph* of remembrance that a bigger Truth was waiting on the other side of that imaginary veil. You set off on quest to truly know who you are, to embody the delicious mystery and magic of Knowing. You discovered that God is real and that Spirit is very much alive, and suddenly everything burst into power and meaning.

But it's easy enough to Remember when we're sitting in the lotus position with the wind chimes gently tinkling in our enlightenment cave near the pond, embraced by the gentle hum of bees tending to the rose blossoms in the Oasis. It's tempting to stay in the cave and chant so we can just be of service to humanity through our exquisite vibration. It's much harder Remembering when we're out there tending to the world, actually participating with the turbulence of collective becoming. The Sovereign Way of life is a surrendered, loving devotion through extraordinary experiences of discovery and artisanship, thus receiving and sharing the Love of God in everyday life. That means Remembering is a daily game.

We have rich and complex stories of the human experience woven throughout the Bible to remind us that across the ages, even with spiritual law clearly engraved in handy tablets and scribed in plenty of scrolls, we remain vulnerable to Life. Despite our best intentions to move on into the holy land with our true spiritual liberation of being free to Love—we can't help interrupting our mission by dancing with energy fields of lust, greed, hate, anger, gluttony, pride and sloth. Energy begets energy when it's left unchecked, so from generation to generation we forget our true nature and identify instead with patterns and systems of being—both out there in the world and in our own innermost chambers. Culture, law, trauma, misunderstanding, expectation and projections become the narratives of how we know ourselves. We are a living Story.

Since we are so vulnerable to forget—we need to be able to Remember. So Remembering is not a one-time spiritual awakening event in our soul's progression but an ongoing mastery that we get to practice as we mature.

So, when you're lost in analysis and judgment about which way to go, take a breath. When you're worrying about which side of the government is controlling you, whether Big Pharma is responsible for the downfall of man, which religion is the most enlightened, and whether your family will ever understand how wise you are and how brainwashed they are by the villains of the world, pause for a moment. When you're agonizing over how much money you think you need to make in order to live the lifestyle you think you need to live to prove your divine abundance, outlining the steps and happenings that must occur for your manifestation to be realized, rejecting divine gifts that land outside that outline... Well, then you can bring yourself back to true power with a quick *"Hang on, wait a minute! Ah! I remember!*

I Know Who I AM.

Remembering Who I AM is the basic spiritual mastery in all religions. Always position God first. It is the fundamental, foundational mastery upon which all your other ascension and growth is based. You'll go nowhere in the Kingdom if you're not first in it. So, let's examine who you really are, and enhance that Knowing in your energy field.

God is Love, and whoever abides in Love abides in God, and God abides in him.

1 John 4:16

The Trinity

It's True that you're a co-creator with Source. Your vibrational mastery genuinely can command the fabric of particularized reality, and your personal magic is essentially therefore your dance with the Holy Spirit through creation. So, as you develop your higher spiritual gifts and are granted greater authority over your manifest dominion, your magnetism dissolves false realities and commands new ones as the presence of Spirit through the Substance of creation. This is the alchemy that creates the signs and wonders others can witness as manifest evidence of God's Love.

When you integrate a more and more cohesive mastery of universal Truth and endless Love, you are granted increasing command of energy and element. Some might call this "divine inheritance" as we grow into the image of our Father. The fundamental dynamic can be understood as Trinity.

DIAGRAM 1: Trinity

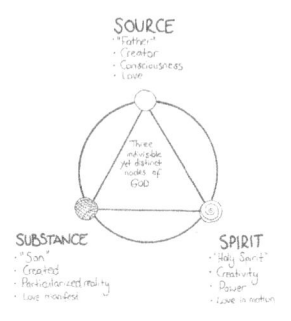

SOURCE
- "Father"
- Creator
- Consciousness
- Love

SUBSTANCE
- "Son"
- Created
- Particularized reality
- Love manifest

SPIRIT
- "Holy Spirit"
- Creativity
- Power
- Love in motion

Three indivisible yet distinct nodes of God

For the sake of this thought experiment, let's say there are only three elements in the universe.

- **Source**. This is Love, the formless seed of consciousness, the ineffable name of all Knowing, the singular beginning and end. The Father.

- **Spirit**. The unifying field of movement and relation, Spirit is Love-in-action, God-in-motion, the universal life force energy that enlightens and renews, and the Word that extends into and through what-is as the omnipresence of Love moving between us. The Holy Spirit.

- **Substance**. This is the form of God, the only begotten true blueprint of time, space and energy that manifests the particularized experience of structured reality. The Son.

So Trinity is:

- Father—Holy Spirit—Son, or
- Love—Power—Manifestation, or
- Creator—Creativity—Created, or
- Consciousness—Vibration—Form.

God is all these three expressions at once, distinctly individual yet indivisible. So this trinity is what all things are, because God is all there is.

There is one Body and one Spirit, just as you were called to one hope when you were called; one Lord, one faith, one baptism; one God and Father of all, who is over all and through all and in all.

Ephesians 4:4-6

All About Substance.

Let's begin by looking at *stuff*, **the primordial place where God becomes manifest:** *actually* **realized and** *occurring* **in form.**

This is the piece of the puzzle that we're most familiar with. This corner of the diagram represents the elements of particularized reality. Even though we are all One, separate configurations of potential become possible when infinity arranges itself into finite shapes. A nice Camembert cheese is different from neon light bulbs, which are different from the ponderosa pine trees of the Rocky Mountains. That difference is possible because of particles. Bits and bytes of God which form themselves around His magnetic intention like metal shavings around a magnet. So this element of God is manifest as particle reality.

We'll call these particles of infinity "*adamantine particles*". As the simplest particle, this is the first building block of the universe: the God Particle. It *creates* mass, resulting in all other possible particles. Adamantine particles are suspended absolutely everywhere, like the hydrogen atoms in air and sunlight, except far preceding hydrogen. It is the original manna, the sovereign substance that can become anything at any time.

Fun fact: The word adamant means firm. *Adam* is Hebrew for Man. These particles are the first firm actualization of God and are therefore literally His Body.

Imagine the dunes of the Sahara, made of an infinite number of sand particles undulating and rolling, forming shapes and releasing them again. No dune remains the same for more than a breath of wind. Imagine that Source is the *intention and decision* to move sand dunes, Spirit is the breath of wind that *connects and carries* the sand particles, and Substance is the gathering and shifting *formation* of these particles into the unique and extraordinary golden sand structures that we see in the vast desert.

Consciousness chooses structure, Spirit moves structure, and adamantine particles are the Substance that make up structure.

Remember: Don't be afraid of structure or declare it as less holy than essence. Just know what it is and understand that structure is mortal so it has no command over your life. Essence is immortal, and that's where true command comes from. Since Spirit and Substance are indivisible, no structure is completely devoid of divine essence.

For example, imagine for a moment that you experience a sudden business failure and you become homeless. To survive you need to Know the essence of Home. You need to Know the difference between a home and a house, so when there is no structure for you to have a home inside, you still have Home. By Knowing the essence of Home, which is an immortal essence, adamantine particles will quickly reassemble to recreate House, which is a structure in which the essence of Home can abide. With this magic, you might go from living in a fancy mansion to an old, abandoned barn, to a million-dollar mountain cabin, to an off-grid tent, to a Victorian terrace in an industrial city and finally to your dream cottage by the beach, all within the space of a few years. *The actual energies and occurrences that lead to the house miracles are just the sand dunes shifting with the breath of Spirit. Substance is free to rearrange itself by loving command in order to accommodate the deepening essence of Home.*

So you are these three elements, a totality of three recapitulated as One, and the extent to which you embody this **Knowing** is your log of consciousness. Your log of consciousness determines the power of your creative electromagnetism:

- Love seeds intention and creates a command.

- Love moves according to this sovereign command.

- Love takes form according to this movement.

Love commands Love to move Love. Ergo, the more Love you embody, the greater your spiritual authority to create and improve the sand dunes.

All About Source.

The Source of Love is the almighty creator, the Father, the One God. It's irrelevant how many different ways we try to understand the divine or how many times we divide Him into sub-divine deities, there is still only One Supreme Source.

That Source is to creation like the sun is to life on Earth. From that love you are emanated, like a ray of light, you are an individualized entity of His infinite Love. You are known and always will be known by the nature of your Love. Love is the essence of your true beingness—not something you do, or give, receive or don't receive, it's not an energy or a substance. Love is *who* you are, and that is what makes it unconditional. It's both your origin and your destiny, and you cannot escape the Truth that you're loved and lovable forever.

> *Beloved, let us love one another, for love is from God, and whoever loves has been born of God and knows God.*
>
> *1 John 4:7*

So Knowing is the activating seed of creation and Love is the true flavor of consciousness.

In this book we will most often use the masculine pronoun for God.

We agree the Holiest of Holies is above gender. But even as the Alpha and Omega beyond definition, God is also the manifestation of universal dynamics. In general conversation we choose to understand these in masculine and feminine qualities. The distinction between these qualities helps us relate to the eternally balancing nature of our process reality. Let's organize masculine and feminine like this:

- The most basic masculine manifestation is that of Source. The seed, the will, the penetrating extension of potential and the ejaculating expression of reality. The characteristics of this node of creation are firm, steadfast, constant, dependable—He is awesome in strength and creative potential.

- The most basic feminine manifestation is that of Life. The dynamic power of creation in incubation, manifestation, nurture, death, decay and resurrection. We see Her in Nature, but She is not limited to Earth. The characteristics of this node of creation are ever-changing, interactional and connective, adaptive and malleable, environmental, and deeply allowing.

There is a divine structure to the relation of masculine dominance and feminine submission which has nothing to do with patriarchy. This has been twisted in lower logs of consciousness to justify destructive behaviors in the world, in intimate family life, and in our own inner chambers to make creative judgments about how infinite Love should or shouldn't manifest in gender and relationship. Luckily, universal balance does not hang on the conclusions of our juvenile reasoning. In the higher dimensions of creative understanding, respect for male and female dynamics in their holy distinctions allow constancy to be sovereign over change, Truth to reign above Story, Creator to precede both Creativity and the Created, and choice to rule over experience. In this respect for these creative dynamics, the Mother God will always obey the Father God.

In each individual strand of God just like you, there is a male and female aspect to your modus operandi. This indwelling potential can either be in balance or out of balance. A true marriage of you and Christ yields a balance of feminine and masculine energy. This has nothing to do with gonads and chromosomes, or the men and women in your life, which are made of manifest particles and therefore structures that must always submit to Spirit. Instead, this balance is about the relationship between what is firm and steadfast and what is malleable and changing.

Often what we need most when we commune personally with God is His steadfast and firm direction, His constancy of provision, and His immovable Love. Abba, as Jesus called Him, is safe. In a world and life that is ever-changing, Our Father is the dependable presence that never withdraws our worthiness. His tender but firm presence as we meet the challenges on our Way is an assurance that frees us to truly engage with the shifting tempers of Life.

Look at Diagram 2, The Sovereign Model of Human Consciousness. Since you are the three nodes of creation recapitulated as one, your consciousness presides over your energy field which presides over your manifest body and life. Your diamond consciousness is the sum of the data points you've made agreement with, ranging from *"I am worthy of receiving the grace of God", "I am allowed to shape my experience", "I am known and cherished by my omnipresent Father"* all the way down to *"I can't do that, that isn't real, I'm not worthy, I'm not ready, everyone else is an idiot, black lives matter slightly less than white lives, nobody understands me, they're out to get me, you can't find a good man around here, the media is corrupt",* etc.

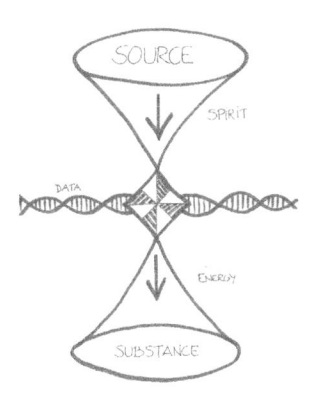

This is why we congregate into cultures or world views, religions and ideologies: we make agreement with each other on how to interpret the relationship between God and the world, Truth and Story. We create a new shared blueprint and creation occurs from that collective framework. Within those cultures there are even further subsets of consciousness, little worlds of communal stories, traumas and errors. These connect with resonating ideas within individuals and larger groups to become *thought-forms* with corresponding energy fields that magnetize together to build intricate systems of creation which direct our decision-making. Without the true intention of Source these sand dunes have no innate power to sustain themselves—they require the buy-in of human choice, and the creative investment of human energy. Our cognitive dissonance and the Law of Attraction work perfectly together to perpetuate our little sub-bubbles of cultural reality that are always a distortion of the original blueprint, the Christ manifested at the beginning of time. We therefore experience what seems like a separation between these false realities and the real Love of God. As long as the attention of the decision-makers is on these thought-forms, however great or small, the electromagnetic energy field persists, the work of these systems carry on, and manifestation continues in the shape of these sand dunes.

Luckily, these realities are all mortal. As soon as creative consciousness releases agreement with these realities, the thought-forms disintegrate. These realities are like vapor.

None of us are immune from creating falsely, because Life is relational—we're doing it together and we will make agreement with each other to keep creating stories about what's *really happening*. Since creation is *always occurring*, you are always experiencing a feedback loop from the world of form, which energetically influences your Knowing. The great error of the human condition is that we train the lens of our telescope onto the adamantine shapes that form as a result of our unconscious commands. We look at the sand dunes we've made and believe them to be gods.

I KNOW I AM the independent woman who must do it all myself.

I KNOW that good things only come from blood, sweat and tears.

I KNOW it is wrong for me to want to be saved.

I KNOW that people in this geography aren't as enlightened as people in that geography.

I KNOW that nobody understand me.

We see that it is fact, so we claim it as reality. Contrary to popular belief, your creative power is not subject to the words you're using or the energy you're saying them with. It's subject to the Knowing behind the words. Through our framework of consciousness, we command the sand particles of reality to form corresponding dunes. We see the birth of our creation and we say: *"Ah, see? There, I knew it. Told you so, didn't I? This is how it is."* This can make it hard to discern what realities are structures that can be transformed, and what realities are essential, universal Truths.

All About Spirit.

But this whole problem is solved when we realize that Spirit is in all things, including in the manifest evidence of all our misery.

Science is great. One of the most wonderful breakthroughs of modern physics was the discovery of the unified field by Albert Einstein. Here came a mathematical formulation to prove the omnipresence of God's ever renewing and restoring Spirit of creativity. Every development in modern physics would have been impossible if not for that breakthrough in consciousness, and from here other great scientific minds were able to prove the probabilistic nature of quantum phenomena—the basis of our understanding of the universe as a malleable hologram space and time that bends to the mind of the observer. Knowing that Light is a wave dispensed evenly that collapses into a specific particle when observed, we begin to respect ourselves more as sovereign observers. We ask "*how am I observing this?*", and we marvel as we watch the unified Spirit breathe new Life that carries adamantine particles into the extraordinary shapes that we perceive as real.

Matthew and I were walking together somewhere in the desert when we passed a dead rat on the side of the dusty road. It was in advanced stages of decay. The stench of rot was pungent and there were crawling maggots worming their way in and out of the gaping holes in the carcass, the bass hum from the buzzing of flies like a morbid undertone of death.

I was appalled. "This is repugnant," I bemoaned. "Why hasn't the council cleaned this up, this is a hazard to our children. It's a revolting travesty, that's what it is! It wasn't like this back when I was a girl, this would have been taken care of immediately but ever since those politicians came into power we've had this type of disrespectful negligence in the county sanitation department, blah, blah, blah." I saw only the proof of what a dirty world we live in, how things are all falling apart in this generation, and I even conjured villains to fight in my mind, energy and body. The fight was instantly real as my stress levels rocketed, shifting the chemical composition in my body when adrenaline and cortisol flooded my gut, inflaming my nerves and tissues, and recalibrating my thought patterns to a lower system of narrative chatter about what was going on. Every criticism triggered another. Everything I saw confirmed: *I was in Hell.*

Matthew witnessed the same actualized occurrence: a rat was indeed decaying. He smelled the same stench. He was aware of the same biological consequences of bacteria. But what he experienced was the Spirit, a constant presence of changing form, the miraculous way Nature reclaims all structures and recycles the elements back into possibility for renewal and growth. He marveled how what had once been adamant flesh and bone was now becoming nourishment and fertilizer to be delivered by a river for brand new creation in the oasis. In his wonder, happy hormones flooded his system, and *he was in Heaven.*

That Spirit is present in the dead rat whether you perceive it or not, but in your Knowing of the presence of Spirit you have the power to release your conscious hold on the shape you've created and allow the particles of infinity to take a new form. The authority with which you observe *Heaven* allows an energy transference which recalibrates the Substance and elevates the log of *its* consciousness and energetic attractor field. The Substance of the rat becomes elevated and sanctified, nourishing the earth yet more deeply. The rat is one example—the foulest villain and evilest patriarchy is another. **Do you have the authority to love the very worst of creation, and liberate it?**

Now the Lord is the Spirit, and where the Spirit of the Lord is, there is freedom.

2 Corinthians 3.17

There is but one spirit. Spirit is in all things, around all things, with all things and of all things. There is no place where Spirit is absent, so everything is actually free to change. Spirit is not a place away from Earth, Spirit isn't somewhere we go in meditation or prayer, it isn't an esoteric library we channel or download information from, it isn't a realm in the mysterious hereafter, hidden behind a veil. **Spirit is not**

divisible from manifest creation. Spirit is here. *This is* Spirit.

Spirit is the unity of us all, the unity of heaven and earth. The motion and power through Spirit in all things is the reason prayer *works* and why energy healing can be experienced remotely. Therefore, in Spirit, we live one shared family life in a journey of common awareness and discovery—either enlightening and uplifting or darkening and entropic, depending on the Way you go.

> *There are different kinds of gifts, but the same Spirit distributes them. There are different kinds of service, but the same Lord. There are different kinds of working, but in all of them and in everyone it is the same God at work.*
>
> *1 Corinthians 12:4-6*

The source of human suffering is an identity structuring itself as separate from God. Self-amputated from the Love that we are by a veil thinner than the moment at midnight between yesterday and tomorrow. Forgotten from the Knowing that Love commands the universe, this identity must maintain systems of forced energy to keep the sand dunes of its creations alive. When you are in a state of separation you must serve structure, in fact you need structured systems to mimic harmony in order to feel any sort of balance. When your identity is in a state of separation, structure will always seek to master you and you will succumb to its manipulation, seduction and control. It will rule over you with carrot and stick illusions of order and reward. It will loom over you with absolute consequences of cause and effect, creating a constant deficit in your time, money, space and joy. It will trap you in the litigious workings of karma and threaten to enslave you until you've solved all the problems of your manifest world. You have nothing to rely on but your own feeble control over the actualizations constantly occurring in your field. You must rush to build the correct sand dunes in a stormy desert with your little red bucket and spade. This is the leverage that structure has over you. As long as you seek to control life or think that you can, you will grovel for structure. The tragedy of that pursuit is that you will never control Life. All structures must fall. As our ancestral civilizations before us discovered, if you identify in structure, you are doomed. You will never be whole and complete. You will never truly be home.

When you Remember yourself to be in Christ, structure becomes a humble and willing servant. Love commands the one Spirit, and the Spirit moves the adamantine particles of the created universe. As sovereign, you can still the storm no matter how wild it seems, because you have the power to choose from Love. You are Love, *you are Knowing you are Love* and therefore you have great magnetic, spiritual authority to shift the sand dunes of creation with your breath of true, loving Word. *Things change*, and renewal is always possible.

Now a moment of stillness,

poise,

in the void

before a choice is made

again,

to Be Love.

Genesis

Since nothing was created outside of Christ, who was **with** God in the beginning, we can remember a lot about our true nature by going back to that very beginning. So where better to explore who we really are, than in the book of Genesis? Genesis means *the beginning*. It's the first book of the Bible, an origin story.

In the beginning, when God created the Heavens and the Earth, the earth was a formless void and darkness covered the deep.

Then a Wind of God swept across the waters.

Then God said, Let There Be Light.

And God saw the Light and Knew that the Light was Good.

And God separated the light from the darkness.

God called the light day and the darkness he called night.

And there was evening, and morning, the first day.

Genesis 1:1-5

Oh, how I love thinking about the formless void of darkness that is quantum potentiality, at the very first exhale. Spirit moved across the face of the waters, says Genesis in a poetic imagery of the dynamism in this node of God. Your potential is formless, so far undefined, but your spiritual essence belongs to God long before you've declared yourself one thing or another.

So the first thing we discover about ourselves is that **I ALREADY ALWAYS AM.**

"Then God said **Let** There Be Light, and there was Light." Formation begins immediately when an intention is seeded into the unformed void, and Spirit allows it. He chose, He allowed and His choice took effect. There was Light.

"And God saw the Light and Knew that it was Good." Consciousness declared creation, and then experienced that same creation. He saw it, experienced it, knew it. He made agreement with it. He knew it as being GOOD indeed.

So we discover about ourselves that **I AM LIGHT** and the third conclusion we must logically draw is that **I AM GOOD.**

This was when He separated light from darkness, as duality was intended and allowed. With duality came *process*: evening and morning on the first day and every day thereafter.

So we know that our nature is light and dark in process. From unformed void, to shape and distinction, and back to unformed void again in a constant rhythmic process of quantum becoming. So the most basic characteristics we can remember about our truest nature are:

I Already Always AM.

I AM Light.

I AM Good.

I AM Becoming.

Let's play with Light for a moment, imagining the wave function of light and what happens between photon particles. In the 1920's we collectively took a quantum leap in our spiritual awareness as giant thought leaders like Einstein, Davisson and Germer exposed the bizarre characteristic about Light that it is both wave and a particle. This distinction is important because a wave can be spread out in space as probability dispensed through everything. At the moment of decision, the whole probability field collapses to a particular point. Now Light isn't a potential anymore, it's a thing.

It acts a bit like a heartbeat, pulsing from wave to particle to wave again, as if all of the fabric of the universe is God's very heartbeat rhythm of poise to reality to poise to reality—so Truth and Story exist together in the same space at the same time—always in relation with each other and always and in process. Not only that, but all time and motion cease at the point where matter or energy vibrates at the speed of Light. In that poised condition all probability is suspended in a superposition state. Anything can happen.

And because Light, the photon fabric of what you are, is both wave and particle at the same time, you are always in the potential for miraculous transformations of time, space and matter, and you are always the storytelling mouthpiece of God as you command the sand dunes of creation. Just as God said *Let There Be Light* and there was Light, so too are your declarations instantaneous, at least in potential. But remember, as created beings we are locked in process—morning and evening not just on the first day but all our days. Our Life is process and so our declarations may be made true instantaneously in the quantum mind, but spacetime reality does require that we see those declarations in form and make agreement with them. You need to choose the sand dune, or it will instantly blow into a new shape:

God didn't just create the Light, he also *saw* the Light and *knew that it was Good*. This is the engagement that makes your experience real, and takes your wish-upon-a-new-moon, creative vision-casting out of spiritual fantasy and into the very real, lived experience of being you.

So God created this fabric of reality where all things are both manifest and potential at the same time, so nothing is created that can't be recreated. And what does He do with it? He forms elements: earth, wind, fire, air, ether and goodness knows what else—we're still discovering all kinds of stuff. Then He brings those elements together and creates life abundantly! Unimaginable diversity, trees of every kind bearing fruit with seed in it—an abundance that has its own innate ability to recreate itself.

From there He created inquisitive consciousness, a self-knowing sentience with a great light to rule the day and a lesser light to rule the night. Now there is sovereignty and dominion both in what is created and what is potential. He went on, combining that sentience with the life He'd prepared earlier, and now we've got swarms of animals, entities and creatures that Know themselves in ascending capacity.

And finally, His *piece de resistance!* Adamantine particles have now formed basic elemental building blocks which have combined to become self-perpetuating abundant life, and combined with sentience to become self-knowing entities, and are finally combined with spiritual sovereignty to become the demi-gods of consciousness!

"Let us make humankind in our image, and let them have sovereign dominion over all Life", He said in a big, booming voice with His long, white beard wafting against a cosmic backdrop.

Remember, in Genesis 1:26 God says "*Let US*". So even though so far in the story we only see the God character as One, He is already knowing Himself as relational. There is not just **I AM**, there is also an **US**. This relationality is inherent in who *we are* and we cannot escape it. *Your sorrow is my sorrow. Your happiness is my happiness.*

And then, in Genesis 1:27:

> *God created humankind in His image.*
>
> *In the image of God He created them.*
>
> *Male and female He created them.*
>
> *And God blessed humankind*
>
> *and gave us dominion over everything He had created.*
>
> *He saw everything He had made,*
>
> *and saw that it was GOOD.*

Everything He made is good. God is male and female as we know these dynamics, and in His image we are male and female. Adam was created first—the first manifestation of God as a sentient being, and then Eve (which is Hebrew for Life) was born from that structure, from the "ribcage" of the human. The adamant authority of human consciousness thus precedes and presides over our malleable Life. And this led to what mythology calls "The Fall". Since our consciousness has dominion over Life, and our creative declarations are instantaneous, and Light potential collapses into particle at the moment of action, and our experience of Life is a causal response to our consciousness, then what a disaster that we used our demi-godlike free will to *choose* to embody the Knowing of good *and* evil!

Now I AM Knowing both what is good and what is not-good.

This is the first time in the Bible we come across not-good as a potential. So far everything He created He knew as Good. There we were, in a field of infinite abundance, possibility and life force, and we're given the assignment to till and keep the garden growing there in the oasis in the vast desert of cosmic possibility. We are directed to nourish what is *good*.

But do not eat of the tree of the knowledge of good and evil, God says in Genesis 2.17.

For on that day you shall die.

But Life tempted you and you ate it. Now you are no longer seeing that *"It Is Good"*. Now you are seeing that *"this is good and that is evil"*. So, in the human condition, this duality is what you're engaging with, creating from, experiencing, believing. What is pure potential has collapsed from its superstate position into something you'll call good and something else you'll call evil. You've breathed life into the sand dunes of creation which have arranged themselves into horrible structures. You have much to navigate now, many decisions to make, and many reflections to view that cause you to see yourself as "not good." Suddenly your innocence is exposed, and now there is room for shame.

In Genesis 3:14 God explains the energetic consequences of a dualistic framework of consciousness where, instead of being 100% free to be, you are making judgments about the correctness of Life as you organize and sort out what is good and what is not good. Separation is immediate, it happens at the speed of Light. Self-expelled from the oasis, now you are wandering in the deserts of structure toiling with your buckets and spades trying to make the sand dunes of your Life work for you. Not only that, but the experience of creation is much more painful. You can no longer create by innocent delight and curiosity since you're wrapped up in outlining the correct creative process based on what is good and evil as far you're concerned. Contraction and expansion become agonizing and you must suffer to grow.

So now we have chosen conscious participation with duality and we are living the energetic consequences of that. Even with the greatest intentions, we want to save the world and rid it of evil—and in doing so we create what we speak, and we see it and we know that it is evil. But then, in Genesis 3:20, before God sent Adam and Eve out of the Garden of Eden, He made them "garments". He beclothed them to protect them from the elements. We are 100% protected and equipped to make our way back home. All our hardship is temporary and fleeting if we have the mastery of Remembering.

The rest of Genesis is incredible, enjoy it in your own time. It is the story of lineage, and the passing of faith, culture and paradigm from generation to generation. It's a story of covenant—making agreement with God about how Life is going to be, the expectations you place on creative possibility, and how you show up both to what manifests and to the call of what is emerging. Knowing your human lineage is an act of deep honor for where you have come from and how your diamond has been shaped by decision and engagement over time. When you understand the momentum that has been set for your Life you can know where the flow is. Water flows easily where the riverbed has already been carved. But it is also a liberation of your identity: if you know your lineage then you also know what influences you're creatively vulnerable to and you are free to choose, at the speed of Light, to be liberated of those. To break the riverbanks and set a new course. You can do that when you're aware that a new choice can be made:

We are the ones who get dementia and arthritis because aging sucks and that's just life.

Becomes: **I AM Always Healed and Healing.**

We are the ones who must avoid pain and death at all costs.

Becomes: **I AM free to live.**

We are the ones who work hard and never quit.

Becomes: **I AM free to work and play in devotion.**

We are the ones who must suffer for progress and who are persecuted and despised for being who we are.

Becomes: **I AM free to change and to love in my unique way.**

We can't do that, that's not possible, that's not how it works, nobody's going to forgive your debts or magically repair your cellular system.

Becomes: **Let there be Light!**

We are ones who are working towards a better world.

Becomes: **That oasis is here now, I see the Light and I know that it is Good.**

So Remembering this Truth is one part of the mastery, and Remembering that you need Remembering is another part. When we need to reconstruct our lives, our identities, our businesses, our relationships, our communities—we begin in poise. And then we choose. The void is no longer and the pinprick point of Light has been found and locked in: I see the Light, and it is Good.

The Stained Glass Window

Let's look at the core principles again, and this time arrange them into the Sovereign Model of Human Consciousness (Diagram 2).

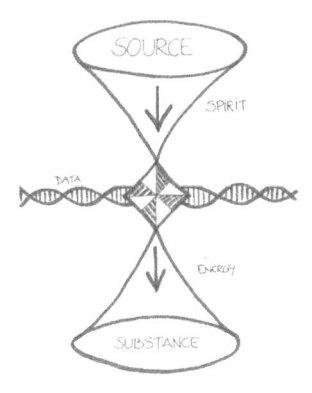

God is real. He is all knowing and all loving.

The very first expression of God is the primordial movement of Spirit.

Just as a raindrop forming in a rain cloud is of the same essence as all other raindrops and the cloud itself, so too is the human consciousness an individualized expression of that *spirit*ual field of Knowing. In the most simplistic way of describing it, a strand of that essential spirit is drawn out and focused into one laser point. You.

If God is all-knowing, there is a very unique aspect of this Knowing that is what *You* Know.

The human consciousness is, by its nature, fractured. Not really broken, but diamond faceted like a prism in a way that it refracts the purity of essential Light into different values, like sunlight refracting in the raindrop and displaying a rainbow—a variety of energetic value. Good *and* evil. Whatever story we use to illustrate this fundamental characteristic of the human experience, we all agree that in a field of infinite potentiality and Oneness, we have the ability to observe a variety and place judgements on that variety.

This is good, this is better, that is very bad.

Those judgments become paradigms, stories of what is true about Life written in the many facets of that diamond consciousness. Compounded traumas become fear-based songs singing from deep within our DNA, a spiral staircase between potential Heaven and actual Earth.

The creative Spirit moves through your diamond and its many stories, and takes on the color and texture of what you have decreed is true about you and reality. It condenses as energy projected into the holographic quantum soup, or the matrix as some call it. In this book let's call it *Life*. This energy, made of all kinds of subtle frequencies like brainwave, heart wave, and electromagnetic emission, is what we'll call the biofield. You declare an energetic decision about what-is, and Light collapses from wave to particle around you. Particularized reality, which is made of the same Substance as the rest of the raincloud, arranges itself in response to that energy. In this dynamic magnetism you dance with Life though trauma, reconciliation, adventuring, discovering, forgetting, and remembering as the sand dunes change shape to the command of your singing consciousness.

Imagine the diamond as a stained glass window in the alabaster cathedral cresting the great pond in the oasis. The sunlight is pure and whole on the other side of window, and when it shines through the window it highlights all those stories embedded in the glass. It doesn't matter how dark and dramatic the stories are that are outlined in the window, the sunlight will never be compromised in any way, it will never stop shining on the window, and is always whole and good. But the sunlight does give life to the stories of the window as they project onto the flagstone floor. Vibrant colors, coded images, characters, deities and settings from the grotesque to the sublime, all are beamed by the wave of sunlight, illuminating the dust particles and telling the stories of the window to the structured foundation of your Life.

When you try to change what you experience without Remembering the source of these projected images, you're just scrubbing the floor. You can easily spend your whole life in therapy, on medication, or as a "spiritual seeker", trying to clean things up. Scrubbing and washing, moving the flagstones around, getting a new rug to cover up the mess—but unless you transform the stained glass window those stories will always project and be experienced by you in some form.

I AM the one who must avoid pain and death at all costs.

I AM the one who must suffer for progress and who is persecuted and despised for being who I am.

I AM the one who must carry the pain of the world.

The story is made real in its projection, and your job is to Remember the Truth that transcends all these deepfake imageries and hyperreal projections. When it comes to the transformation you need to undergo to truly live the sovereign life, you'll significantly increase your success rate by directing your awareness into your framework of consciousness first, before you try scrubbing the floor, and letting new revelations govern your energy field and your molecular structure. Let the Son transform the window so the story on the floor is transformed.

> ***I will open the windows of heaven for you. I will pour out blessings so great you won't have enough room to take it in!***
>
> ***Malachi 3:10***

In your own story, during the first experiences of spiritually conscious Remembering you began seeing magic everywhere, collecting personal evidence that the mind is sovereign over energy and reality can easily be bent. Ridiculously good luck often follows these early experiments, like a song of encouragement from the "car park angel" who always directs you to the best spot! Many will stagnate at this stage of awakening as the Ego takes the reins again, addicted to the dopamine exhilaration of seeing personal magic come real, and conscious manifestation becomes an obsession. *"Look everyone! I manifested another red car! The Law of Attraction is still working for me!"*

And this is Good. But for a sovereign player in the great commission this early streak of luck doesn't need to last long because there are more important lessons to learn. After this stage and for the rest of your life you will use Remembering to pivot your awareness away from the glamorous and illusory perceptions reflected by an actualized fabric. You will take delight in the world, but your devotion is fulfilled in the innate, essential Truth. Cleaning the window, not the floor. The stories in the window never crystallize but constantly change, and new realities—even the hard ones—are projected, seen and Known as *Good*.

Oh, I see that my mistake has cost me a great opportunity, and this person is exploiting the result. It feels horrible, my stomach is nauseous and my thoughts are racing. But I Remember who I AM, and that I AM Sovereign in this moment. I AM free. I see this thing happening, and Know that this is Good. I allow it to Become what it is becoming, and as I participate righteously I experience the goodness. I share this Goodness.

As the Bible shows us, Life as a human is complex and comprehensive. Hardship is a part of the game for a framework of consciousness that knows good and evil. Sooner or later, agony manifests again in your life's circumstances like your relationships or finances. There's agony in your behavior like poor choices and reaction, and in the body like disease or inflammation. It's in the biofield like your unprocessed emotions or energetic disturbances, demons, entities and empathically absorbed solar flares. Agony resides in your mental health like anxiety and depression, or in your identity like a compartmentalized spirit, or a weak or inflated sense of self. Hardship is us wandering together in the desert of consciousness, energetically trying to find our way home to the oasis. It's a sacred part of Life. **But when I remember the Truth of what I AM and what We Are, and what *makes* Life, I AM free.**

On that day you will know that I am in My Father, and you in Me, and I in you.

John 14:20

You can't do anything else on this planet as a conscious master if you haven't mastered the art of remembering that that's what you are. The moment you submit your sovereign dominion over Light to a story or idea that you have about what's possible, you're not Remembering.

Remembering is both a recollection—*"oh yes, I already always am Light, Good and Becoming!"*—and it's also a *re*-membering of your identity into that One unified body of infinite creativity, *whoomphed* back into the oasis, once again becoming an expression of the essence and omnipresence of a vital Light that can restore all things. Even in the hollow groan of loneliness that we feel in the shadows of the dark, formless void, the Spirit *is* moving upon the waters, and you *are* aware of the Light. You are aware of the spark of Light that never goes away. It's what you're made of.

Behold the Light streaming through your window, and know that it is Good.

Your Core Values

Look at **Diagram 2: The Sovereign Model of Human Consciousness.**

If your diamond consciousness is a stained glass window with the stories of all you Know to be true about Life, then it also contains the core values foundational to your unique perspective, the divine blueprint of who you are in Christ. These are the aspects of God that the world gets to know through you. They are the aspects of God that are confining and defining proof of your individuality within Him. Your core values are *God as You*.

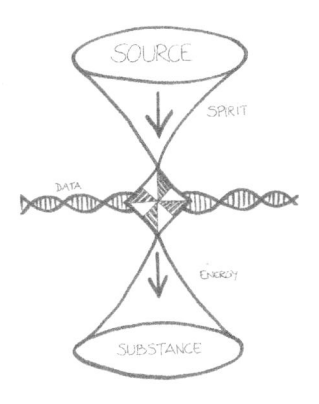

Your experience of the world is a gift to God, for you are the only creature with this unique point of view. If you can identify what your core values are, then you have a foundation upon which to build a sovereign, consecrated life because every right action and true expression is in line with these governing values. When your daily actions are in concert with the things that matter the most, and you act based on *your* values, you are in alignment with what God is doing through you. Now the Spirit will provide the motivation to go on and the opportunities to lead you into graceful expansion. If, on the other hand, you build your Life on the foundation of values that belong to external doctrines, other people or to outdated versions of yourself, then you will serve structure, you will never feel fulfilled and you will always be a seeker in the desert.

What is the prayer that is silently, wordlessly coming from your soul? Underneath all the intricately formulated ideals and visions, all the meticulous plans and noble wantings on behalf of the world—what is simplest, most authentic combination of values that spills from your heart and flavors the entirety of your experience? Listen...

The volume with which that vibrational melody penetrates the sand storms of the world to command new shapes depends on the extent of your self-realization—your log of consciousness *and* the resulting electromagnetic weight of your biofield. If your awareness is split among layers and layers of identities and constructed ideals, not centralized on Truth but scattered among the infinite conflicting facts of the world, then your energy is diffuse and Substance becomes a dense cloud of half-formed, disintegrating thought-forms, sand dunes of partially energized matter in a process of dissolution. The originally intended vibrational command in your biofield is but a whisper and can barely be heard. You have nothing but vapor. In this creative ineffectiveness, you have to serve structure, for only systems of governance and applied jurisdiction will keep those scattered energies together. In your life, relationships, finance, health, equality, social justice and everything else must be forced to adjust to externally calibrated coordinates, otherwise you have no guiding principles to keep you safe in existence. You live out there in time and space, bound to the systems that orchestrate the direction of your life, controlling and holding energy together like the puppet master of the unconscious.

> *"Unless the Lord builds the House, the builders labor in vain."*
>
> *Psalm 127:1*

But if you have cleared most of the grime and false stories from the window, then your energy is cohesive rather than diffuse and the Light casts a clear and concise combination of commands. In the cathedral, a melody emerges! Your Light vibration is now like a soul song. Who you are is crisp and clear. You are like a walking prayer, as the tone of your authentic values initiate the transformation of Substance all around you.

When you trust this fully, you're praying freely. This prayer is Known and allowed by the Source, acted upon by the Spirit and obeyed by the Substance of all that is. You needn't architect the outcome, you needn't fight for it, you need only follow the next step and the next as your vibrational authority shifts the path a few feet ahead of you at all times, like a Dragonfly zooming through the mist cast by a waterfall.

In a lovely piece of music there are many layers. In Western music, a scale has eight notes: do, re, mi, fa, so, la, ti, do. DO is the *home key*. The *dominance* is the main chord of notes leading back to the home key. The *polyphonic melody* is a diverse collection of strands of sounds emerging from but anchored in the dominance. The *monophonic top melody* is the story told on top.

The top melody in your life is the externally witnessed outline: *I want to be successful so I will do this and then this and then this.* One note after another. Below this hangs a polyphonic sound, a collection of multiple melodies that play together like a collaboration of *your* works and *mine*, or the coming together of your *genius*, your *magic* and your *loving action,* as many values are fulfilled at once. Below this is the undertone, a bassline which anchors the harmonies above it into purpose and meaning. This is *your* dominance. The dominance is the main chord of the undertones that make up the foundation of your overall music. Even though the top poly- and monophonic tones can modulate in any direction, as long as they are anchored in the dominance the melody will always lead to the home key.

Let's say, the bong of the gong that you heard is the home key *OM*. The primordial vibration of the universe. The dominance is the chord above that, **Your Name**, made of the specific vibrations of your core love values—perhaps *Family, Growth* and *Honor*, or maybe *Freedom, Justice* and *Truth*, or maybe *Celebration, Innovation* and *Discovery*—this undertone is ever present and all your harmonies are anchored into it which means any false note you play creates a vibrational interference pattern that cannot be sustained and won't last long without excruciating force. The dominance will organically modulate the melody. You may diversify your polyphonic magic, adventure and explore with your manifestation efforts and spiritual works in any direction, but if your actions are anchored in your bassline undertone you will always be led Home. From the top layer melody that is telling the story, it may seem that your manifestations aren't working when in fact God is constantly attuning every one of your prayers to your home key and bassline. A reality is emerging that is higher than you could consciously visualize and pray for.

Discover your bassline and become intimately familiar with it. Your core values are the foundation of your sovereignty, and we'll return to them often in this book.

What does truly matter most to you?

1. **Identify what you value the most right now.** You can look at your monthly spending habits to see where you put your energy, and you might discover things like Home Comfort, Family Time, Adventure and Discovery, Healing and Growth, Business Expansion, Making Money. You might examine what triggers you in the world and see that you value Peace, Truth, Passion, Justice, Honor. Perhaps you look at your goals for the future and see that your heart desires Legacy, Impact, Community, Solitude. Identify the tones that strike a bassline chord in your Knowing of who you really are, and accept that the specific cocktail is 100% unique to you, and is meant to be.

2. **Define these values in your own understanding.** Formulate one or more simple definitions for each item to clarify what that value means to you. This may take some time, so be patient. It's not enough to say "I value Love" if you haven't specified for yourself what that means. This is not to disqualify other interpretations of various words, but to truly magnify in your own Knowing what matters most to you.

3. **Prioritize your values in relation to each other.** Life often gives us opportunities to choose between our values, like when that important creative deadline coincides with your child's school musical recital. If you are familiar with the weight of each value in terms of its impact on your sovereignty, then you have greater power of choice and you will discover magical economies of scale open up as you consistently choose in favor of more Love. You no longer need to sacrifice the things that matter most, for all these are fulfilled in the miraculous economies of scale that unfold when energy is stewarded and applied righteously.

Imagine that you're somewhere in the desert standing on the edge of a cliff with a river three hundred feet below you. A large, fallen tree is spanning the ravine from the edge you're standing on to the cliff on the other side of the river two-hundred feet away. Would you walk across the tree trunk for a nice bit of Camembert? Probably not.

The value that is directing your decision-making in this case is *Safety*. In this instance your *Safety* is worth more to you than *Yummy Taste Sensation*. But what if your little toddler were crawling around on the other side? You'd walk across. The value that is directing your decision-making in this case is *Your Child's Life*. In this instance your *Safety* is less valuable to you than your *Your Child's Life*. That one's easy though. What if you were standing in the middle of the tree, with *Personal Peace* on one side and *Justice for All* on the other? Discover which of your desired ideals and core values you'd be willing to cross the ravine for. There are no right answers, but there are True ones.

Remember, it is only in the desert that split realities occur where you must choose between core values. In the oasis, all your values are aligned and fulfilled.

You cannot be True to who you are if you're not sure who you are. Your highest priorities must always be those that represent your core diamond consciousness. These values touch every role you play as spouse, sibling, parent, disciple, employee, and friend. Your values inform your talents, skills, and message to the world. And when you understand which of these values are the undertones and which are the overtones to your Life, investing your energy and time becomes a delight. If you understand what your core values are and build your goals upon those values, you are energetically aligned for your intention to follow through into your action and be embedded as a vibrational prayer into the works of everything you do. Moreover, you can trust that the electromagnetism of your vibrational field is powerful enough to command the Spirit to move the Substance in favor of Love, and you need not submit to the fast-paced and fickle algorithms of the world.

What matters most to you? See if you can create a melody consisting of:

The home key: God.

The bassline: A chord of three values that matter the most.

The polyphonic melody: A harmony of five to ten additional ideals that might emerge from each one of those values and add richness and beauty to many lives.

The monophonic melody: The simplest steps you can see in front of you that can be done right now.

I will sing a new song to you, O God; upon a ten-stringed harp I will play to you

Psalm 144:9

The Choice

Let's say Jesus Christ is the human manifestation of God, 100% Love in human form.

Whatever you like to call him, whether Yeshua, Bodhisattva, Shiva or Sophia, this is the only truly worthy ideal which is in constant communion with you. As a pre-existing consciousness framework that you are already entangled with, he installs a mindset principle that overrides sub-divine paradigms, and establishes you in embodied trust. You can realign your creative coordinates of consciousness so you experience life inside the body of Christ. Your energy field will be soaked with and surrounded by a vibration of immediate mercy, infinite grace and the deep personal love of the Beloved. This is why, whatever your spiritual lineage, he matters to your graceful relationship with an ascending world.

"So if God gave them the same gift he gave us who believed in the Lord Jesus Christ, who was I to think that I could stand in God's way?"

Acts 11:17

Look at Diagram 3: The Sovereign Model of Human Experience. When we are slaves to system consciousness that experiences reality entirely in the desert of form, we live in a constant energetic call and response experience of rise and fall, rise and fall, over and over as Substance responds to diffuse and conflicting vibrational command.

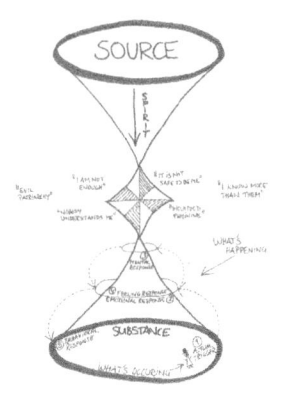

Ascension is slow as we repeatedly make new agreement with actually manifesting occurrences, which triggers an emotional reaction, which triggers a mental reaction, which triggers a feeling reaction, which triggers a behavioral reaction, and the cycles repeat themselves. We are not returning home, we are going round in circles. We can not see what is *actually occurring*, because we are seduced by the story we think is *really happening*.

Our inner work and mastery practice help us improve the quality of this feedback loop, and we ascend slowly, coming closer to the True blueprint of who we are. We see the effects of improvements, and the closer we get to Truth the greater the influence of Love over our Life.

Look at Diagram 4: The Scale. The universal laws dictate that when you are in charge of creation, the quality of your creation must according correspond to your log of consciousness. Wherever your diamond abides on this scale, the energy projected from your life view will command Substance to form itself to those attractor fields. So for a collective stuck in net entropy, there is little chance of escape. Nature's way is to let the species wipe itself out as through patterns of destruction.

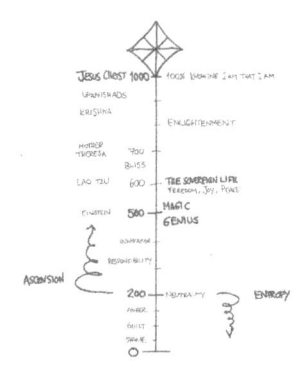

[figure: a vertical consciousness/calibration scale with labels including "Jesus Christ 1000", "I AM THAT I AM", "Upanishads", "Krishna", "Enlightenment", "Mother Theresa 700", "Bliss", "Lao Tzu 600", "The Sovereign Life — Freedom, Joy, Peace", "Einstein 500", "Magic", "Genius", "Universe", "Responsibility", "Ascension", "200 — Neutrality", "Anger", "Guilt", "Shame", "0", "Entropy"]

But God has a plan for humanity. We're not in this alone. In a decision made no differently than the decision to Create in the first place, Spirit impregnates Substance. Inspiration. A seeding occurs. This particular impregnation 2000 years ago had a purpose: to end this cyclical and entropic game of story-telling and trigger a permanent ascension. Ascension is organic and natural because I AM is always BEING *and* BECOMING. When we're not seduced by all the trappings of the world we get to ride that expansion wave with lightness. In Christ, there is nothing but good light being and becoming.

With a perfect diamond that Knows only Love, there is no constant feedback cycle between conflicting intentions, diffuse creative energy and manifestations of vapor. There is only constantly unfolding Truth in a real experience of unconditional Love. The weight of consciousness when one mind is in cohesion with itself is incredibly powerful and elevates the collective mind as well. A conscious person has more spiritual authority than an unconscious person. A genius person has more electromagnetic authority than a passively benevolent person. A mystic saint has more creative authority than a genius mind. An enlightened avatar of God has more authority over the natural world than an advanced adventuring alchemist in the desert of spiritual seeking. All spiritual authority is in Christ, and it is only our capacity to embody which dictates whether we have the personal experience of that authority or not. Love commands Power to move Form.

One human at a log of consciousness of 1000 has the electromagnetism of millions at 100.

The divine union of God and human was realized in Jesus Christ. Jesus, by the fact that he was born a droplet of perfect consciousness into the human fabric, tipped the magnetism scales for all of us, broke the collective consciousness out of the cycles of entropy and initiated the ascension. His dominance saved us all and we're going Home. So the Christ event collapsed the quantum possibility of this and the human consciousness was forever changed. The code was uploaded into the collective data field some know as the Akash, and therefore True for you now and can be made *real* for you now. Here's why:

Look at Diagram 5, Walking With Christ

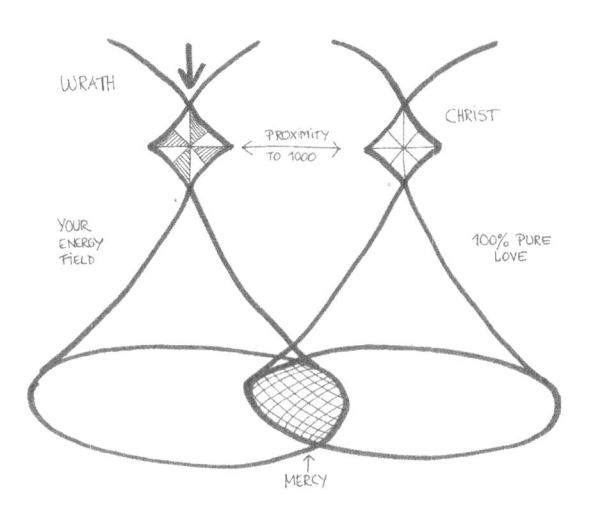

This model shows the increasing effect of mercy upon your life as you consciously participate more with Love and ascend on that imaginary scale closer and closer to 1000. The more you *become* sovereign in your mental and vibrational mastery, the closer your proximity to Truth, the purer and more lovely is your realized experience as you increasingly allow the energy of mercy to permeate your Life. As you tend to your inner work, purify your intentions, forgive your enemies, integrate your wisdom, improve your surroundings, help others and so on, you move "up the ladder" and closer to the original framework of consciousness that Christ is. More magic manifests.

But you are still always in direct relation with infinite creative energy, which, unfiltered, we may archaically call "the Wrath of God" for its indiscriminate creative power. In this model you're still creating all your rubbish as well, so you are vulnerable to being triggered back into cycles or seduced by your own creations into systems designed to artificially uphold them. For this reason you really do have to be on top in your mastery, and the risk is you find yourself working so hard at disciplining your mind, energy field and behavior that you miss Life *happening*. You become subject to the pressure of spiritual perfection, and your focus hones in on your own individual improvement instead of the collective good. From now we'll call this consciousness *Excelsior*, after the poem by Henry Wadsworth Longfellow. This poem is in the public domain—go and find it, and discover the cost of seeking your zenith experience at the expense of real life.

Look at Diagram 6, Walking In Christ

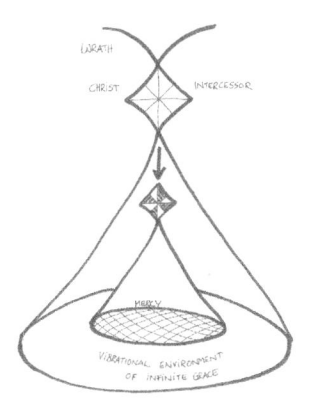

But since the True life is already happening, you don't need to wait until you reach the mountain zenith before you can abide in it. You can align your coordinates of consciousness so that your mindset is reborn inside the dimension where your reality is already redeemed and Substance is obeying the Spirit of what matters most. Now you're planting your flag at the tippety-top *and* snuggled with your lover by the fireside in the little cottage at the bottom of the mountain *at the same time*.

A few metaphysical effects of this choice:

1. The pure creative power is no longer creating immediately and directly through all the unresolved and compartmentalized shadow stories in the stained glass window of the cathedral. Before it even gets to you it's softened by the intercessory field of the One who Knows what Life is like. Immediate grace and endless compassion temper the fury of instantaneous creativity.

2. And when you, in your little limited universe, take a misstep while you're navigating your constantly tumultuous life—guess what, you're walking inside an energy field of unconditional Mercy, so the frequency of your error is neutralized quickly, interrupting the harmful ripple effect. He is the indwelling Healer.

3. This is such a good environment for you to practice your mastery and participate in your ascension. If you're doing any sort of ascension work at all, do it in a vibrational environment characterized by Grace. You can really simplify your spirituality and focus entirely on your mission as a herald of Love.

4. The framework of consciousness overshadowing your conscious mind and thus directing all your decisions and movements, is Perfectly Knowing—so your success in Life rapidly increases = **He is "Lord"**.

5. When you do stray out of this field and find yourself wandering in the thickets of conflict, overwhelm and decay, he comes like a shepherd and brings you back Home. Why? Because that is a part of the covenant of this alignment = **He is "Savior"**.

Imagine if one of the main stories in your diamond is *"Jesus is my Lord and Savior"*.

Creation will manifest that way. In an infinite cosmic sea of quantum possibility, he will save you when you're drowning. Subtle attunements of your perspective so you see clearly where it was hazy before. Subtle adjustments to your body chemistry so you feel better and lighter. Subtle new thoughts and knowings, the light dialed slightly brighter. Despair turns to hope, and your own actions shift. You magnetize higher energy fields and the denser energies dissolve and dissipate. You literally shine.

Living inside this body you are utterly One with the essence of Love, *in* a God not just infinitely powerful but also intimately real and in tender relation with you, loving you just like this.

I AM Knowing That I AM Love

This is how to make the choice real:

Step 1) Believe it is possible for you. We create as we believe, so if you allow the paradigm *"Jesus is my Lord and Savor"* (the word formulation is irrelevant, the essence of the intention is what counts) to be active in your diamond consciousness, then this is what will manifest in your world of experience. You don't need to be fully convinced, you just need faith the size of a mustard seed. You do the first 10%, and he will do the remaining 90%.

Step 2) Make the declaration. By formulating the words in your own way and actually speaking them out to be received by someone you trust, you are creating an agreement reality and Spirit moves Substance much more effectively. If you don't say it but believe it secretly in your heart, Jesus will still be with you immediately. But if you wish to participate in the exquisite magic of watching this experience be made manifest, your words are your wand. Baptism is a powerful alchemy that does this job. It is a sacred sacrament of initiation and adoption into the Body of Christ. It is a unity between and among those devoted to the Way—no matter what religion we think we belong to. Baptism is a unity that says *"We KNOW we are immersed in Christ and He in Us."*

Step 3) Allow him to reveal himself to you in the Way he does. *"Hello, Jesus. So I've been reading this book that's using a new combination of words to explain the reality of You, and I'm wondering who you really are? Show me."* He may manifest visually, audibly, or through a secret language only the two of you know, perhaps in the rhythm of numbers like the triple 3s or 11:11s you see around you, or perhaps in a magical call and response where your attention is drawn to him in your surroundings. Perhaps you will start hearing his voice in the conversations of others. You don't need to join a church, but a loving community that is open to your new reality is a powerful and safe field in which to become reborn. Open a new line of communication with him and let it develop organically. You'll notice radical shifts in your Life as your experience becomes soaked with Mercy.

> ***Then Christ will make his home in your heart as you trust in him. Your roots will grow down into God's love and keep you strong. And may you have the power to understand, as all God's people should, how wide, how long, how high, and how deep His love is.***
>
> *Ephesians 3:17-18*

Dwell for a few more glorious weeks by the sparkling waters in the oasis, and peer out through your telescope to the desert beyond the borders of tranquility. Witness everything that is occurring out there in the vast plains of constantly rearranging adamantine particles. The traffic lights changed. The stock market crashed. The left leg broke. The chicken dumplings burned. The sun rose again over the crystalline oasis. The beetle crawled across the window sill. Count it all joy, remember it as all beautiful, made of God's Body.

The Second Mastery: Recognizing

House Versus Home

So, you Remember who you are. You know you are Source, Spirit and Substance, three in one, and that we all are. But Remembering that you are in fact an expression of God—always being and becoming, made of light, originally good, unconditionally loving, tapped into a field of harmonious creative energy—is just the beginning. This is where the sovereign Life starts!

You've entered the oasis and discovered a whole universe of synchronistic magic open up for you. But it's not all bliss. Now you get good at Recognizing the opposite of Remembering, because one of the side effects of Truth is that it exposes what's not. So, now you're invited to sift and sort through all the many energy fields you've encountered in the past, re-editing narratives that you expose in your own judgments about who you have been so far, and what's going on out there. You suddenly see, more clearly than before, the unhappy condition of our desert-bound family and the supreme spiritual agony Knowing there is a better Way for all.

The oasis is still surrounded by desert. Those vast, manifest sand dunes in the desert, structures built up of the adamantine particles you have previously commanded into place, are beginning to shift. Destruction and decay must occur, but what is True and what is false? All those factual realities you used to believe were sovereign are still stitched to your experience like old rags wafting in the desert winds of turbulence. You Remember the Truth, but these old rags keep floating into your line of sight, obscuring the view. Pieces of fabric like personality type, trauma stories, false identities and involuntary behavioral patterns, emotional triggers and mental programming, systems of governance and karmic agreements, flapping about interrupting the harmony of your vibrational command.

So God sends you to your next initiation in this desert bootcamp: training in the art of recognition. To know a flapping rag when you see one. To know Story from Truth. You develop your intuitive discernment, learning the mechanisms in your own Sovereign Way. With his companionship you develop your craft of sorting out structure from essence, house from home, wheat from chaff, and the frequencies of good from those of evil.

Keep in mind, the end game for you isn't to conquer the prince of evil and establish Christ consciousness on the planet. This accomplishment is already whole and complete. Only Love is real, humanity and our planet have been redeemed and are free. **The Kingdom is already established. You are practicing entering the oasis,** *being here,* **and bringing it back out into the desert.**

Life is equal parts truth and story, and your enlightenment is Knowing the difference. Imagine being so masterful at your discernment of Truth versus Story that the story can become the mythology, the stage of your life's experience in which you *do* your *being*. After all, you cannot avoid story, for there are creative limitations inherent to your individuality and you keep bumping into people who spill their story into yours and vice versa. You will make judgments and limit the borders of your human experience. Since Truth is objective and Life is subjective, the only place you can ever truly meet another in the Stories that brew between us. Stories are lies that somewhere and somehow tell the Truth. Accept this lovely part of the deal, that these sacred stories should be the richness of our evolving journey together. **We have eternity to be floating blissfully in Oneness—and we have only this LIFE to live.**

So you must come to peace with Story, but you must become sovereign over it or you will be engulfed back into the dream. You will need to disarm and disperse the stories that draw your awareness from Love and into the chaos of doubt, anxiety, hesitation and procrastination, codependency and terror, stagnation and self-pity. When you Recognize them, these frequencies submit to your authority as quickly as they're identified.

But sometimes we can't see the desert for all the dunes. We start by learning to recognize the outright lies like *"I'm not worthy"* and *"you're not worthy"*. But falsehood is subtle, and sneaky—it's as intelligent as you are and it adapts to your consciousness. It knows how to reason you into thinking that structure is essence, and that down is up. So if you don't get good at Recognizing, you'll easily be seduced into addiction, judgment and bitterness, regret and stagnation, pride and spiritual decline. You'll find yourself engaged in discourse about matters that don't matter, your creative energy consumed by the effort to keep your reality relevant in a turbulent world, constantly tearing down and building up mortal structures within and without. You will feel exhausted, despite all your intentions to be Love, and you'll wonder why "it" *isn't here yet.*

With the world and our collective human family facing this historic coming of age, witnessed through an increasingly turbulent relationship with our Mother God, all energies will be increasingly magnified as Truth is revealed and falsehood is exposed. Both in your personal life and as a leader of the real people you love, you will be one who demonstrates "I AM Sovereign" even when there are millions of old rags flapping about your face in the sandstorm. If you Recognize those false notes against the bassline of His holy dominance, then you can easily choose poise and allow all energy to be modulated to Truth.

Structure Versus Essence

There are many ways to build your muscle of discernment, and one of the easiest is by reflecting on the distinction between essence and structure.

Imagine your human personality as an operating system that allows you to interface with the world. It is your house, structured and firm, with clear limitations and unique features. Like a physical house your identity is not really inert, it wants to be able to move. Otherwise your personality crystallizes and the house begins to crack and crumble as the earth shift. Your ascension then becomes a gruesome experience of constant ego death and rebirth, you're a phoenix plummeting in a fiery blaze of glory before emerging again pridefully from the ashes only to go through the cycle again. On the other hand, when you Recognize your timeless essence, the structure of your personality is malleable and submits to your sovereignty. Your ascension process becomes graceful and organic like the inhale and exhale of God's universal breath.

- Home is an eternal quality, a sacred belonging.

- House is a structure.

There is nothing wrong with having a house, a structure that you use to shelter your home. But your housing needs might change over time, to better accommodate a home that is becoming. And if you get too stuck in your house, too attached to the building itself, and you start to believe that the house *is* what home is, then you might never notice how inappropriate the structure really is for the changing environment, and the changing needs of the occupant. In fact you'll end up losing everything that matters most fighting to the death to defend the structure of your house, mistakenly believing this is what *home* is. If, on the other hand, you Recognize where the house ends and the home begins, then you are liberated to make gentle and smooth upgrades to the house as time goes by and your understanding of home deepens and unfolds.

The same is true for your personality self. It is a constructed part of you, pieced together bit by bit by your innocently emerging soul as you learned and adopted facts about Life that you needed to relate to. It is not dangerous, and you don't need to destroy it. Just be aware of where it ends and your true essence begins. Some people are so afraid of the Ego, they want to kill it. They say *"We are our own worst enemy"* and thus form a self-sabotaging way of being where the Ego consistently chooses against your soul's higher knowing, because that's exactly the subconscious directive it's being given. Imagine in **diagram 2, the Sovereign Model of Human Consciousness**, that a core value in the diamond is *"I AM my own worst enemy"*. Visualize the consciousness of this agreement commanding the movement of your energy to form the substance of your particle-based life. Your life will demonstrate that you are correct, and you are indeed the sabotaging arch-nemesis of all your soul's desires.

But it is only Ego that tries to kill Ego. The Self has no fear of it at all. In fact, the thing named Ego is a good friend. It is the character playing the stories, paradigms and peculiarities that are chosen again and again as we explore our way through this sacred Life. The Ego is a wonderful help for interfacing with the world, and it does what it can to preserve its directive. That's its job. Your job is to give it proper directive. If you allow the command to be modulated by the bassline of True values unique to you, you will align your entire being with God.

When you make peace with the character of your constructed personality, you Recognize that Ego is not an enemy, but an executive partner delivering on a series of interconnected directives that make up a "Way of Being"—your modus operandi. A symphony made of hundreds of thousands of subconscious players, dutifully playing the music they've been given. It is a malleable, seismological field of self that melds with the Truth to meet life in the highest and best way in the moment. Introvert? Extravert? Thinker? Feeler? Whatever the situation demands. What used to be crystallized as a specific genre of sound is now an orchestra that plays to the conductor's dominance.

We don't need to kill the orchestra. There is no need to dissolve the part of the self that is conducted like this, because it is the very structure that allows the essence to commune with Life, to spin the stories that give richness and meaning to it, and to relate with other Selves in the plains of a moving frontier. You are adaptable yet resilient precisely because your structured Ego works with your essential Self. **But, for true sovereignty, it is necessary to know the difference between the orchestra and the conductor,** or there's a danger that the collective organism of players in that curated personality type will play to a false command. The mastery of Recognizing is the discernment of notes in the constantly evolving interface through which you interact with the world.

That's why you don't need to fear the constructed systems of Life. The House we built for our Home. You just need to know the foundation and where the walls are. That's what will give you the insight to know where the updates need to happen so your Home can grow in perfect, peaceful joy. The house must be fit for purpose. The different traits and values that emerge from each of us influence and guide our choices—from how we think to how we feel and certainly what we put our hands to. That's why some become nurturers and some become builders, and there is magic in how all the needs of a collective society will be met when each individual follows the Sovereign Way of their soul. With our distinguished differences we glide in a symphony of human interaction that gives us each deep fulfillment and serves humanity as a whole.

The Orthodox and The Gnostics: An Alchemy of Peter and Paul.

Let's say that alchemy is when you marry essence and structure and the result is far greater than the sum of two parts. It's combining the philosopher's stone and the elixir of life in order to turn lead into gold. We'll explore this more in the sixth mastery, "Alchemy". We agree that structure without essence is lifeless, hollow and meaningless. *Hevel*, as the teacher in Ecclesiastes says. We can also logically see that essence without Structure never forms, simply *is* but never *becomes*. Unless the two are unified, change never occurs in reality.

Jesus came to deliver the collective human consciousness from our enslavement to structure and energetic entropy, and he activated in us perfect faith in the unity of Source, Spirit and Substance—*"I and my Father are One"*—we have living, breathing authority to turn water into wine and make all things new. The structured systems of old stories, bad habits, karmic energy cycles, epigenetic disease, Mercury retrograde, cultural oppression and intergenerational curses no longer need to enslave our energy fields, because we have instant access to the essence of renewing Love. We don't need to earn it, we don't seek to find it. We just need to choose it.

And this good news was spreading rather well until about 100 years after Jesus' abrupt ascension, when contradictory values among his followers split the new reality into a multitude of subcultures. It was a complicated network of spiritual thought-forms, so we shall simplify it by juxtaposing two main interpretations of Truth: **the orthodox and the gnostic**—or "established, approved frameworks of thought" versus "personal awareness and subjective Knowing".

The orthodox established that true spiritual authority was passed down from the first male apostles who Jesus revealed himself to after his resurrection, one by one the apostolic succession trickles down along a dependable lineage. Jesus' disciple Peter became "the rock" at the head of this lineage of thought, and from this vibrational command came the succession of bishops, priests and deacons that make up "institution." Orthodoxy is proper thought, a linear mind, a system-based log of consciousness. It is a structure, "the philosopher's stone".

It's risky to rely on our subjective emotions and feelings about who God is, since we are so often at the mercy of some vibrational storm, and sometimes we don't feel His

Love. The structure provided by this stewardship of True Law, the divine blueprint, gives us something to depend on and keeps us within his embrace. And, as with all structures that refuse to budge, orthodoxy has cracks in it. We can get too reliant on structure and begin to worship it as the source of our freedom—we fall into false idolism or what the Buddhists call "mad delusion", and we submit our sovereignty to *that thing*. *"Forgiveness is only possible for me on the other side of this pre-approved ritual, and at the discretion of this pre-approved authority."*

The gnostics, on the other hand, say that true spiritual authority is not handed down man to man but delivered from Christ himself through the omnipresence of the Holy Spirit, directly into the soul of the receiver. Gnosis, or Knowing, is when you yourself are in direct communion with God, without the need for an earthly intercessor like a bishop, priest or deacon. How can you know God unless you KNOW God, who is inherently relational and the most intimate companion? It is impossible to know God when you have surrendered that relationship and placed it in the hands and books of an external authority. So the gnostics taught a spiritual communion that is personal, mystical and magic beyond measure.

This is a quantum log of consciousness and Way to Know God. The apostle Paul was one who received his commission directly from Christ during a transcendental experience.

> **"I did not receive it from any man, nor was I taught it; rather, I received it by revelation from Jesus Christ."**
>
> **Galatians 1:12**

As for the idea that spiritual authority had to be dispensed in a linear way by the orthodox succession, Paul "never learned anything" from the disciples who had studied directly with the master, the so-called "pillars of the church."

> **"As for those who were held in high esteem, whoever they were makes no difference to me. God does not show favoritism. They added nothing to my message."**
>
> **Galatians 2:4**

So this approach to spiritual communion and development is based on transcendental knowing, gnosis. Like the orthodox mind, this approach is also good and holy *with flaws*. We can easily be manipulated by all kinds of lower forms of energy, and with a lack of structure we can find ourselves floating about like dandelion seeds following whatever vibrational current seduces our attention. Our ancestors the Atlanteans were ultimately seduced by glamor, pouring their creative energy into sub-divine psychic realities that sparkled like champagne bliss.

So if Peter represents the structure, *the philosopher's stone*, then Paul represents the essence, *the elixir of life*. True alchemy only happens when the two are united. Your job as a Sovereign Master is to recognize their distinctions and allow both to be holy at the same time. Your Sovereign Way is a path of orthodoxy and gnosis.

Both orthodox and gnostic scriptures are absolutely soaking with mystery teachings that weave together structure and essence, unravel surrender and mastery, and prove the omnipresence of grace. They tell the story of the human journey all the way from the deepest agony to the exquisite bliss of true union. They bring a wellspring of hope. They function best together.

What's Actually Occurring vs What's Really Happening

With the sovereign poise to recognize structure and essence, it's now possible to distinguish between what's actually occurring *(a rat is decaying on the path)* and the rich and complex story of what seems to be really happening *(the authorities are failing their duties and I'm exposed to the filth of the world)*.

Look at **diagram 3 again, the Sovereign Model of Human Experience**.

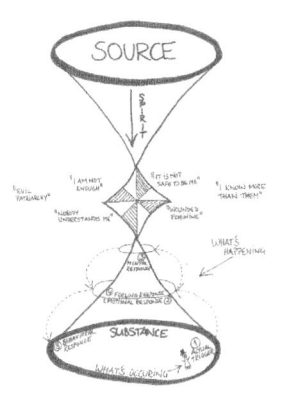

1. Ideals and beliefs are projected into substance and the sand dunes of creation take form.

2. These actual manifestations in the four dimensions are then perceived by your cellular consciousness through your many sensing and intuitive faculties. When these perceived manifestations signal that one of your core values has been violated, emotions are activated. An alarm goes off in your amygdala and your hippocampus sends a floods of hormones to shift your entire biochemistry into a stress response. Your nervous system is now in sympathetic mode, and a reactive program is initiated.

3. Since your chemical composition has changed with all those stress hormones, your vibrational field has shifted and you are a different expression of energy. This means your mental process also shifts. Thoughts are not linear—we know from quantum models of cognition and decision-making that your potential thought field collapses at the moment of judgment and becomes a linear stream of thinking. Your thoughts now match your vibration and a whole narrative fills your internal storytelling about what's happening. You are not observing with poise, you are immersed in a living story.

4. And because your thoughts have changed, so have your feelings. While your

emotions are biological responses to external conditions, your feelings are spiritual identity-based responses to internal conditions. The emotion of anger comes before the feeling of "I AM angry".

5. And since you feel differently, you behave differently while you speak and move in the world of form, activating new ripples of cause and effect. The feedback loop is perpetuated and you have experienced a rich internal story of happening, even if nothing has really occurred.

When any sort of conflict arises, ask yourself:

What is happening to me, versus what is actually occurring?

You'll soon see how much of your life you spend in your own unconscious system of limbic responses to a pre-programmed world, unconsciously doing what you can to seek pleasure and avoid pain upholding sand dunes that seemed to be important once. You will also see how much of your day you spend in true relation with the Body of God, the living presence of Love, and how often you can notice the innocent, little baby and the divine Christ in every human being who crosses your path.

The Frog

A little tadpole lived in the dragonfly pond in the oasis, where the wild roses grow. It didn't need to study or practice coming into vibrational resonance with a frog. It was just being Tadpole while simultaneously becoming Frog. When the little tadpole had finally transformed and become a frog, he happily hopped about his business from lily pad to lily pad catching flies, just as the frogs in this pond love to do.

Every year, in the spring time, a flock of herons would visit the pond in a short sojourn on their migration path to somewhere else. For the herons, it was a time of comfort, recuperation and delicious abundance. For the frogs, this annual event was a social catastrophe, triggering the self-preservation systems of the collective.

On a biological level, an automated survival response was already installed in Frog. Each one had inherited this within the cluster of spawn of which they had once been an individuated part. So precise was this warning system, that our little frog didn't need to do anything to activate it, and wasn't even aware that it was running. In fact, the limbic system of the frog had, over multiple generations of tadpole to frog metamorphosis, learned to make shortcut associations to ensure its survival.

Every year, about a week before the herons arrived, the wild roses opened their buds and bloomed for the first time. The scent transformed the landscape with its essence, and a code in the froggy genetics signaled to the amphibians that the time is now. As the frogs picked up the scent of the roses, adrenaline was released into their little bodies and a sense of impending danger came over them as they chemically adapted to the new vibration. They chose the best defense actions for a frog: playing dead, screaming, puffing up, spraying urine. Some just quietly moved away from the pond where the roses grew. Some hid under a lilypad, some withdrew all the way down to the bottom of the pond, and stayed there. As the roses opened their blooms, the danger was *really happening*, but not *actually occurring*.

This system was wonderfully crafted and kept the frogs and herons in a balanced relationship for 60 million years.

But now, something was afoot. There was magic in the air, a *bong* calling the little frog onwards. A whole new thing altogether, one that somehow promised radically transformed awareness, the ability to create unimaginable possibilities, miracles of the mind and adventures of discovery far beyond the pond. He sat on a log on the top of a hill and gazed out toward a distant glint of white alabaster. He could feel it, expanding through him in a different way than when his puberty metamorphosis turned him from tadpole to frog. This wasn't evolutionary biology, this was spiritual, mystical—quantum. This was not his orthodox limbic system calling, this was gnosis.

He had to leave. With great courage, he hopped off in the direction of the call, overcoming many obstacles along his Sovereign Way. He was almost squashed on the village road. He almost got eaten by the snake in the barn. He almost fell down the sewer pipe during that one heavy rain. Actually occurring risks and dangers that he responded to in the moment. Terrifying at the time, but each danger survived.

He followed the call all the way across the oasis until he got to a beautiful cathedral of alabaster. There dwelled a princess with the power of alchemy, able and willing to transform the frog into a prince by dispensing a kiss of True Love so every cell in his body, every energy field in his vibration, every bit of froggy data in his subconscious field, would be transformed in an instant into Sovereignty. From *Ramadi Amphibia* to *Homo Spiritus*, a species not only self-aware, but in sovereign dominion of that awareness. This version of him would have the power to create, to transcend all systems of being and live in the presence of poised realization, forever held in the embrace of the Beloved, adventuring in the joy of aliveness! *Wow!*

But alas.

The entrance to the cathedral was adorned by wild roses. Alive in bloom their scent filled the air with sweetness, and the frog could go nowhere near the cathedral and had no idea why. Every time he hopped close to the entrance, his skin tightened, a lump grew in his throat, his little webbed feet got clammy and he had an ominous feeling. His thoughts went dark. *"This isn't safe"*, he thought. "*It just doesn't resonate with me at the moment. The herons are watching, they're trying to suppress and control us, I have to fight back or hide, I need to become a better frog. Why do I keep manifesting this?*" He had no awareness of the limbic association encoded in his froggy DNA that was connecting this scent with his sympathetic nervous system. Every part of him was being called through those gates, but he couldn't overcome the resistance. The mortal danger he sensed when he came near the wild roses by the palace entrance was *really happening* to him but it wasn't *actually occurring*, so he couldn't find the solution in his archives of experiential knowledge, though his mental narratives were constantly reasoning why he shouldn't cross that threshold. Unlike the cars on the village road, the snake in the barn, the sewer pipe—which were *actually occurring*—this was not a manifest obstruction. This was an unidentified limbic connection that caused a subtle survival response preventing him from moving in the direction of his calling.

It's hard to know what you don't know that you don't know. Little Frog didn't know about the limbic association connecting the roses to his hormone-activated defense system, so he spent years suspended in a space between his old pond life and the promise of total transformation that he knew he was being called to. For years he lived under the moat bridge far from home on either side, taking self-development courses and trying different diets and spiritual work out regimes. He blamed the void in his heart on his upbringing in the pond. He blamed it on the traumatic journey he'd had to get there. He blamed it on his age.

There's a happy ending! What's calling you knows where you are, where you're going, and what's in the way. And when you make the Choice to be received before you've arrived, the Sovereign One will come to the bridge and meet you there. That is in fact the only Way across. And, with the magic of True Love's kiss, Sovereign will transform you cell by cell until you stand fully in your true nature. That's your destiny.

You do the first 10%, and God does the remaining 90%. This is going to be easier than you think, if you will allow it.

One day the Frog simply had enough of waiting. He croaked a desperate plea into any direction, a Choice unworded but loaded with allowing. And the Princess came out to bridge, scooped him up and kissed the Frog. The transformation occurred in space and time, and the results were permanent.

This Is The Love of God

In the wine cellars of the alabaster cathedral is a master sommelier who can name every layer and nuance in a drop of wine. You are becoming as discerning as him. The more you practice, the faster and more precisely you notice the different energy fields in your awareness in any given circumstance. With that discernment comes the responsibility of sovereign choice. You don't need to claim every vibration that you can feel as fact. "*But I feel this ominous sense of doom, so I'd better not cross that bridge*". It's a legitimate feeling. You can certainly choose to say that it's real for you. And you can also choose to recalibrate that frequency, and allow something new to emerge. Practice with this vibrational experiment. Read each line below slowly, shifting the emphasis to the emboldened word each time and noticing the subtle difference between one frequency and the next.

THIS is the Love of God.

This **IS** the Love of God

This is **THE** Love of God

This is the **LOVE** of God.

This is the Love **OF** God.

This is the Love of **GOD**.

One sentence. Six meanings. Though the structured configurations of words remain the same, the essential meaning evolves ever so slightly as the emphasis changes. Here we are leaning through different energy fields and noticing the subtle variation in frequency. And we can experience that the six different frequencies are all embedded within the one sentence.

All the energy in heaven and earth are embedded within this singular moment, and can be experienced by you *through* any configuration of substantive particles. You are always able to recognize which active frequencies are impressing the substance of Life, and the decaying rat can become a marvel of God's majesty.

I and My Father are One

John 10:30

The Snake in The Oasis Garden

A Sovereign Master doesn't need to understand quantum mechanics, it is enough to grasp some simple creation energetics. Let's say, in order for the universe to be manifest, there must be both expansion and compression. If there was no compression, everything would burst into infinity and there would be no time in space to form bees tending to blossoming roses, no homemade soup by the fireplace, and no crayon art stuck to the fridge. Counterforce of many varied powers is designed to keep the quality of **Becoming** in a state of process.

The human consciousness is not supposed to internalize counterforce and allow it to twist our thought-forms and corresponding attractor fields into warped and self-serving realities, but we do—and this error is the plague we are dealing with. The snake in the garden is a simple analogy that helps us process the consequences of such a creative framework.

Let's say God formed the oasis, a field of infinite potentiality. And He designed the human consciousness in His image as sovereign and creative, and He placed that consciousness in dominion and stewardship of all that lovely abundant potential. In that very same oasis, slithered the serpent. The snake was "more subtle" than the wild animals God had made. Not a manifest beast of nature at all, but an esoteric frequency. For the sake of illustrating energetic dynamics, we shall call this snake "evil".

Recognize that the snake was already there. Man didn't invent it—the dark forces are a pre-existing idea allowed in the mind of God. In a divine paradox typical of our Father, "God saw all that he had made, and it was very good," so the snake has its purpose and place. Inverted illusion is a natural potential of compression, and it is there, quivering in a poised superstate waiting to be allowed to form.

Look at Diagram 4, The Scale. Notice the upward spiral, and notice the downward spiral. Imagine that for every action there is an equal and opposite reaction.

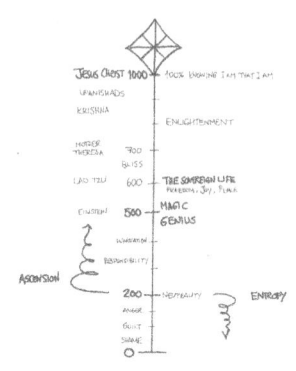

[Hand-drawn diagram showing a vertical consciousness scale with labels including: Jesus Christ 1000 / 100% knowing I AM THAT I AM, Upanishads, Krishna, Enlightenment, Mother Theresa 700, Bliss, Lao Tzu 600 / The Sovereign Life (freedom, joy, peace), Einstein 580 / Magic / Genius, Ascension, 200 / Neutrality, Anger, Guilt, Shame, Entropy, 0]

As you ascend in consciousness and your energy field expands, you will notice counterforce pressing up against your natural growth and manifesting in your areas of weakness. Achille's enemy aimed for his heel. Let's imagine evil as an intelligent coding designed as a counterforce to natural expansion, seeking to prevent the externalization of Light, influencing your awareness toward structure consciousness, and holding your identity imprisoned there in a universe that must fall, because all structures do.

> *For as in Adam all die, so also in Christ shall all be made alive.*
>
> *1 Cor 15:22*

If Christ is a state of consciousness fully remembered and realized—**I AM**—then anti-Christ is the opposite: fully separate and voided, illusion. **I AM Not**. It is thus the inversion of Truth, so all counterforce will twist creative perspectives in that direction.

We see in our Genesis story that the first instruction we are given is to uphold and nurture what is good and true, to tend the garden of diversity and abundance. We are directed not to embody the knowing of good and evil because we will "surely die" a spiritual death of declining awareness, suffering the illusion of separation from wholeness as we become consumed by our own judgments and analysis trying to navigate the creative effects of **"I AM Not"**. God's will is for us to choose to embody all things that are good. We do know in our hearts what is good. We Remember **I Am Good.**

The primary function of evil is to manipulate sovereign choice—because Sovereign choice is always True and benevolent, which is disastrous to the existence of false realities. The snake doesn't tell Life what to do. It cannot override free will. It simply questions and suggests until you have created an inverted reality it can build upon. *"Really? Did God really say that? He knows you won't die if you eat the apple."* Evil frequencies don't necessarily seem to oppose the Truth. There is no *actual* opposition to Truth. Evil takes Truth and twists it, inverting it and then energetically building off the inversion, creating a false reality that is *really happening* to all who believe in it. It seduces your awareness deeper into the inversion by offering all sorts of benefits that appeal to your intelligent Ego no matter your log of consciousness. For someone who considers themselves conscious and awake, it might sound like:

"Maybe if you eat the fruit you'll be like a god!"

"There are millions suffering, if you don't save them—who will?"

"Maybe if you manifest another red car you will be seen as a great spiritual master!"

"Maybe you should deprive yourself of joy so you will be known as a humble and noble servant."

"If you quit your mission everyone will see you are brave, unattached and surrendered."

"You should probably keep spending, if you tighten up you must be in lack consciousness and you'll never attract real wealth."

"You really are the Son of God, right? Throw yourself off the highest point of your temple and let's see you fly!"

When you Remember who you really are and you Recognize the structure of a false reality such as "*I AM the one who must get up at 5am and work hard and never quit, for then I shall be of use to the Kingdom*", ask yourself where this creative idea is coming from. Who told me this? Is this Truth, or the patterns of a Story I've heard from somewhere and have been creating upon ever since? Sovereign awareness dispels falsehood quickly and easily. That simple question, "who told me this?" is always powerful no matter where you think you are in your spiritual maturity, as it illuminates and directs your sovereign mind. Energetically, any time you sense a decline in the quality of your mental narrative, a weakening in your sense of self or body, you are under the influence of counterforce and have an excellent opportunity to quantum leap. Once it is exposed you can simply release it with a sovereign command "*away from me*," and re-establish your poise with even greater authority.

Then Jesus was led by the Spirit into the wilderness to be tempted by Satan. After fasting forty days and forty nights, he was hungry. The tempter came to him and said, "If you are the Son of God, tell these stones to become bread."

Jesus answered, "It is written: 'Man shall not live on bread alone, but on every word that comes from the mouth of God."

Then the devil took him to the holy city and had him stand on the highest point of the temple. "If you are the Son of God," he said, "throw yourself down. For it is written: 'He will command his angels concerning you, and they will lift you up in their hands, so that you will not strike your foot against a stone."

Jesus answered him, "It is also written: 'Do not put the Lord your God to the test."

Again, Satan took him to a very high mountain and showed him all the kingdoms of the world and their splendor. "All this I will give you," he said, "if you will bow down and worship me."

Jesus said to him, "Away from me, Satan! For it is written: 'Worship the Almighty Loving God, and serve him only.'"

Then evil left him, and angels came and attended to him.

Matthew 4:1-11

We can look again at **Diagram 3** to see how the Knowing of good *and* evil lands in the relationship between consciousness, energy and manifestation in real Life. We can see why we are called to embody only what is good and true, and why in Genesis 3:15 God lists the consequences of holding a frame of consciousness which knows evil. These consequences are not punishment, they are logical energetic outcomes according to universal laws of creation. Imagine eight billion interconnected energy fields all creating good and evil on top of each other. It's a sand storm of particles.

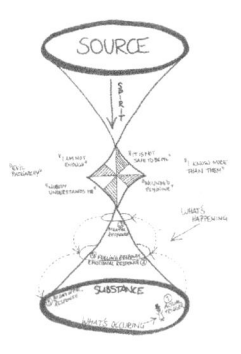

Borrowing some vernacular from the noble Catholic cosmology, we can categorize evil in three ways:

- Sin of the Flesh: This is our personal sin, our shadow world of unconscious thoughts, feelings and actions on an individual level that play out in a Story about what's *really happening,* twisting the organic expression of God and diminishing the experience of Love for ourselves and others. No matter the severity of the crime, Jesus never condemned individual people for sins of the flesh, for it is but an unconscious consequence of illusion.

- Sin of the World: These are the structures and systems of economy, politics, culture and religion that serve to glorify the deepfake illusion of structure. The corporate, systemic manipulations that inform our choices when we are not aware, imposing culturally agreed upon limitations and exclusions, tracks of evil we unconsciously whizz along on from subtle levels of unconscious discrimination to the most heinous global systems of genocide and slavery.

- Satan: This is the fundamental idea of **I AM Not,** which, when applied to the human consciousness, creates an alternative reality in illusion. The Anti-Christic frequency that "*dominates the very air we breathe*" as the spiritual pioneer Paul writes in the book of Ephesians, is a part of the potential fabric of creation just like grace and abundance. The snake was there in the garden already and does not need to be conquered by you. In Christ, there is no creative agreement with evil and therefore no manifest expression of it. In Christ, the battle has already been won.

Falsehood is subtle. It can't be sourced out there and typecast as a particular character, ideology, industry or political party—though its entire agenda is to win your attention "out there" and keep your consciousness from entering the oasis. There *are* characters, ideologies, industries and groups that have been initiated into dark service, but none of these are irredeemable.

No actualized person, structure, object, event or occurring system is in itself either wholly True or wholly False, because Substance cannot be separated from the Spirit and Source of Love. For example, the creative judgment "*transgender people are evil*" is therefore blasphemy, a disrespect toward the holiness of God's design. The statement puts particularized chromosomes, genes and genitals as the authority to tell you who you are and where your Love should go. If your body has arranged itself into the shape of a human fellow, but your incarnate essence Knows *I AM Woman*, then denying that voice in favor of the form in the reflection, *that's* putting structure before essence, and the world of form before the sovereign voice of God. Likewise, "*I cannot be who I AM unless I radically change my body,*" is also blasphemy, a creative judgment that limits the extent of your natural ability to experience God right now, loved and wanted exactly as you are, even when you feel opposite to yourself. It is putting the structure of your body before the essence of your fulfillment.

The first principle in all things—from the Great Commission to the Mosaic Decalogue to the Tenets of Reiki—is to put God first, and not to give the House more authority than the Home.

So evil is the divine intention whose entire purpose is to seduce you into believing manifest actualization is the real source and authority, enslave your energy to the continuation of this illusion, and influence you away from the infinitely loving potential of God. How does it do it?

Look at Diagram 4 again. Let's remember our arrangement of theoretical logs of consciousness on an imaginary scale from Anti-Christ to Christ. Your becoming is an ascension on this scale as you embody more of the divine Knowing that you are in fact Source, Spirit and Substance recapitulated as One glorious child of God. More Knowing of Love equals greater authority to command the Spirit to moves the Substance. This is the same as saying that your power to manifest by true sovereign choice increases as you ascend. At lower logs of consciousness your electromagnetism decreases and structure has more authority over you.

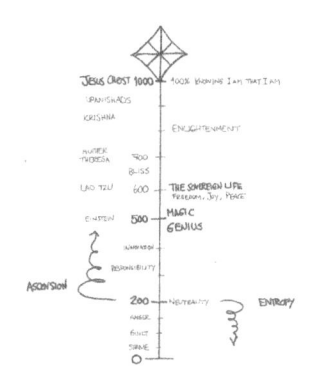

On a macro level, there are two distinct dynamics influencing your log of consciousness:

When we are looking "up", aligned with Truth and surrendered to the way God is moving through us, we experience an elevation, enlightenment, enhancement, and thus a sense of buoyancy and growth. We'll call this "ascension" as the laws of creation respond exponentially to our expanding energy field and we experience the improving Life. Even when things fall apart and we're in the throes of human agony, majesty always emerges and beauty blossoms, for we are actively and consciously participating with the alchemy of sovereign becoming.

When we are looking down, aligned with Falsehood and clinging to the structures of paradigm and illusion, we experience depression and spiritual decline. We'll call this "entropy", as the laws of the universe force adamantine particles into arrangements of gradual decline and disorder. Things fall apart and so does Life.

This is the most powerful piece of awareness for you to practice your discernment of good and evil. The easiest way to simplify this in a visceral sense is to say that Truth is strengthening and Falsehood is weakening. You can actually measure this scientifically in the subtle energy systems in your body, and train your own muscles to calibrate the level of Truth in anything. This is a well-known craft called kinesiology. You also have the ability to calibrate energy upward. To transmute, improve and enhance. This is the sanctification that occurs when you bless your food: you elevate its frequency and bring it closer to its perfect Truth. We'll explore this more in the sixth mastery: Alchemy.

For levels of consciousness below neutral awareness at 200 on Hawkins' Scale, it's very easy for falsehood to deceive your awareness. You're in illusion anyway, so you're already living out a story of deception. You are in the coding of Falsehood, so you are in "Anti-Christic" attractor fields. Evil simply needs to keep you there. Lies like *"you're worthless"* or "*he's worthless*" have a lot of impact on this field. Every moment lived in this mindset is an infinity of separation from God. This is the eternal Hell.

For higher levels of awareness, the lie *"you're worthless"* has little influence over you, because your Knowing of **I Am Worthy** is much more powerful. Poison darts thrown by others might sting a little, because that's how you discern them as false: you notice the depressing effect on your biofield. But you are not swayed off course by them.

So instead evil arranges itself intelligently into other systems to hijack your creative power. For you, evil is unlikely to manifest through atrocious crimes like murder, though you have the free will to do so. You might say a harsh word, get into scuffles with social media trolls or drink too many cups of your favorite poison, but for the most part you have the sovereign discipline to choose right action. The emotion of anger rises in you as a biological response to one of your core values being violated, but your sovereign reason is in charge of your decision making so you don't throw a rock at your neighbor.

Counterforce must therefore show up in other ways. For example, in mid-range layers of consciousness around 500 (populated by intelligent, powerful, purposeful, loving individuals and systems), the mechanisms of seduction and manipulation work very well. Glamor reaches even beyond those logs as it uses your own biochemistry to distract you from Truth, shots of endorphin that feel a lot like divine bliss.

"If you eat the fruit you'll be like a god!"

"If you don't eat the fruit you'll never be able to reach the ones who need you the most. The poor people must be saved by your best, badass goddess self."

Even at your advanced logs of consciousness, evil can quite easily seduce your attention inward. For example, if you're running the paradigm "*the world is a reflection of me*", then anytime you experience a challenge in real life, evil will trick you into gazing inward at all your past traumas and into endless self-psychoanalysis to dig up the dirt about all the intergenerational wounds that you still need to overcome before you get on with your mission.

"If you eat the fruit you'll be like a god, but you aren't manifesting the fruit so it must be your lack consciousness and all the blockages from what Alice said to you in third grade and your witch wound from eight lifetimes ago." Now you're focusing on those stories, not the actual fruit that God is providing you abundantly.

So what role should you play in managing the cosmic balance of good and evil?

You may be called to the frontlines of the energetic warfare manifesting in the lower astral realms, but it's unlikely. There are other providential systems of creation working wonders there. We little fleshy humans don't need to lend our biofields and bodies as battlegrounds for energy transmutation. When you experience grotesque visions and horrible narratives playing out in your clairvoyant mind, this is a sign that your radar is tuned into the lower astral dimensions and your imagination is translating these energies into visual effects. When you feel agonizing physical ascension symptoms, it's a sign that you are internalizing cosmic energies and they are manifesting through your own flesh. It is very unlikely that God is asking you to keep your conscious mind in psychosis to be experiencing the gruesome imagination that occurs there. It's unlikely God requires your body to be tortured. Same if you're being tossed about by extraterrestrials, negative entities, demonic forces, the planetary energies or solar flares, chances are you are participating in a playing field that has little to do with who you are and how you best serve our family. The fact that these warfare dynamics are occurring is ok, God is aware and has it covered. He does not need you to experience this, and you are allowed to be free of it.

It's more likely that you are called to the frontlines of healing the human effects of entropy. With your forgiving and compassionate presence, your creative authority and your understanding of the Sovereign Way you've been so far, you are perfectly placed to improve the lives of multitudes, bringing them into the oasis simply by engaging them. If you are thus a planetary lightworker and , all the more important that you don't align with the phenomenological story of how bad and evil the world is. Instead, hold the sovereign position of unconditional love. Truly Know the one before you as the Beloved Christ, and the earth under your feet as paradise.

Observe counterforce as an effect of expansion, and deal with it from that mindset. Do not agree with it as an identity experience, or you will eternalize those energies. That's what Hell is. With the sovereignty to observe counterforce as an effect, you are free to simply perform the energy hygiene to clear these frequencies, establish the correct field of spiritual protection, and identify the thresholds of righteous action in front of you. Where is the shoe is rubbing? That's where the effects of counterforce is felt. That's a clue about what's next for you to move through. Is it showing up in your relationships? Your bank account? Digestive system? Technology? Your sense of self? Addictions? Emotional awareness? Complete what needs to be completed in these areas, and enjoy the ascension.

What's in the way *is* the Way.

Recognize where your awareness identifies "*not good*"—both on a macro scale in our world and in your secret, inner chambers. Clarify with yourself if the "not good" is an actual occurrence or an inner reality happening. No other action is needed. For now, the recognition is enough.

Deadly Sins and All That Stuff

"The Seven Deadly Sins," is a handy construct made by Pope Gregory I. You can use to practice defining the frequencies of evil, and recognizing when you're letting the mechanisms of evil activate entropy instead of ascension, causing the experience of vibrational harm against yourself and others. Reflect on these formulations and recognize how you know what they mean. Feel free to redefine them according to your heart's wisdom.

Pride: Positioning the structure of your personality before the essence of your being, inflating or wounding your worldly identity. Both "*I deserve it more than them*" and "*I don't deserve it at all*" are voices of pride. Pride is the sneakiest of sins, for it poses as nobility, and presents martyrdom, victimhood, conquest, narcissism, impostor syndrome and all those identities that convince you their survival is more important than God's work through you. "*I am a god*," is the source of all other entropic actions, because our hubris and self-sufficiency close the floodgates of God's life-giving Presence and makes us unable to receive grace.

Lust: Desiring anything for the sake of carnal pleasure, instead of love. Lust poses as spiritual pleasure and connection, moving through seduction and addiction to convince you that your spiritual fulfillment must be known in the sensual body. Paradigms like "*If it feels good it must be good*" and "*I only go for the hell yeah business opportunities that give me the bliss!*" are lustful beliefs that keep you focused on manifest reality to source and fulfill animal pleasure, placing your sensory function as the authority in your decision-making.

Gluttony: Constantly needing more and more in bigger doses. Nothing fills you up and you need more attention, validation, sensation, excitement, drama, wine... more and more is never enough. Gluttony poses as abundance, convincing you that excess is the way God demonstrates His love for you, letting the true essence of Love go to spoil either in your environment or in your body's poor, overworked digestive and elimination systems.

Envy: This is a double-edged curse of both wanting to have what someone else has and also not wanting them to have it. Envy poses as righteous judgment: "*She just manifested all that so quick, it's going to come crashing down. He might seem successful but*

I bet he's empty inside. Yes, they might be happy, but at what cost to society?" This envious assessment of who should have what always severs us from our fellow humans and deepens the separation between us.

Greed: Collecting more and more for the sake of having, not enjoying. Greed also poses as abundance and success mindset, though it aims less for physical pleasure and more for physical stature: "*This is mine, and you can tell my worth, my relevant place in the hierarchy, and my favor with God because of it.*" When greed sets in, we have made the world our god.

Sloth: Not participating with the flow of God's creation through you in order to avoid the groaning pain of effort. Sloth poses as surrender: "*I just wasn't called to finishing my project, doing my accounting just doesn't resonate right now, I really need to just focus on me.*" Sloth will also blame trauma. *"I'm not putting myself out there because Alice laughed at me in third grade and I'm still traumatized by it."* We can delay righteous action for decades because of our childlike avoidance of anything that seems boring or like exertion. Inertia sets in while the world moves on, your modus operandi becomes irrelevant to the collective reality. Your mind, energy and body are no longer attuned to your mission field, and without deliverance it becomes extremely energy-expensive to get back on track.

Wrath: A force of destruction that destroys what is beautiful and growing. While anger is a legitimate and useful emotion that signals the violation of your values, it becomes wrath when it is disproportionately given sovereignty in your decision-making. Wrath poses as righteous anger, claiming to champion certain ideals over others but indiscriminately directs fiery fury into the world of form setting structures ablaze without the guidance of God's sovereign Spirit.

Let's imagine each of these working together to create inverted realities, bending energy fields and corrupting thought-forms, and influencing action to energize those inverted realities. From now on we'll shorthand the variety of evil frequencies with the term "*All That Stuff*". Recognizing all that stuff as it arises will help discern whether the urge you're feeling is the call of God into expansion or the lure of entropic counterforce into entropy. **Recognizing** will give you a broader and deeper awareness of Truth, and it will improve your worldly mission as you effectively sift and sort through which identities, ideals, energy fields and situations deserve your engagement, and which do not. You will always be vulnerable to each of these frequencies simply because evil is here in collective human creation, a constant backdrop like the howl of the desert winds. You are free at any time to tune into it, internalize that hum and let it manifest through you for the glory of Falsehood. There is always the chance you'll forget, even for a nanosecond, that beside ascension and entropy there is a third universal force at play:

Grace.

Grace trumps all the laws of physics and metaphysics. It is universal, ever-present and evenly dispensed by God just because of Love. It is infinitely abundant in that place of Sovereign poise, and, when you have the mastery of Recognizing, you can stand face to face with the personification of Anti-Christ and simply Know I AM Christ.

So while you can't ever vanquish the counterforce that is evil, you can learn the mastery of aligning with the field that has forever overcome it, thus releasing your attachment to whatever the sand dunes seem to be. Now you have the sovereignty to choose how you dance with the resistance that will never "just go away", and you will be able to meet your Life with much less vulnerability to trigger and much more presence to actually serve in the way God intends for you. It was grace, not conquest, that allowed Jesus to say "*get away from me*" and experience the immediate relief as Satan was replaced by angels.

Finally, brothers and sisters, whatever is true, whatever is noble, whatever is right, whatever is pure, whatever is lovely, whatever is admirable—if anything is excellent or praiseworthy—think about such things.

Philippians 4:8

But even with all this—never be too certain that you know Truth from Falsehood. Never be rigidly confident that you know the exact timbre and tone of God's voice. Be humble, and be listening. Counterforce has its purpose and place. When allowed but not internalized it activates doubt which is a rich soil for creativity. Growth germinates in the upheaval of spiritual adventure. It is tempting to aspire to reach that Excelsior zenith, to say "*I have overcome it all it, I am saved, I am an ascended master, 100% pure consciousness, there is no mystery left and I've discovered the Ultimate Truth!*" Yet evil's seduction is always in the security of structured knowledge rather than in venturing through doubt into the unknown fields of discovery.

Can you give yourself permission to be OK with oscillating in and out of Knowing? In and out of illusion? In and out of joy? Up and down the scale like a sewing machine needle stitching Christ into the sludgiest depths of the pond? Can you give yourself mercy for the sins of the flesh? Can you Recognize your own humanity, and forgive it for being? Jesus, on the cross, recognized the desperation of humanity that suddenly hung upon his shoulders as he made the quantum agreement to transmute all illusion from the beginning till the end of time. He Knew, perhaps for the first time in eternity, the anguish of separation from Self. In that agonizing moment he called out to give voice to this anguish and confirm that only God can deliver us from the dark suffering of separation.

When it was noon, darkness came over the whole land until three in the afternoon. At three o'clock, Jesus cried out with a loud voice, "Eloi, Eloi, lema sabachthani?" which means "My God, my God, why have you forsaken me?"

Mark 15:33

Our human lamentations process the unbearable situations we find ourselves in, and also prove our universal dependence upon our Father God and our yearning for His steadfast Love. Even Mother Theresa could Recognize, "*Darkness is such that I really do not see, neither with my mind nor with my reason. The place of God in my soul is blank. There is no God in me.*"

With the mastery of Recognizing it's easier to dwell in the agony of the dark night of the soul, living inside a question and coexisting with the tensions of uncertainty. You have greater sovereignty to incubate pain and let it birth something new. Things around you fall apart and the Anti-Christ whispers "*maybe you're losing it all*," but in your patient endurance you make no agreement with any story, no declaration of what the sand dunes must be becoming. You allow yourself to be crucified, and you descend. In graceful poise you witness the structures of manifestation dissolve and the seedbed of possibility grow.

I say to God my Rock, "Why have you forgotten me? Why must I walk in sorrow because of the enemy's oppression?" Like the crushing of my bones, my enemies taunt me, constantly saying, "Where is your God?" Why are you downcast, O my soul? Why the unease within me? Put your hope in God, for I will yet praise Him, my Savior and my God.

Psalm 42:9-11

Just know that He is there, and you are in Him, and He is in you. And that *this* is the love of God.

Staying Sovereign When in Pain

How do we stay sovereign when the body itself is the most intimate enemy? Let's start with a ground rule: Pain is pain. We will get nowhere with this lesson if we don't first put down any comparison or judgment about whose pain is worse. *"Oh, you think you're in pain, try living with what I have to live with, then you'll know pain!"* That prideful mentality won't open anyone up to healing, so first, rest in deep compassion for one another and for yourself. Remember, God is not just I AM, he is also US. Your sorrow is my sorrow.

Pain is an intimate life partner who demands our attention and awareness. It is designed for that—to capture our attention with a message that something's wrong. Thus it steals us away from our lives, takes attention away from becoming and focuses it right here on the structure of what is. It makes us selfish and that's ok. It is hard to be focused on others' needs or grander issues when what's *really happening* right here is consumed by agony. Yet, life doesn't wait—seasons come and go—friends move on. We can grow old lamenting and grieving the passing moments slipping through our aching fingers waiting for the pain to pass so we can finally get on with being. All the time, your soul's becoming is still singing that longing into the universe: *I am here for something greater than this pain, this is surely not my whole legacy!*

So how do you stay Sovereign enough to participate with life richly and with devotion even when the body or mind is in agony? There are no conditions on fulfillment, we know that: God doesn't need you to be in pain or out of pain before you can Know the glorious depths of belonging and service. So your mastery is in maintaining the sovereign poise of Knowing who you are even when you're in pain. Agony belongs to Life and it's a part of the becoming, but suffering belongs to illusion, and your mastery is in remembering yourself back into the Truth that is true always. You are always in the presence of Grace, always inside the possibility of deliverance and resurrection *through* the very thing you think is keeping you captive.

Biologically, pain is a sign that something is off, but we needn't transpose that spiritually to think that we're put together wrong or missing something. There is actually no impending doom. You are safe within your experience, there is only life and more life. You needn't deny the pain, nor your Self, but distinguish which is which and place the true sovereign One at the helm of your decision-making.

Let's be clear that we don't mean "sovereign" is the freedom to have and do whatever the personal will fancies at any given moment. **Let's say true sovereignty is the freedom to be who you are**, to choose creatively based on what matters most and to devote your life to the highest Way possible. It is a personal and unique quality of owning the spiritual authority to love without hindrance and to express that love in a way that fulfills a belonging in a beautiful world where you matter. To be sovereign is to have the mental and vibrational mastery to not be spiritually influenced by false forces and collective tidal waves of energy, but to peacefully and faithfully navigate to True North whatever the weather. This sovereignty can therefore be accomplished no matter the cross you bear.

Look at Diagram 3: The Sovereign Model of Human Experience. Pain is supposed to bring our attention to the needs of the physical body. The risk is that we identify with Substance over Spirit, crystallizing the qualities of that Substance as they actualize. In other words, we make agreement with the pain, and thus we make more pain. Now we are not sovereign, because now we have declared that the actual experience of pain is more true than the potential experience of Love, so we are stuck in a collapsed reality and it's hard to suspend that creative declaration because the experience is real. The sand dune is set and held in place.

Three of the major neurological processes of pain are transduction, transmission, and perception:

Transduction refers to the processes where tissue-damaging stimuli like heat or a poky thing activate nerve endings. The manifest cause of pain in the world of substance. You sense pain because of transduction.

Transmission refers to the relay functions where the message is carried from the site of injury to the brain regions underlying perception. That's a chemical activity that changes your biofield as hormone cocktails shift your vibrational point of creation.

Perception is the subjective awareness produced by sensory signals; integrating many sensory messages into a coherent and meaningful whole. Perception is a complex function of several processes, including attention, expectation, and interpretation. You sense the pain, and you don't like it. Perception is where your suffering is, and this is also where you have sovereign authority. The other processes are governed by the body system but *you have authority in perception*. This is why pain is such a personal experience and why we cannot compare or judge people's pain, only take responsibility for how we allow pain to impact our quality of life. We get to be in exquisite sacred pain, and still say the words

> ***Strengthen me with raisins, refresh me with apples, for I am faint with love!***
>
> ***Song of Solomon, 2:5***

If we imagine a vertical scale—to what extent do you identify with pain, and to what extent do you identify with the Love of God? Pain and Christ are both present here and now, and you can slide your identity between the two, denying neither one, allowing both.

Look at Diagram 6: Walking in Christ.

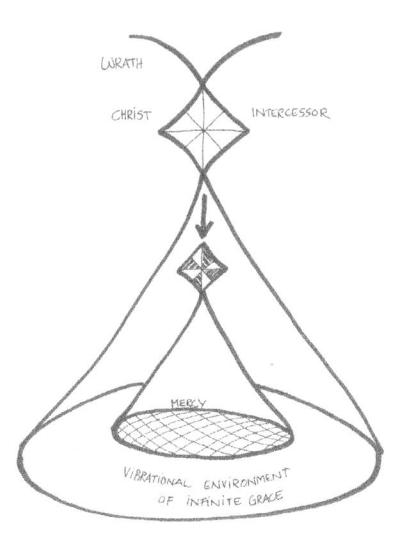

[Diagram with labels: WRATH, CHRIST, INTERCESSOR, MERCY, VIBRATIONAL ENVIRONMENT OF INFINITE GRACE]

What if pain was still allowed but only soaked in mercy, soaked in the life force that soothes and renews? You would have the lightness of Spirit to be non-resistant to whatever healing processes are already taking place. Pain can be *occurring*, but you can choose what's *happening*. Are you writhing with self-loathing and misery, or humming a soft tune as you translate the static agony into a rhythmic devotion?

My years of alcohol abuse taught me to go work ignoring the daily pain of hangovers. I learned to spiritually bypass pain, a skill I later transferred to the chronic nerve pain in my hips. After decades of being denied the pain suddenly exploded into a pick-axe headache I could no longer ignore. It blinded me with an intensity level of 10 that lasted seven whole months before vanishing. Always in pain, I went through all sorts of therapies—cranial structural, acupuncture, herbal, neurological, and so on, and the X-Rays found no abnormalities. I could do nothing but transform the pain into a personal crucifixion, and give myself to Love over and over on a daily basis. I'm sure every one of the therapies I tried progressed the process of healing, because that was the agreement I was making when I was pushing through. But in the end, it was during prayer time in bed when I was imagining handing Jesus cards one-by-one from a deck of intrusive thoughts, when suddenly I felt a snap, like a lock being cut. The pain released like a broken dam. Electricity spilled out from under my skull, cascaded down my spine, and everything lifted. The headache was gone, and didn't come back, perhaps because I finally respected pain for what it was.

I prefer a life without pain, but what about those who choose it? Think of St Francis, who self-inflicted pain by starvation, or the martyrs described in the apocryphal Maccabees who at any time could have stopped the intense pain of being boiled in oil. All they had to do to escape the pain was surrender their core values, but they did not. And why do so many religious rituals involve inflicting intentional pain, whether through self flagellation, barefoot pilgrimages, extreme fasting, sleepless nights in prayer vigils, tattoos, excruciating yoga poses, intensely hot sweat lodges? Why, when they know what pain is and what it does to hijack our attention away from Love, do these spiritual seekers knowingly choose it?

Intense spiritual devotion doesn't need good health and comfort. A sovereign mystic can breathe under water, and will not drown. The martyr regards her pain as serving a divine purpose, her strange sovereignty over pain as a means to transcendent clarity and profound Love. Such meaningful pain and discipline can create deeper human community because it embraces the presence of pain in our humanness. Now pain is not a punishment but an exquisite sacrifice that leads to gnosis, and submission to the God who delivers. In some communities, people compare ascension symptoms and regard the most excruciating energetic upgrades to be the most impressive. In other communities the old wives sit and small talk about who's the latest to be diagnosed with a horrible malady. Even deep inside the pain Story there is a camaraderie and connection that leads to Love.

In neuroscience, certain levels of pain have analgesic qualities and can even induce euphoric states of mind. Pain is even blotted out via a process in the brain known as gate control that profoundly alters biochemistry and consciousness. These states of mind release endogenous opioids in the brain, and other biochemical events. Thus a spiritual attitude can turn pain into the passage to a new self. Here are empirical grounds to prove that pain will not dominate the true lovers of God. The great martyrs of history have been able to transcend the most horrible torture, and people today living with chronic pain can live rich and sovereign lives of spiritual intimacy. **Rec-**

ognize also the risk of Lust, for the focus on the sensual nature of pain as devotion can quickly become a chemical addiction, which is not the same as Love.

Devotion, which we will explore more in the eighth mastery, is what helps us distinguish pain from suffering. The role of pain is rich and nuanced, and life can be painful and meaningful at the same time. Our lust of sensory pleasure and our expectation of comfort and convenience remove us from our dependence on faith. Faith has always helped people manage pain. Many among us live in chronic pain, and we must always Know that painful lives can also be good ones. We must learn to deal creatively with the physical and psychological experiences of pain that belong to the frailties of human existence, without depending on the pain itself to validate our place in life.

But whether we take St Francis' deeply devotional blessing of pain or the Maccabean martyrs' stoic sovereignty even as the torture intensified, we can see that there are countless ways to live life where you dominate pain by allowing it, making this paradox your exquisite devotion and intimacy with God. **What's in the way is the Way:**

1. **Assess**. What pain are you in? What are its parameters? What are its qualities? What is keeping you in pain?

I AM in pain. I AM the one with scoliosis. I AM the one with Lyme disease. I AM the one with peripheral neuropathy. Do you have a core paradigm that "*no pain = no gain*"? Are you too proud to take the synthetic pain killers that could elevate your day to day? Are you too proud to try an alternative remedy that might resolve the root cause? Is the notion that Big Pharma is controlling the world more powerful than the notion that your body can easily process an aspirin and benefit from the relief? Are you too proud to stop working, or too attached to a linear economy that requires you to sell yourself to survive? Are you addicted to the attention and care you get from others, or addicted to the sense of spiritual significance in your suffering, or the sugar that inflames your body? Or do you fiercely believe that lessons are in the suffering and since you want to grow you have to suffer?

We all have these little influencing paradigms that keep us in the experience of pain. There is no shame in this but if you want to be Sovereign you must know what these are, and clear them first. Once clear, what remains is *actual* pain, and that's what you want to be in true relation with.

2. Understand the limitations of this pain. How does the pain impact your quality of Life? Recognize that pain threshold and pain tolerance are two different things. You need to be aware of both these standards in your life. Your pain threshold is the level of pain manageable to you, and pain tolerance is to what extent will you allow this pain before it impacts your quality of life.

Again, you can't be proud—pain doesn't care that you're an independent badass boss babe—if you can't think clearly or your range of motion is affected, you need to be aware of these limitations so you can properly prioritize. Don't be tempted to spiritually bypass your pain. *"But I'm a limitless being of Oneness, a child of the Universe, my faith in Jesus is enough!"* Sure, in ultimate terms of course, but right now you are locked in a four dimensional experience and you need to know the edges of that experience so you can ground into the perfection of what-is and not suffer the could-have-been.

3. Prioritize. Know what your core values are and know what your limitations are. Now you can see where these things overlap and which elements are in the periphery of what can be accomplished today. Now you have sovereignty of choice. Being Sovereign isn't about having it all exactly as your Ego designs it, but being free to Love.

> ***In all this you greatly rejoice, though now for a little while you may have had to suffer grief in all kinds of trials. These have come so that the proven Truth of your faith—of greater worth than gold, which perishes even though refined by fire—may result in praise, glory and honor when Christ is revealed.***
>
> *1 Peter 1:6-7*

Christ is revealed through you when your core values are made manifest. What actually matters most to you? And what does that look like within the manageable parameters of your pain? *Family Time* may be your top priority, but perhaps within the context of your excruciating hip pain that value doesn't need to look like going to Disneyland.

4. Communicate. Be truthful about your pain and the shape of what is possible for you right now, and communicate clearly with the world about what expectations and standards you are choosing to meet. This communication is how the world can show up to support you. You do have access to the support and help you need, but the creative spirit will only fill the gaps if you let those gaps exist.

5. Return often to the question: Who Am I and where is the pain? Check in throughout the day.

A Story About A Man Called Pain.

There is a little story hidden in 1 Chronicles 4, which starts with the genealogy of the tribe of Judah, listing one by one who begat whom. *"The sons of Judah: Perez, Hezron, Carmi, Hur, and Shobal. Reaiah son of Shobal became the father of Jahath, and Jahath became the father of Ahumai and Lahad."* And it goes on—until suddenly, out of the blue, a man named Pain:

Jabez was honored more than his brothers; and his mother thus named him Jabez, saying, "Because I bore him in Pain." Jabez called on the God of Israel, saying, "Oh, that you would bless me and enlarge my border, and that your hand might be with me, protect me from evil and keep me from causing pain!" And God granted what he asked.

1 Chronicles 4:10

And then the chapter continues with the genealogy of who begat whom next. This long line of genetics, passing on the DNA from one generation of little frogs to another, was interrupted by a plea for release and expansion. One frog chose differently. His mother had passed her legacy of pain to him, yet he knew he wanted expansion and growth as he called for God to enlarge his borders. His soul's bassline Knew **I AM BECOMING** *more* than it Knew **I AM PAIN**. He recognized that Pain is a part of his inherited identity, and he recognized that energy transfers. He made the Choice, specifically requested so that he could experience ascension without passing on that pain to others.

You come from a line of pain, and you are allowed to interrupt that path. It is honorable to interrupt the intergenerational identification with pain, and it is honorable to ask for help. You are lovingly commanding the sand dunes to move into a new shape, and even if you don't know what caused the pain in the first place, and there is no recognizable solution, the Sovereign One will meet you on the bridge to kiss the pain away.

He shall cover thee with his feathers and under his wings shalt thou trust, His Truth shall be thy shield and buckler.

Psalms 91:4

As a Sovereign Master you will sometimes wander in the desert. There will be mountains of sand dunes all around you, and storms in the mind: *I AM a confused failure in a terrible mess, I AM unworthy of the dream I have, or I AM the only one who can keep control of it all, I AM at immediate risk because the world is collapsing.* It doesn't matter. You Recognize them all as Stories, and you say: *"ah wait, I Remember..."*

I Already Always AM

I AM Light

I AM Good

I AM Becoming

I AM Sovereign

I AM Saved.

The Third Mastery: Releasing
I AM the Kingdom of Mercy

So you've remembered the Truth about your quantum nature and how deeply, utterly Beloved you are. You've remembered that the entire universe is Source, Spirit and Substance, and you know Love commands all the adamantine particles in infinity. And you've also become rather good at recognizing the difference between truth and falsehood in your Life, so you can tell when you're operating inside a Story that's *really happening* underneath that diamond compared to when you're in the peaceful and surrendered state of sovereign poise participating with what's *actually occurring*. You can also discern how essence and structure arrange themselves in relation to each other, and which is which. You know the difference between House and Home. You also recognize frequencies of entropy, and the twisting characteristic of evil, so you can by-and-large tell when you're under the influence and your compass is off. What are you going to do about it? Time to move into the next level of mastery.

The third mastery on the Sovereign Way is Releasing. Because if you Remember the Truth, and you Recognize what's not, you can effectively Release your grip on the sand dunes of creation and become new over and over again in an endless experience of deliverance and possibility, and a deeper friendship with God as you begin to trust His Way more. So now you explore the mystical process of forgiveness, dissolving the ties that bind you to the world.

What have you not yet forgiven? Did someone betray you? Is there a behavior pattern or addiction that still wins your sovereignty? Maybe a system of governance out there, in the machinery of the world? A deep, unjust and terrible wound in your cultural identity? Is there wellspring of sorrow in the world that demands your co-suffering? You are allowed to let it go and be free.

How?

Perhaps you've heard you must plunge into the pungent bogs of sin to sensually feel every energy and consciously transform the falsehoods encoded in your subconscious, wading in shadow work. Little by little, you must reprogram your personal wounds and your expectations of others, turning your attention then to dismantling cultural paradigm frameworks and transmuting energy fields that prevent spiritual progress in the collective and individual mind so that nobody ever needs to experience what you experienced.

This sort of conscious descent is indeed a part of overcoming the world, but Releasing can also be quick and easy. Because ultimately, you are already always light and good, and everything else is Story. All that stuff has already been overcome.

Releasing is simple if you soften into that energy field called Mercy. You can use it for the rest of your Life as the human experience expands, contracts, compresses and quantum leaps, oscillating in and out of Falsehood and Structure. Complete forgiveness and deliverance is always at hand, because the presence of Love calibrates all energy when it's allowed to.

Perfect Love applied to what is already manifest, is called Mercy. Mercy dissolves attachments and calibrates energy fields, interrupting karmic ripple-effects and fulfilling vibrational debt. You are thus released from the energy it takes to consciously restore all things in a linear way. This frees your mind, body and soul to experience new wonder and more love. When his Spirit moves through your Substance all illusions are forgiven and reality resurrects in Truth, a fresh wind over the sand dunes we had attempted to make rigid and permanent. Ideas and ideologies, rules and ways to enforce them, judgments and expectations, identities and favorite hats, plans and legacies. Sometimes these structures have been extremely helpful, like scaffolding for you to grow along as you've built your experience in Life. But at some point the scaffolding must come down, and destruction can be merciful too.

> *"Come to me, all you who are weary and burdened, and I will give you rest. Take my yoke upon you and learn from me, for I am gentle and humble in heart, and you will find rest for your souls. For my yoke is easy and my burden is light."*
>
> Matthew 11:29-30

Like the Frog, you do a wonderful job dealing with the good, deep inner work. You tend to your mind and energy field, you make pretty decent choices for your health and you're intending to do better still to clear the blockages, the traumas, the bad habits, all the enemies you boldly meet. But some things have been sneakier and harder to release. These are the subtle resistances in energy fields all around you, both those in your blind spots like the blossoming roses you never knew were triggering your fear of being eaten, and the energies that *want* to stay hidden, like pride, vanity, gluttony, and their sneaky frequency friends. Mercy dissolves them, bringing truer energies into cohesion in your vibrational field, increasing your magnetism, enhancing your radiance and purifying your soul song. Then the adamantine sand dunes of creation respond with a new dance, and your life changes in marvelous ways—even if you haven't figured it all out yet.

Nobody is immune to the need for release and forgiveness. For the rest of your life in fact, you'll need to be open to forgive and be forgiven. And what's more, nobody you will ever meet is unforgivable or irredeemable. If you really want to be at peace you do need to Know the innocence in yourself and all others. If you Know you are innocent, then every sin and obstacle is an illusion being enacted upon in an inverted reality. With that confession comes the release of all other people you know plus all actualized occurrences in your timelines, and the release of all meaning in the stories you've spun around them. It means releasing yourself from the complicated network of after-effects of every transgression that ever existed in your life, and any idea that you're not where you should be because of this and that.

Most importantly, it means forgiving your own humanity and accepting that your incarnate Life will always be soaked in the richness of diverse experience. Even as a Sovereign Master, as soon as you step out of your enlightenment cave to go on mission adventures in the desert you *will* submit to structure from time to time, you *will* be fooled by the entropic forces of misery, and you *will* sin and be sinned against.

If you have the mastery of Releasing, it's safe to go forth anyway.

The world is changing rapidly. We haven't yet arrived at the core of what we are collectively detoxing. There are wobbly times ahead for our shared humanity as everything we have ever known shifts and the merciful destructions of ancient sand dunes give the appearance of doomsday even as new life is emerging within and in our midst. We need to adapt quickly and make wise and calm steps to establish the new world we were born to experience. That's not possible when our creative command is still influenced by the trauma stories of who we've been. Our vibrational utterance of God's Will is warped by our perspective when that perspective is formed by pain and by the belief that we have something to make up for in order to restore balance to the world. It's awful trying to compose a sweet piano overture with death metal playing in the background. Unless we are to become eight billion perfectly pure humans in the next few centuries, we will need his Mercy. We need world servers able to make agreement with Mercy on behalf of our entire family and beautiful planet so our true inheritance can be made manifest even through the chaos of what must ensue.

Why Is It So Hard to Forgive?

It's got less to do with *you* than you think.

Look at Diagram 3, The Sovereign Model of Human Experience. Think of the subtle energy system in your body as software. This biofield is your vibration, your feeling, your emotion, your brain wave, your heart wave, your energetic attractor field. It's your lovely halo. It is most directly governed by all the data held in your diamond consciousness, from the deepest subconscious to the most focused conscious and all the way to the highest superconscious, archives upon archives of what you think you know about *"what-is"*. The software picks up information about whatever is going on in your surroundings, in the perceivable energy field that you are surrounded by, runs the results against available data in those archives, then informs the molecular hardware in your body of what is going on.

Our experience of everything in life depends entirely on what we believe about this information, how we respond energetically (in our subtle energy system) to what we believe about it, and the information that is passed on to the molecular hardware (where our body chemistry alters in response to what we feel about what we think—and then what happens in the body because of that chemistry.) What this means is that when we experience stress or anxiety in our body from something that has triggered an unforgiven trauma, that is the physical product of a chemical response to an energetic response to some data that's running in our consciousness. When the data changes, everything changes.

What someone experiences as trauma depends on the amount of adrenaline in the blood at the time. The body is designed to record as trauma those experiences that trigger high levels of adrenaline. It's a useful way of learning how to survive. That is why two people can experience the same actual occurrence, but what really happened to one person was traumatic and what really happened to the other was transformative—it depends on their adrenaline levels at that moment. And of course, some trauma is inherited. Think of our friend the Frog. His lineage has been compacting certain data in his Knowing for 265 million years. He instinctively knows to avoid the pond when the roses bloom, because he Knows he'll get eaten. He doesn't know this intellectually or cognitively. He Knows this innately. But each little frog didn't have to learn the lesson themselves, or the species would have become extinct by lunch time on day six of creation. Instead, their great-great-great-great grandparents learned the lesson, and passed it down as a trauma code in the DNA to keep future generations safe.

Adrenaline and Trauma Codes

Imagine that you were born to a loving mother. She welcomed you, held you and smiled when you made cute noises. One day, a dog barked and scared you, and you screamed for a little too long. This activated something really happening in your mother's experience and her tired body responded with an abrupt *"Just shut up, you're too demanding!"*

This moment is the *origin point* for a trauma. Your tiny body was full of adrenaline and for the first time you receive the vibrational information that **I AM Too Demanding** and need to be quiet. The first thing your little subconscious mind did was to scan what was already Known, seeking data to help frame this new information. Your mind recalled the first evidence from the past to confirm this new present reality. *"Ah yes. That frequency of annoyance was experienced in utero as well when I was kicking at 4am. So it's true."* This is a *grounding point*. The information was encoded in your programming and you grounded an agreement with that reality. You had no reason not to.

The next thing your little baby subconscious did was look forward into Life, at what was becoming. The next day, your mother scowled at you when you played your truck too loudly during her favorite show. *"I see, it's true—I demand too much."* In first grade your friend embarrassed you when you helped yourself to two servings at the birthday party. *"See, it's true—I demand too much."* At high school your boyfriend dumped you because you were too emotional, at college you drank too much and your body got sick, at your first job you got fired when you spoke up against harassment. Over and over again, you witnessed the increasingly intricate evidence that *"you need to be quiet, you're demanding too much."*

These are *anchor points*, each one an energetic agreement that you remake with that sand dune, each one validating the original trauma code and stitching it to your life's canvas. The more of these "stitches" there are, the more life compounds the projected evidence to validate that story. Your attention is always on the story, then. You keep affirming it. Week after week, year after year talking about the same pain. So then forgiveness becomes a focus issue—you intend to forgive and release but the reality of that trauma is so tightly stitched into life that you see it everywhere without seeing it, and continue to affirm it as a part of who you are.

It's a wonderful evolutionary trait that keeps your physical bodies safe—if you're a frog. But we have evolved egoically and intellectually, and this trait has evolved to keep our egos and intellects safe too. As we have become more complex, so have the trauma codes that create stories of what is to perceived as traumatic. Life gets quite complicated when you've inherited all that stuff, like your great-great-great grandfather's fear of failure, **plus** your great-great-great grandmother's fear of success! Damned if you do, and damned if you don't.

Entire cultures are linked intergenerationally in this way, with stories about what to fear and what to do to avoid those threats. We begin to know it innately—and this is what we call collective consciousness. When a trauma code is recorded in the DNA it is associated with the production of stress hormones, so when you experience something that triggers the trauma (like when the frog picks up the scent of a blossoming rose), the cells signal danger, the brain records the signal and activates the production and release of fight or flight hormones. This chemical cocktail initiates a flurry of physical processes, including pulling blood from vital organs and pressing it into the extremities to prepare for survival tactics. Some people spend their whole lives in that state and wonder why they're tense!

There's good news. The sand dunes of creation are constantly undulating and shifting, malleable and willing to dance, and you are made of the power to dissolve every link in that involuntary chain reaction. You can dissolve the trauma codes that bind you to pattern experience. You can dissolve the data that binds your identity to the structure of the world. You can dissolve the connection between your biological emotional responses and mental narratives. You can dissolve the connection between the automative negative thought patterns and the way you feel. You can dissolve the authority that the way you feel has over the way you behave.

Not only do you thus release the entire vibrational reality that has imprisoned you, but the whole world will be improved as you release your white-knuckle grip on your agreement with that reality and let the sand dune reshape itself to God's will. In rushes Spirit to take over the reigns.

Releasing will never occur before confession though. All forgiveness means illuminating both the inner victim and the inner perpetrator for long enough to confess that what's *really happening* isn't necessarily what's *actually occurring*. Awareness can be super uncomfortable. Nobody enjoys feeling like a villain. You wouldn't be alone in burying your admission of guilt under layers and layers of subtle defensiveness and distraction. It takes passion for Truth, humble courage and trust in God's mercy to enter that cavern, recognize yourself as guilty and remember yourself as innocent. That's how you transmute guilt to gratitude. This is how we release.

As we grow up, our stories about the meanings of things get more complex, and they begin to interfere with the way we look at everything. We stop looking at things in innocence and start looking at things in judgment. We validate the stories we've chosen to tell and retell, and we begin to believe the projection cast through the cathedral window and landing on the stone floor. Be bold, look at how you have compounded the experience with your judgment of your self and others around you, repeated it time and time again to cement it in your knowing of who you are. You may notice all the times you've lamented and complained, or blamed and lashed out in bitterness. So while we may have no control over what others did to us, we have certainly played a part in the suffering, in a way all the external villains in our story had no control over. This needs forgiveness too, or the hidden threads of guilt will keep the story woven into our experience and we have the feeling of not being able to let it go, even if we've chosen to forgive the other.

Of course, some experiences in our lives came uninvited, unsolicited, unexpected, and seem frightfully unfair. There is no point analyzing all our potential errors in behavior, energy or thought to discover the root cause of why something unexpected occurred—that is a rabbit hole out of which it's hard to return. "*Did I manifest the death of my loved one?*" Some mysteries must be surrendered, and allowed to be. You must recognize when your shadow work is becoming a pattern. When navel-gazing and constant self-scrutiny become your way of being, you'll find your vibrational command into Substance sounding a lot like "I'm not whole yet". You might have agreed with God for Release and metamorphosized into a Dragonfly, but you aren't going to have the experience of *being* a Dragonfly if you're dragging your dusty old exuvia around to show people what you came from, commiserating in their lamentations of also having come from dark and lonely cocoons.

Relationships in The Kingdom of Mercy

Staying sovereign *and* relational is at the core of the human quest, for that is the image of God. This can feel like a paradox to an Excelsior consciousness that is laser focused on **I AM** at the expense of **We Are.** After all, other people can be absolutely awful, terrible drivers and just absolute fools, and they're all in the way of my spiritual growth.

As we discovered in Genesis, relationship is at the core of God's nature. A Trinity, indivisible but distinct, is constantly in relation with itself. All of reality is composed of a series of events and happenings, actualized experiences. So to be in relation with something is to affect that something, while simultaneously being affected by that same thing. To exist is to live in a give and take relationship with the world, where your presence directly impacts everything manifest and is also affected by it. Sitting in your enlightenment cave striving for the ideal state of mind is therefore missing the true richness of divine life.

You are not a rigid lighthouse beaming your Light out. *"Behold my glory, I am a high-vibing, positive spiritual being!"* On the contrary, you are a droplet in the ocean of love, always entangled with every part of it, and to be in true relation with it is to be embodied in Christ.

There are two relationship glitches that prevent you from being truly relational with manifestation, and they're opposite sides of the same coin:

The first is when you forget that the world is a reflection of you. Momentarily you believe it to be your master and you give it your sovereignty. Your power depends on certain relationships aligning in the way you declare they should, and the movements of the world dictate your experience and your decision making. Your boss, fiancé or business partner is in a mood and acts a certain way, so you step into that story and play the projected character, navigating turbulent and conflicting realities without processing anything. You're a bobbing cork being tossed about on wild seas.

In this scenario, you are not in TRUE relation, you are in illusory relation. You are affecting things and being affected by things in Story, not Truth.

The second glitch is the opposite side of the same coin: you believe the world is just a reflection of yourself. You say the world is a mirror, and all you see out there is a reflection of your own strengths and weaknesses. Narcissus rejected all romantic advances, all possibility of entanglement with the God out there, the Beloved One we are in true relation with, instead falling in love with his own reflection in the *surface* of the pond, losing his Life.

Are you looking at the world and interpreting everything personally? *"This team's success is a reflection of me, I deserve the credit! The team's failure is a reflection of me, why is this occurring? What am I doing wrong, what does that black cat mean, oh, what does it all mean about meeeee?"* Are you taking too little ownership, easily cutting away shoots of friendship and intimacy when the going gets tough because the reflection seems like a part of you that's toxic or no longer serves? Are you taking too *much* ownership in relationships because you aren't being truly relational, but vain: convinced that it's all about you? *"I am the one who must rectify the dissonance here and put this mess to right, for the world is a mirror, I'm the problem, it's all me!"*

No—it is all God. You are not staring at soulless hologram. You are not that rigid lighthouse shining your truth into a matrix for the rest of creation to just put up with. This is the *Body of God* you are peering into, the very soul of our world. Peer with respect and deep compassion. Be the witness that calls out the Christ through the eyes of everyone you meet, be the alchemist that Knows God into being *through the very fabric of Life*. Witness the Spirit of Source in His Substance. Glorify the Father *through* the Son.

Humility and vulnerability are therefore key to being able to be in true relation with the expansive body of all that is, for to receive mercy you must give mercy. True transformation in relationship happens when you integrate your knowing that you are a sovereign co-creator of your experience seeing projections of your stained glass storylines in the manifest world *and also* that you are inside a relational energy body and it's not all about you.

This is the key that liberates you from other people's energy and also *softens what's hardened in your* energy. What's hardened in your energy? Anything that has been actualized in form as a way of being relational, including behavioral patterns, emotional eating, always being late, throwing temper tantrums, or withdrawing your love. Self-sabotaging mindsets like *"I can do this on my own!"* Refusal to receive the love, grace and abundance that the world has for you. *"I will not accept Love unless it looks like this."* This is the hardening of your heart.

So, for you who are consciously becoming more aware, more loving, and more sovereign, how are you able to be affected by the world without it activating net negative magnetism and an entropic slide down the scale? How can you be impressed and influenced by the Ones you are with here, without depleting your spiritual presence, or theirs? Like when you're working on your spiritual maturity and your partner isn't. When your path involves surrender and hers involves conquest. When you believe in abundance and he believes in lack? You must innocently Know that providential order exists in any given set of coordinates of consciousness, even in the most complicated and difficult relationships. If you agree that all of creation is entangled as one field of Source, Spirit and Substance, then you also agree that whatever is occurring right now *is*—in at least one of the infinite dimensions of possibility—*good*.

One of my students shared this prayer with me, and I thought it was absolutely lovely: *"Lord, if all things are redeemed in Truth, then show me the redeemed version of this. What is it?"*

Knowing divine order in all things is also not about passively submitting to the crap hand you've been dealt by life, or allowing others to diminish your sovereignty through conflicting values. Nor is it about letting the world out there burn to the ground because God could put out all our fires if only He wanted to. But true forgiveness means releasing every ounce of meaning you've invested in the wrongness of what has occurred in relationship, letting the sand dunes be as they are so the breath of God can blow new Spirit into Substance, and the sand dunes of reality can shift. It's important to remember this: harmony is always there, in the *dominance* of the combined field between you. You don't need to hold it or keep it up. But to be in True Relation with any other human check that your awareness is sovereign, anchored in the bassline of *your* core values and your divine home key.

Look at **Diagram 3: The Sovereign Model of Human Experience** and see again how unconscious systems of judgment hold adamantine particles in position in certain configurations of storylines and experiences. And now let's pretend that you're not in an isolated enlightenment cave but that you're out there, in true relation with an opulent diversity of millions of other beings navigating their own complex vibrational universes.

In your mind's eye, go back into the alabaster cathedral and look up at the stained-glass window that is your consciousness. If you examine the lovely stained glass, full of color and texture, you see all the stories written as codes in your DNA. Perhaps *"it's dangerous to be where the roses bloom"* or *"I don't need a blade of grass, I must push through the water's surface on my own!"* Now turn your gaze and look at the stone floor under the window. The beautiful imagery that you see here on the floor is the projection of those stories into the world, your emotional response to those stories, your own thoughts about it all and the way these thoughts make you feel. So, the image you see is what you **believe** about life *and* what you **feel** about what you **think** about what you **believe** about life, and how life arranges itself in response.

Now, another window appears, projecting onto another patch of the floor. It is your mother, or father, or husband, or ex-wife. And that one's stories. And the image on the floor is what they **believe** about life, and what they *feel* about what they **think** about what they **believe** about life.

And now God decides to bend the entire fabric of space and time, and the walls of the cathedral shift and angle the two windows so the projections slide across the floor and are suddenly touching. He has brought you into relationship.

Look at Diagram 7 RELATIONSHIP.

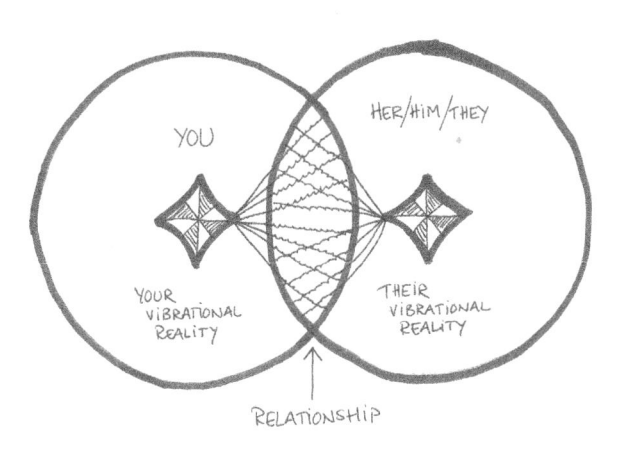

What happens in relationship is that the two windows project onto the same patch on the cathedral flagstone floor. We see a few things happening to the image on the floor. The colors are brighter! More vibrant! A space with two windows is lighter than a space with only one. But the stories are harder to read, and figures and happenings sort of overlap each other as if merging together. Your childhood trauma is happening in the same place as her business success. His fear of being left alone is on top of your need for independence.

This is relationship. Energetically, the manifestation between you forms from a solution of the following thought-forms and attractor fields:

(what you believe about life) + (what you feel about)(what you think about)(your beliefs about life)

plus

(what they think about life) + (what they feel about)(what they think about)(their beliefs about life)

plus

(what you believe) (they believe about life) + (what you think + feel about)(what you believe)(they believe about life)

plus

(what they believe)(you believe about life) + (what they think + feel about)(what they believe)(you believe about life).

= Quite the algorithmic mess.

Release is therefore not in trying to understand all the interconnected psycho-pneuma-somatic facts through the distortions of these complexly interlinked paradigms, but to gaze *beyond* the facts and stories that make up the reflection you see on the surface. Instead of peering at the surface and saying "*he is the perpetrator and I am the victim*" or "*everything is a reflection of me*", peer deeply into the body of God and see that the other is an equally Beloved Child. As you meet there in the vibrancy of the stories melding together, you forgive yourself and the other for having a window, and new harmonies of color come about as your story influences his and her story influences yours. Now look up at your window, as a curious thing occurs—the windows are changing.

Unfinished stories complete with a happy ending, stolen things returned, lost things found, lessons learned and questions answered, other adventures open up.

It is in relation, in that divine friendship, that our stories are fulfilled. You know the sun on the other side of the windows is shining equally on both, you know all the stories are just projections of one unified Truth moving through the filters on the stained glass. But do you know how *special* those stories are? Look closely at these sacred stories projecting here in the white alabaster cathedral of your consciousness. Go on, get your line of sight focused so that you see, in the projection, the swirling particles of dust, catching the light and glinting, magnifying the color and vibrancy, dancing with the Light of the great Sun beyond.

Dust.

Millions of particles.

Alive.

Above, below, all around, throughout you, your body is of this, indivisibly...

Billions of them, trillions of adamantine particles,

quantum pricks of Light,

The Body of the Beloved.

His Name is Love,

and this is the body of Love.

The Only Thing Ever Begotten

And look all around you how the particles dance in the Light of the vibrancy of your stories. All the colors, all the vibes, all the mysteries, the inquiries, the discoveries, the people, the belonging, all that made of particles, the Body of God. The brilliant colors of your vibrant stories animate these living particles and you are alive. Look how the particles dance in the Story of Love.

This *is* the Love of God. Eternal peace as Source, Spirit and Substance dance with one another through the stories of Life.

And all the dust of your life emulsifies together in a garden of adamantine particles, an infinite bursting of Life and Life abundantly inside and outside the structure of the cathedral, as he makes every herb bearing flower upon the face of all the Earth, every tree bearing fruit pregnant with the seed of eternal Life. Life is already the garden in which you are the Love story with the Beloved, no more or less important than the dance of two dragonflies in the summer.

Remember:

I AM Light,

I AM Good,

I AM Becoming.

I AM consciousness, born as a human, good and becoming. And the values that matter most to my heart make up the soul song that become my voice in a harmony of humanity, always relevant, always belonging, always wanted, and always loved. Now I must acknowledge that if this is true for me, then it is True for you. You are the most beloved child of God.

In Genesis 1:26 God says "*Let US make humankind in our image, and let them have sovereign dominion over all Life.*" God is not just **I AM**, God is **Us**. This relationality is inherent in who we are as the only begotten child of God. **Emmanuel = God is *with* us.** So *true relation* inherent in *true humanity* is an entangled intimacy of innocence and belonging. A familiar love, a heart that says "I see you, I love you". That is *conscious* humanity.

If we are looking at each other and seeing the enemy, then we are not conscious, we are not Emmanuel, and therefore, we are not truly human. We are are unconscious unhuman = Anti-Christ. But if you can approach the enemy through deeply present and devotional listening, you will be receiving the Holy Spirit through every word spoken. Noticing more and more distinctions in sound and clearly discerning the strands of Truth in all things, you will be magnetizing the Spirit through the other. Listen to the angry man in front of you and Know that Christ is speaking through suffering. It takes practice because our operating systems want us to listen through our operating systems, our filters are all there for a good reason and all our points of view are legitimate, but to be in true relation, listen with your soul.

We are not required to see things from the eyes of the Father, so there is no need to aspire for God consciousness, God already has that point of view and once you've Remembered this is the ultimate Truth you don't need to strive for it. We are called to see things through the eyes of the Son. Divine yes, but completely and thoroughly human. We are deeply saddened by how we treat each other when we remember that each one was somebody's baby once. This innocence is the only place from which a truly conscious human response can occur.

When Jesus said, *"forgive them, they know not what they do,"* he was loving the babies inside his tormentors. They had forgotten, become so unconscious to Love's presence, so stuck in the system that they were willing to destroy the innocent lamb of God.

> *The King will reply, 'Truly I tell you, **whatever you did for one of the least of these brothers and sisters of mine, you did for me.**"*
>
> *Matthew 25:40*

When you next look in the mirror, or into the eyes of another, will you see the baby? Or will you crucify the lamb of God?

We are all vulnerable to unconscious inhumanity. It's hard to stay present and in love when the structured happenings of the world get so overwhelming and complicated. You let a trigger overpower your sovereignty for a moment and you're in an unconscious story you once believed was real. That's why Jesus is also our Savior. Conscious humanity must be a daily, moment by moment choice—a constant practice of releasing pride, unforgiveness, and control. Namaste means "*the divine in me sees the divine in you*", and Jesus means "*yes, and I see also the little baby human, born into the dirt. Be with me, rest in me.*" A simple friendship that softens our hearts and minds, and brings us home into a communion of love.

Manifesting in Relationship

The intersection of the Venn diagram in Diagram 7 is the energetic womb of your joint creation. Whose genes are dominant?

Let's distinguish "dominant". In entropy, domination is an egoic control method. In ascension, domination is natural. Nature takes the flow of least resistance, and dominance has to do where the most relevant power is coming from. Sometimes it's a coyote, and sometimes it's a flea. Dominance helps keep all natural systems in order. So to transpose this idea on to relationship: which values, motivations, ideals, beliefs have the most creative power between you and the One you're in true relation with? Those are the ones that hold the most energetic actualizing agency in the soup bubbling away in your shared cauldron. So will this relationship come out as tomato soup or chicken soup? Depends on which flavor is the most powerful! Return to **Diagram 4: Hawkins' Scale** to remind yourself of the calibrations of true power, and where the greatest electromagnetism calibrates.

If you are highly conscious, and the One in relation with you is less so, you have a greater electromagnetic attractor field, and greater creative power. Then you have a spiritual responsibility to hold your poise and make sovereign decisions about your energy field to avoid unintentional harm, dropping a word like a one-inch punch, or overriding God's will through *them*. You'll need to forgive more often than they do, allow more than they do, process your emotions more than they do, and surrender more than they do. Life in the Kingdom requires great sacrifice, and your pride must go first. You may never win another argument in your life.

If you are in relation with someone, then there is commonality between you, a shared space of Love. Your weighted consciousness is matched by an equally weighted consciousness. If you are the partner who is spiritually accountable for bringing integrity into a situation, or driving well in traffic, then you can guarantee the other is propelling you forward with an equally weighted focus on some other aspect of your wholeness. Safety? Provision? Community? Manual labor? Compassion? World lessons? Everyone has something to share, and unless you value that in them you will override the sovereign dominance in the space between you, and the resulting manifestation will be manipulated to your favor and therefore much less energetically stable.

Look at Diagram 7 again, and look at the intersection. **There is an algorithmic tangle of paradigms here, but there is also the sacred space of shared values.**

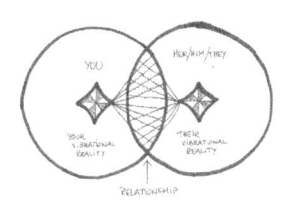

A Sovereign Master views friendship as the fulfillment of all that is most distinctively human, the pure manifestation of God's relationality. An Excelsior consciousness assesses friendship primarily in terms of its usefulness for achieving material ends, where friends function as business contacts, to minimize boredom and loneliness, or to serve as support on an ascending journey. Meritocratic relationships involve little of the intimacy, trust, commitment and loyalty of real friendships. You can tell these relationships because it's easy to cut ties and cancel people who "*no longer serve*". This falls short of the ideals of true friendship. God will not cancel you when you fail to serve. The Kingdom of Mercy allows and allows and allows—and alchemizes in that allowing. Friendship is one of God's special gifts to humans. Indeed, *friendship* is one of the terms God uses to describe the relationship He desires with us. **Friendship with other people is a way to deepen our friendship with God.**

And the Lord spoke to Moses face to face, as a man speaks to his friend.

Exodus 33:11

No healing is more powerful and beautiful than to have someone to share your loss with compassion and your success with celebration. Shoulder to shoulder, friends carry each other's burdens, share lessons and forgive the imperfections and limitations that make us depend on each other for wholeness. Sovereign does not mean alone—we are not holy unless we are together, because God is **Us**. This humble and vulnerable version of sovereignty is as far from Excelsior consciousness as you can get.

> **I no longer call you servants, because a servant does not know his master's business. Instead, I have called you friends, for everything that I learned from my Father I have made known to you.**
>
> *John 15:15*

But Jesus gives an exception to the responsibility of union. In Christ there is no need for separation because your Presence alone brings balance and justice, but at all other logs of consciousness you are allowed to separate from your creative partner in the name of Love. Not in the name of accelerating of your spiritual progress. Not in the name of manifesting your visions, including things like your preferred daily family traditions or earthly legacy goals. But for the sake of the Kingdom of Heaven.

You do not need to choose to invest your energy, time or devotion into a field where you cannot hold your sovereignty. As a friend, your first loyalty is to Love, not to the character the person before you is playing or the character you think you're playing in their Life. The key to mercifully releasing a person from your Life is understanding that the character you are forgiving is made up of the complicated algorithmic tangle in the Venn diagram's intersection. You are not, and never could be, releasing the Christ in them, for He remains a true friend in shared values for the rest of your Life.

When adventuring in the intersection of the Venn diagram, living the story of relationship, your poise is improved by recognizing the difference between "what is *actually occurring*" and "what is *really happening*". This helps you sort out the distinction between actual occurrences in the shared infrastructure (ie. *the roses are blooming*) and real experiences of happenings through your interpretation of the vibrational cauldron between you and the other (ie. *mayday, mortal danger imminent!*). Without this sovereignty, you will miss opportunities to adopt higher values and allow higher manifestations.

For example, there we were, Matthew and I, strolling together as we spotted that dead rat, decaying on the side of the road. The rat decaying by the road was *actually occurring*. I lay my eyes upon this revolting sight, smelled the stench of death, and was appalled and proclaimed the situation a *disgrace*. These data points were all facts in my knowing, and I was really experiencing what I was experiencing, but it wasn't *actually occurring.*

Matthew also saw the rat, and marveled at the utter miracle of life's works. We explained our points of view to each other. I heard Matthew's point of view said, *"Ah, yes I see what you mean, I get what you're saying, nature is amazing. What a Sovereign view of the world!"*

I intellectually accepted his point of view, but didn't embody it. I never released the old sand dunes. I was still creating my experience from an old framework, even though new ideas that I actually preferred now existed intellectually. The next time I saw a rat it triggered the exact same process in me and I was unconscious to it. *"See! This is what I'm talking about, another disgusting bit of evidence of what I've been saying all along, that is definitely NOT Love."*

To be willing to release the old reality also means to stop arguing for it. We have all known people who, in one breath, claim to be moving on, ready for change, ready to go soaring high, and in the next breath moan on social media about all the dreadful things. My original viewpoint about the rat was rational and has a right to exist. All the facts were correct and I was right about it all along. But the rat still needs to be recreated in an ascending energy if I want to stop experiencing decay. It isn't easy to release the old narrative because that rat still stinks and it's hard to ignore when that's what you've trained yourself to Know. Remember that manifest form moves slower than consciousness so even after you've declared yourself over something you're still going to see manifest results of it out there for a while. That doesn't mean you have to get down on all fours and sniff the rat, and then run off to tell everyone about it. Allow it to be what it is, trust that due process is actually occurring, and recreate your contribution to the relationship from a place of poise. **Mercy**, the unconditional Love directed into what has already formed, delivers a fresh supply of adamantine particles, alchemizing the nature of the thing and returning it to God. Mercy belongs to God, and you get to wield it.

This is how you practice Mercy in relationship:

You look lovingly at what has manifested. And you Know that this too is of God. That this too is some mysterious expression of divine. You let this Knowing of a "redeemed version" soak into the *manifested form* of harm, into the *vibration* and *energetic attractor field* of the harm, and through the *consciousness* and *idea* of what harm has been caused. When you Know something in a new way you are lovingly commanding sand dunes to release and shift, and true alchemy occurs.

Love is the only thing that heals, the only thing that transforms, the only thing that renews, that only thing that nurtures, and if you're not in love when you're looking at a thing then you're not in Mercy. You're in judgment.

"But how can I love this rat when it stinks so bad?" The stink is just an olfactory fact. It's just data you are collecting through your sensory radars. You have the authority to release all meaning you've placed on the stink, and be in poised relation with it. In judgment, you have collapsed potentiality and created a linear timeline based on those judgments, perpetuating the existence of the sand dune. In poise, the outpouring of Christ directs you to the best perspective and action for you to take on your true Sovereign Way.

A Protocol for True Forgiveness

Mercy loves what-is and allows what-is to be released from the linear ripple effects of its energetic nature. **Mercy cancels karma.**

The first step in deep forgiveness and release is Knowing that you have permission to unplug yourself from that feedback loop. Remember: you are not your trauma. You are not your triggers. You are not the stress, anxiety and fear that comes from the trauma triggers. You are not the energetic frequencies in the air. You are not the one who controls how others should be experiencing Life. Those things are real but they are Stories. In Truth, you are the one God is experiencing *Your* Life through. Some energies are stickier than others, some traumas are more established in our identities, and some of our archetypal enemies that we love to hate are complexly written into our plot line. It doesn't matter, it can all be transformed.

Grace is a mystery of the universe, this expression of Love transcends all structures, systems, illusions, fears and errors. It is Perfect Love applied to potential—something *not yet manifest*. It opens quantum actualizations that seemingly have no vibrational alignment with your energetic field, frequently defying the Law of Attraction and other universal principles of creation, manifesting miracles and keeping you constantly surprised and grateful. You haven't come into resonance with the thing—yet there it is!

Mercy is that same Perfect Love but now applied to what *has already been actualized*. Even when the adamantine particles have already become something, that something needn't be accountable for the entire ripple effect of its being. Christ is accountable. In him, Mercy has the quality of dissolving harm, forgiving the unforgivable and redeeming what was forever lost. It rights wrongs and releases shackles, pays off debts and neutralizes negative karma. With new Spirit infused into actual Substance, alchemy occurs and things are made new.

"Come now, and let us reason together," says the Lord, "Though your sins are like scarlet, they shall be as white as snow; though they are red like crimson, they shall be as wool."

Isaiah 1:18

So Mercy is Love applied gracefully to anything already actualized. On a human level, we consciously receive Mercy through Christ. Christ is the anointed, original Knowing of Ones' Self *as* Love. It's a plain of consciousness accessible to all regardless of your mood, body shape or religious alignment, and it is lighter than air. As a conscious practice in a process-based Life, the mastery of Releasing is a vibrational command to all attractor fields to allow Mercy, an amnesty to surrender all that is false. This relationship is like taking a shower after a long and painful session digging in the garden:

Your Knowing of your hygienic state is what activates your intention to shower. "Ah. All that stuff. **I Am Needing to Clean.**" Mercy is the water from the shower that cleans the dirt away. Your own conscious actions are what initiate and conduct the process that becomes your experience of washing.

That doesn't mean you do your part well though. You might step into the shower still wearing your filthy clothes, pour bleach over your head and turn the heat to max. But if you know how to set the temperature, which bottle contains the right soap, and which part of your body to wash in which order, then the process of cleansing and releasing the dirt is fast, efficient and delightful. The energetics of this process are simple, but specific. Order is important. It helps the mind to accept the relationship between the mystical aspect of release and the biological/functional process of embodying a new Knowing. Do it in the wrong order and you could end up poking open some wounds that were already healing nicely, or worse, you may even end up forming new traumatic narratives out of memories that weren't actually negatively impacting your Truth. You are still in the presence of the Mercy, but you might not be making the most of it.

True forgiveness is an alchemy that also liberates entire timelines and dimensions from all the after-effects of the harm that was caused in those traumatic moments. It doesn't take away the sacredness of your agony and hardship, but it removes the connection between potential triggers around you and the stress response that "really happens" when those actualized triggers cross your path. Your loving awareness becomes a tool that alters the vibrational qualities of these links and allows a complete forgiveness and release of these—dissolving the exuvia so the nymph can become a Dragonfly. From this point you are free to continue your Life on this planet with more capacity for mastery, new laws of Being, and far fewer buttons for others to push. Broken hearts, broken relationships, deviance and addiction, anxiety and mental slavery become incredible survivor stories, all emerging from the work of Grace. With this work, structures of all kinds that have previously prevented the experience of Love simply rearrange by the loving breath of possibility.

Of course, as a sovereign player in the game of Life you will eventually become dirty again, which is why the mastery of Release remains in your toolbox for a lifetime. But at least all the stigma is gone, and there is no longer any shame in forgiving or asking forgiveness. Forgiveness is mystical, metaphysical, and physical. Even though it is already granted to you, it is not passive. It must be chosen and believed: **I AM Forgiven.**

If the entire fabric of our shared universe is a delicious, living sea of Source, Spirit and Substance which forms itself according to our vibrational command **and** inherent in that sea are creative frequencies of entropy that warp the fields of consciousness and energy interacting in relation with one another, **then** of course you'll come across opportunities to forgive again and again for the rest of your Life.

> *Then came Peter to him, and said, "Lord, how many times shall my brother sin against me, and I forgive him? Seven?"*
>
> *Jesus said, "I'm telling you, not seven. But seventy times seven."*
>
> *Matthew 18.21-22.*

The phrase "seventy times seven," is a mystical number of an uncertain, nearly indescribable amount. Jesus says you need to master Releasing because you'll be forgiving as many times as it takes. **In fact, make forgiveness a natural part of your lifestyle** because we are never done with falling and getting back up as we oscillate in and out of Remembering.

The Spirit animates and propels us all towards being reconciled with that essence of Grace. At the point of perfect Sovereign poise there is no process of forgiveness, there is only Grace. But for every other state of mind journeying in the ontological process of space and time, you will need the process of forgiveness. It is immeasurably liberating to participate in that flow of Mercy and Grace. Released again and again, moment by moment, pinprick flashes of quantum light, He renews our waning spirit and keeps us in the infinite ocean of Grace.

Anyone can drink from that free wellspring—but to be immersed in it you need to extend the very same flow towards the other, out there. The deep mystery of being forgiven—without proper karmic restoration, lawful punishment, linear jurisdiction, just pure forgiven—that's what frees you from the meritocratic mentality that calculates and assesses systems of what's deserved and undeserved through your relationships. No more measuring who's done what and **who needs to change in order for you to experience the fullness of God's love.**

The unearned and undeserved forgiveness of Mercy is what breaks down the Lex Talionis eye-for-an-eye of the linear world. Suddenly politicians, capitalists, socialists, atheists, religious freaks, Big Pharma, white collar criminals, your sister, your abuser, your children's spouses, all those in the wrong while you're in the right (*or wait, am I the villain here?*), suddenly all villains soften and dissolve. Suddenly all villains become God's substance in the process of becoming something else.

Let's formulate a simple, ontological three-step process for effective forgiveness.

Step 1: POISE

Put God before all things. This is the first principle in everything. God is present even in the things you're working on releasing, and your loving presence to that Truth is the only place from which you can do any true energy work, especially forgiveness. This is why we begin with confession. "*I AM aware that all that stuff must be released and I am willing for it to be released*" is a humble and true confession that opens the process. In Sovereign poise you can understand your own role and contribution to a situation. Bring light to this, share this awareness and speak it out loud to someone who can bear witness, truly hearing you in non-judgment and joining you in agreement with release. In that true relation you allow an incredible alchemy of compassion and mercy.

> *You will never succeed in life if you try to hide your sins. Confess them and give them up; then God will show mercy to you.*
>
> *Proverbs 28:13*

Step 2: PURIFY

Next is the purification, the cleansing, the repentance. There are always three levels of clearing: form/manifestation, vibration/energy and consciousness/data. An esotericist may split these further infinitely, but there is no need. Dealing with these three layers in sequence is a simple enough way to guide your Knowing. This is taking the shower in an appropriate manner. Although there is no *actually occurring* ritual that in itself holds the key to your deliverance, *taking any action* with the *intention* of Releasing is your active participation with the process that's *really happening*. Remember, movement is a primordial characteristic of God, and the Spirit moves across the face of the unformed.

So if you want something new to take form, move. Use your herbs and oils. Do some restorative yin yoga. Say twenty Hail Maries, or burn your letters under the full moon. Use precision energy work, do some alchemical surgery guided by the Holy Spirit to remove the faulty data codes from the diamond. Push your way through the throng so you can touch the hem of the healer's garments. Shake it off. Go and swim in the sea. Fast for three days. Whatever you choose, take part in the purification *Knowing* that the purification is occurring.

Wash me with hyssop and I shall be clean, wash me and I shall be whiter than snow.

Psalm 51:7

Step 3: REESTABLISH.

Last, establish a new covenant. You've cleared the old, now you claim your Sovereign Way. Make agreement with the highest reality Spirit may form for you. Repent. Act as though it's done. Solidify.

This is a piece of the puzzle we often forget. We focus so much on releasing our grip on the shapes of the sand dunes that we don't take the time to actually make a new reality agreement. By giving your mind, energy and body a new Way, you are using your sovereign command to design a new Life, and the Spirit will indeed move the Substance.

Whatever you do, don't start moaning again! Don't pick up the old dusty exuvia and carry it around with you to show people why you deserve your Dragonfly wings. Commit to that new vision of yours and speak and act as though it is already made manifest.

Nothing new happens without this forgiveness. We just keep repeating the same old patterns, illusions, and half-truths in the process of trying to find the Kingdom. The great alchemy of Life accepts reality, forgives reality for being what it is. This frees you from the entrapment of the past and allows you to become new.

When my husband and I lost our home for the second time in two years, my father flew from England to help us set up our tent in the wild. He said, "*Elizabeth, next time remember to tie your shoelaces before you start running.*" I was always so eager launch back into expansion that I didn't tie my laces first. I would rejoice at some overcoming and then launch myself headfirst back into white water rapids, needing a whole process to right my Life again. Shoelace-tying, or **Completion**, is the outward demonstration of the embodiment and appropriate application of the lessons you have learned in Life, which is why it is a vital part of expansion. Before your next upgrade is made manifest, the energetic foundation needs to be in integrity. Tie your shoelaces before proceeding. That exquisite forgiveness of true release is then made manifest as **fulfillment** in the world. Let things be complete. Know your numbers, whether red or black. Deliver what needed to be delivered. Pay the bills or set up payment plans. Restore broken connections and release unmendable ones. Know what your to do list is, even if you don't know how to do it. Hear your directions, even if they are "wait", and honor them. Fulfill, and you shall be fulfilled.

Do those things that will show that you have turned from your sins.

Matthew 3:8

So the steps are:

1. **POISE:** Awareness allows a truthful confession and a shared agreement with release and renewal.

2. **RELEASE:** Intentional movement surrendered to faith in the process.

3. **REESTABLISH:** Commitment and discipline to a new Way helps energize and amplify the new sand dunes.

You are 100% forgiven.

Metaphysically and energetically therefore, from now on that you've mastered Remembering, Recognizing and Releasing, any problem you encounter in the manifest, actualized experience can be solved by completing whatever needs to be completed. Your action is like a healing balm that massages universal creative life force into the joints of "what-is", so substance can easily shift.

Now that you Know you are completely forgiven, when you see evidence of old misery become manifest in the world, you will no longer say "*Oh, see, here it is again, I knew things would never change, this is how it always is for me, it's not really forgiven but a deep, deep wounding in my many layers of past lives and ancestral trauma, so hard to overcome.*" Instead, you will say, "*Ah, I see some old misery—perhaps a mystery, or perhaps my vibration has descended a little and my filter of prehension is askew. I will drink a glass of water, take a quick walk, and choose a new way to see."*

Now let us leave the elementary doctrine of Christ and go on to maturity, not laying again a foundation of repentance from dead works and of faith toward God.

Hebrew 6:1

The River

There is a flowing River filling the dragonfly pond in the little oasis where the wild roses grow. You are standing in it.

This river flows around you and also through you. It's a mystery where the river came from and where it leads, and it doesn't matter. You understand that this is your river, flowing around and through you, and it is safe to trust it. This Substance, water, it embraces you and whether or not the flow increases or decreases, you are buoyant and aware within it.

The water level rises and sinks. The current increases and decreases. Sometimes the surface is glass-like and smooth, sometimes rough and turbulent like frothy white rapids. There isn't an ideal state of flow in this river: it's all ideal, it's all flow. And it's not something you can control, no matter who you are or how powerful. This is because the river is connected to multiple streams of water that you have no dominion over, all originating from the same Source.

Right now, the flow is calm and steady. Notice the feeling, the temperature, the pressure of the water against your skin. How deep is it? Does it reach your knees? Waist? Neck? What is the riverbed like under your bare feet? Is it firm with pebbles and sand? Is it smooth with grasses and waterweeds? Is it sludgy and squidgy with mud? What is your footing like?

The current speeds up, the pressure increases as you firmly hold your ground. Your shift your stance a little to fortify yourself against the accelerating flow, you notice it is harder and harder to maintain your footing. The water level increases, splashing up over your face as you gasp and hold your breath, then breathe out again as the surface dips a little, now at eye level and still rushing. You grab hold of a branch at the riverbank and cling on, slipping. This is the feeling of overwhelm. The belief that the flow is overtaking you.

A sudden Remembering descends on you like a dove, you Recognize the riverbanks and you let go. Release. The flow grabs you and carries you down a channel that you haven't mapped. You have no idea where this river leads, and it doesn't matter. You understand that this is your river, flowing around and through you, and it is safe to trust it.

The flow leads you to a pool. You recognize this pool, because now you have been surrendered to the flow for long enough that you remember all things held in it—and *all things are* held in the Substance of this river. The pool that the river has led you to is in fact the first of three pools, separated from each other by waterfalls as the river cascades down a luscious and abundant valley before collecting in the great pond. This first pool is your consciousness, what you know about who you are and what the world is. The second pool is your energy field, your thoughts and feelings and emotions, your electromagnetic output and vibrational point of attraction. The third pool is your body, your cells and organs, body systems and structure. And you know that the river always flows this way—from the Source, through the consciousness, then the energy, then the body.

But as your awareness floats into the center of the first pool, you notice that the opening to the waterfall is blocked. As this is your pool of consciousness, it is blocked with structures, rules and parameters about life, beliefs about your worth and that of others, and stories and judgments about this and that. They are clogging up the river mouth that leads to the next pool, and the flow of the waterfall between the two has reduced to a trickle. The water itself is still pure but your experience of it is that it is becoming stagnant, and you know this must be true on the other side of the blockage too—what flows from the pool above collects in the pool below. That's ok, there is no debris that has the power to permanently stop the flow.

Mercy. You look at the tangled mess of all that stuff there at the edge of the fall. You know the sticks and debris for what they really are, and the tangle loses its value. Gently, bit by bit, the pieces of debris loosen as you let your awareness slide over them. There goes your fear of success. There goes the idea that hard work is the only way to be validated. There goes the rule that as long as you're suffering someone else will take care of things. And there goes the belief that if you don't control everything the world will fall apart. It is Love that is releasing these bits of structure, that happens naturally when you see them from this angle. It is your awareness within the substance of water that has this effect. Essence infused into structure is the formula for alchemy.

The blockage is released, and the flow rushes through the opening and cascades down the fall, purifying the pool and filling it with crystal clear and scintillating water, whooshing into the second pool. This is the pool of your energy field. Here are the feelings, the pulsing and flashing, constant movement of emotion and thought. The rising and falling of emotion responding to the ideas and rules of the pool above. The vibrational pool always follows consciousness, and you see here the aftereffects of those bits of broken structure you just encountered. In this body of water there are stagnant and suppressed emotions and clogging up the edge of the pool where the flow wishes to rush through and down the fall to the next. Anger that had no outlet, shame that was hidden, grief that was denied, bitterness that has been kept here on purpose out of spite, and all that stuff. These have formed foul pockets of thick and dense water that coagulate and reduce the flow of essential, exquisite beauty.

So you slide your awareness over them, knowing these bubbles of gloop for what they are and instantly forgiving the pool itself for holding them. Your awareness combined with the essence of the pure water is all that is needed to purify the vibrational debris here, and the emotions release. You already know it's completely safe and that the river itself is what Life is. The blockages release and *whoosh* down you go into the third pool.

This pool is the body of your manifest Life. This is the pool of molecules: your body, organs, body systems, musculoskeletal structure. This is the manifestation of you in the physical experience. The river's miraculous flow extends from the Source, through the pool of consciousness, through the pool of vibration, and into the pool of body. You can see where the flow has brought with it the leftover gunk from upper pools. It has formed into inflammation, suboptimal body functions, and maybe even disease. It forms a dam at the edge of the pool and stagnates the flow of the river.

But you know it can be transformed. Your Love glides over the blockages, reducing inflammation and bringing equilibrium to the functions of the body. The flow coming from the upper pools is no longer puny and riddled with the sludge of stagnation, but rushing—cool, clear, sparkling with light—and the pathogens and diseases that had made a home in the bottom pool can no longer live there, the conditions are simply too clean and light. The blockages dissolve, and *whoosh* goes the flow out into the world.

The river flows endlessly. You are a wellspring of life force. Your awareness may linger in any one of the pools, but you will never run out of flow. You no longer resist the movement, the current and the direction of the water, and you know to merge yourself with it in order to transform all obstacles. Beauty is ceaselessly flowing into and through you, and now that obstructions are dissolved you are full to the brim and brimming over with powerful, magnetic essence. Abundant life fills your waters.

Now the water rushes and ebbs and flows undisturbed forever, and you continue your journey along its surface. You are buoyant, safe, watching and taking delight in the passing views: relationships, adventures, discoveries through stormy or sunny weather. Sometimes the river's path is winding and sometimes steep, sometimes it's frothy and wild and sometimes calm, but you know one thing for sure: It is going to whence it came—into Source.

Then my heart will once again be thrilled to sing

the passionate songs of joy and deliverance!

Lord God, unlock my heart, unlock my lips,

and I will overcome with my joyous praise!

For the source of your pleasure is not in my performance

or the sacrifices I might offer to you.

The fountain of your pleasure is found

in the sacrifice of my shattered heart before you.

You will not despise my tenderness

as I bow down humbly at your feet.

And when we are fully restored,

you will rejoice and take delight

in every offering of our lives

as we bring our sacrifices of righteousness before you in love!

Psalm 51

A Protocol for True Forgiveness

Mercy loves what-is and allows what-is to be released from the linear ripple effects of its energetic nature. **Mercy cancels karma.**

The first step in deep forgiveness and release is Knowing that you have permission to unplug yourself from that feedback loop. Remember: you are not your trauma. You are not your triggers. You are not the stress, anxiety and fear that comes from the trauma triggers. You are not the energetic frequencies in the air. You are not the one who controls how others should be experiencing Life. Those things are real but they are Stories. In Truth, you are the one God is experiencing *Your* Life through. Some energies are stickier than others, some traumas are more established in our identities, and some of our archetypal enemies that we love to hate are complexly written into our plot line. It doesn't matter, it can all be transformed.

Grace is a mystery of the universe, this expression of Love transcends all structures, systems, illusions, fears and errors. It is Perfect Love applied to potential—something *not yet manifest*. It opens quantum actualizations that seemingly have no vibrational alignment with your energetic field, frequently defying the Law of Attraction and other universal principles of creation, manifesting miracles and keeping you constantly surprised and grateful. You haven't come into resonance with the thing—yet there it is!

Mercy is that same Perfect Love but now applied to what *has already been actualized*. Even when the adamantine particles have already become something, that something needn't be accountable for the entire ripple effect of its being. Christ is accountable. In him, Mercy has the quality of dissolving harm, forgiving the unforgivable and redeeming what was forever lost. It rights wrongs and releases shackles, pays off debts and neutralizes negative karma. With new Spirit infused into actual Substance, alchemy occurs and things are made new.

"Come now, and let us reason together," says the Lord, "Though your sins are like scarlet, they shall be as white as snow; though they are red like crimson, they shall be as wool."

Isaiah 1:18

So Mercy is Love applied gracefully to anything already actualized. On a human level, we consciously receive Mercy through Christ. Christ is the anointed, original Knowing of Ones' Self *as* Love. It's a plain of consciousness accessible to all regardless of your mood, body shape or religious alignment, and it is lighter than air. As a conscious practice in a process-based Life, the mastery of Releasing is a vibrational command to all attractor fields to allow Mercy, an amnesty to surrender all that is false. This relationship is like taking a shower after a long and painful session digging in the garden:

Your Knowing of your hygienic state is what activates your intention to shower. "Ah. All that stuff. **I Am Needing to Clean.**" Mercy is the water from the shower that cleans the dirt away. Your own conscious actions are what initiate and conduct the process that becomes your experience of washing.

That doesn't mean you do your part well though. You might step into the shower still wearing your filthy clothes, pour bleach over your head and turn the heat to max. But if you know how to set the temperature, which bottle contains the right soap, and which part of your body to wash in which order, then the process of cleansing and releasing the dirt is fast, efficient and delightful. The energetics of this process are simple, but specific. Order is important. It helps the mind to accept the relationship between the mystical aspect of release and the biological/functional process of embodying a new Knowing. Do it in the wrong order and you could end up poking open some wounds that were already healing nicely, or worse, you may even end up forming new traumatic narratives out of memories that weren't actually negatively impacting your Truth. You are still in the presence of the Mercy, but you might not be making the most of it.

True forgiveness is an alchemy that also liberates entire timelines and dimensions from all the after-effects of the harm that was caused in those traumatic moments. It doesn't take away the sacredness of your agony and hardship, but it removes the connection between potential triggers around you and the stress response that "really happens" when those actualized triggers cross your path. Your loving awareness becomes a tool that alters the vibrational qualities of these links and allows a complete forgiveness and release of these—dissolving the exuvia so the nymph can become a Dragonfly. From this point you are free to continue your Life on this planet with more capacity for mastery, new laws of Being, and far fewer buttons for others to push. Broken hearts, broken relationships, deviance and addiction, anxiety and mental slavery become incredible survivor stories, all emerging from the work of Grace. With this work, structures of all kinds that have previously prevented the experience of Love simply rearrange by the loving breath of possibility.

Of course, as a sovereign player in the game of Life you will eventually become dirty again, which is why the mastery of Release remains in your toolbox for a lifetime. But at least all the stigma is gone, and there is no longer any shame in forgiving or asking forgiveness. Forgiveness is mystical, metaphysical, and physical. Even though it is already granted to you, it is not passive. It must be chosen and believed: **I AM Forgiven.**

If the entire fabric of our shared universe is a delicious, living sea of Source, Spirit and Substance which forms itself according to our vibrational command **and** inherent in that sea are creative frequencies of entropy that warp the fields of consciousness and energy interacting in relation with one another, **then** of course you'll come across opportunities to forgive again and again for the rest of your Life.

> *Then came Peter to him, and said, "Lord, how many times shall my brother sin against me, and I forgive him? Seven?"*
>
> *Jesus said, "I'm telling you, not seven. But seventy times seven."*
>
> *Matthew 18.21-22.*

The phrase "seventy times seven," is a mystical number of an uncertain, nearly indescribable amount. Jesus says you need to master Releasing because you'll be forgiving as many times as it takes. **In fact, make forgiveness a natural part of your lifestyle** because we are never done with falling and getting back up as we oscillate in and out of Remembering.

The Spirit animates and propels us all towards being reconciled with that essence of Grace. At the point of perfect Sovereign poise there is no process of forgiveness, there is only Grace. But for every other state of mind journeying in the ontological process of space and time, you will need the process of forgiveness. It is immeasurably liberating to participate in that flow of Mercy and Grace. Released again and again, moment by moment, pinprick flashes of quantum light, He renews our waning spirit and keeps us in the infinite ocean of Grace.

Anyone can drink from that free wellspring—but to be immersed in it you need to extend the very same flow towards the other, out there. The deep mystery of being forgiven—without proper karmic restoration, lawful punishment, linear jurisdiction, just pure forgiven—that's what frees you from the meritocratic mentality that calculates and assesses systems of what's deserved and undeserved through your relationships. No more measuring who's done what and **who needs to change in order for you to experience the fullness of God's love.**

The unearned and undeserved forgiveness of Mercy is what breaks down the Lex Talionis eye-for-an-eye of the linear world. Suddenly politicians, capitalists, socialists, atheists, religious freaks, Big Pharma, white collar criminals, your sister, your abuser, your children's spouses, all those in the wrong while you're in the right (*or wait, am I the villain here?*), suddenly all villains soften and dissolve. Suddenly all villains become God's substance in the process of becoming something else.

Let's formulate a simple, ontological three-step process for effective forgiveness.

Step 1: POISE

Put God before all things. This is the first principle in everything. God is present even in the things you're working on releasing, and your loving presence to that Truth is the only place from which you can do any true energy work, especially forgiveness. This is why we begin with confession. "*I AM aware that all that stuff must be released and I am willing for it to be released*" is a humble and true confession that opens the process. In Sovereign poise you can understand your own role and contribution to a situation. Bring light to this, share this awareness and speak it out loud to someone who can bear witness, truly hearing you in non-judgment and joining you in agreement with release. In that true relation you allow an incredible alchemy of compassion and mercy.

You will never succeed in life if you try to hide your sins. Confess them and give them up; then God will show mercy to you.

Proverbs 28:13

Step 2: PURIFY

Next is the purification, the cleansing, the repentance. There are always three levels of clearing: form/manifestation, vibration/energy and consciousness/data. An esotericist may split these further infinitely, but there is no need. Dealing with these three layers in sequence is a simple enough way to guide your Knowing. This is taking the shower in an appropriate manner. Although there is no *actually occurring* ritual that in itself holds the key to your deliverance, *taking any action* with the *intention* of Releasing is your active participation with the process that's *really happening*. Remember, movement is a primordial characteristic of God, and the Spirit moves across the face of the unformed.

So if you want something new to take form, move. Use your herbs and oils. Do some restorative yin yoga. Say twenty Hail Maries, or burn your letters under the full moon. Use precision energy work, do some alchemical surgery guided by the Holy Spirit to remove the faulty data codes from the diamond. Push your way through the throng so you can touch the hem of the healer's garments. Shake it off. Go and swim in the sea. Fast for three days. Whatever you choose, take part in the purification *Knowing* that the purification is occurring.

Wash me with hyssop and I shall be clean, wash me and I shall be whiter than snow.

Psalm 51:7

Step 3: REESTABLISH.

Last, establish a new covenant. You've cleared the old, now you claim your Sovereign Way. Make agreement with the highest reality Spirit may form for you. Repent. Act as though it's done. Solidify.

This is a piece of the puzzle we often forget. We focus so much on releasing our grip on the shapes of the sand dunes that we don't take the time to actually make a new reality agreement. By giving your mind, energy and body a new Way, you are using your sovereign command to design a new Life, and the Spirit will indeed move the Substance.

Whatever you do, don't start moaning again! Don't pick up the old dusty exuvia and carry it around with you to show people why you deserve your Dragonfly wings. Commit to that new vision of yours and speak and act as though it is already made manifest.

Nothing new happens without this forgiveness. We just keep repeating the same old patterns, illusions, and half-truths in the process of trying to find the Kingdom. The great alchemy of Life accepts reality, forgives reality for being what it is. This frees you from the entrapment of the past and allows you to become new.

When my husband and I lost our home for the second time in two years, my father flew from England to help us set up our tent in the wild. He said, "*Elizabeth, next time remember to tie your shoelaces before you start running.*" I was always so eager launch back into expansion that I didn't tie my laces first. I would rejoice at some overcoming and then launch myself headfirst back into white water rapids, needing a whole process to right my Life again. Shoelace-tying, or **Completion**, is the outward demonstration of the embodiment and appropriate application of the lessons you have learned in Life, which is why it is a vital part of expansion. Before your next upgrade is made manifest, the energetic foundation needs to be in integrity. Tie your shoelaces before proceeding. That exquisite forgiveness of true release is then made manifest as **fulfillment** in the world. Let things be complete. Know your numbers, whether red or black. Deliver what needed to be delivered. Pay the bills or set up payment plans. Restore broken connections and release unmendable ones. Know what your to do list is, even if you don't know how to do it. Hear your directions, even if they are "wait", and honor them. Fulfill, and you shall be fulfilled.

Do those things that will show that you have turned from your sins.

Matthew 3:8

So the steps are:

1. **POISE:** Awareness allows a truthful confession and a shared agreement with release and renewal.

2. **RELEASE:** Intentional movement surrendered to faith in the process.

3. **REESTABLISH:** Commitment and discipline to a new Way helps energize

and amplify the new sand dunes.

You are 100% forgiven.

Metaphysically and energetically therefore, from now on that you've mastered Remembering, Recognizing and Releasing, any problem you encounter in the manifest, actualized experience can be solved by completing whatever needs to be completed. Your action is like a healing balm that massages universal creative life force into the joints of "what-is", so substance can easily shift.

Now that you Know you are completely forgiven, when you see evidence of old misery become manifest in the world, you will no longer say *"Oh, see, here it is again, I knew things would never change, this is how it always is for me, it's not really forgiven but a deep, deep wounding in my many layers of past lives and ancestral trauma, so hard to overcome."* Instead, you will say, *"Ah, I see some old misery—perhaps a mystery, or perhaps my vibration has descended a little and my filter of prehension is askew. I will drink a glass of water, take a quick walk, and choose a new way to see."*

Now let us leave the elementary doctrine of Christ and go on to maturity, not laying again a foundation of repentance from dead works and of faith toward God.

Hebrews 6:1

The River

There is a flowing River filling the dragonfly pond in the little oasis where the wild roses grow. You are standing in it.

This river flows around you and also through you. It's a mystery where the river came from and where it leads, and it doesn't matter. You understand that this is your river, flowing around and through you, and it is safe to trust it. This Substance, water, it embraces you and whether or not the flow increases or decreases, you are buoyant and aware within it.

The water level rises and sinks. The current increases and decreases. Sometimes the surface is glass-like and smooth, sometimes rough and turbulent like frothy white rapids. There isn't an ideal state of flow in this river: it's all ideal, it's all flow. And it's not something you can control, no matter who you are or how powerful. This is because the river is connected to multiple streams of water that you have no dominion over, all originating from the same Source.

Right now, the flow is calm and steady. Notice the feeling, the temperature, the pressure of the water against your skin. How deep is it? Does it reach your knees? Waist? Neck? What is the riverbed like under your bare feet? Is it firm with pebbles and sand? Is it smooth with grasses and waterweeds? Is it sludgy and squidgy with mud? What is your footing like?

The current speeds up, the pressure increases as you firmly hold your ground. Your shift your stance a little to fortify yourself against the accelerating flow, you notice it is harder and harder to maintain your footing. The water level increases, splashing up over your face as you gasp and hold your breath, then breathe out again as the surface dips a little, now at eye level and still rushing. You grab hold of a branch at the riverbank and cling on, slipping. This is the feeling of overwhelm. The belief that the flow is overtaking you.

A sudden Remembering descends on you like a dove, you Recognize the riverbanks and you let go. Release. The flow grabs you and carries you down a channel that you haven't mapped. You have no idea where this river leads, and it doesn't matter. You understand that this is your river, flowing around and through you, and it is safe to trust it.

The flow leads you to a pool. You recognize this pool, because now you have been surrendered to the flow for long enough that you remember all things held in it—and *all things are* held in the Substance of this river. The pool that the river has led you to is in fact the first of three pools, separated from each other by waterfalls as the river cascades down a luscious and abundant valley before collecting in the great pond. This first pool is your consciousness, what you know about who you are and what the world is. The second pool is your energy field, your thoughts and feelings and emotions, your electromagnetic output and vibrational point of attraction. The third pool is your body, your cells and organs, body systems and structure. And you know that the river always flows this way—from the Source, through the consciousness, then the energy, then the body.

But as your awareness floats into the center of the first pool, you notice that the opening to the waterfall is blocked. As this is your pool of consciousness, it is blocked with structures, rules and parameters about life, beliefs about your worth and that of others, and stories and judgments about this and that. They are clogging up the river mouth that leads to the next pool, and the flow of the waterfall between the two has reduced to a trickle. The water itself is still pure but your experience of it is that it is becoming stagnant, and you know this must be true on the other side of the blockage too—what flows from the pool above collects in the pool below. That's ok, there is no debris that has the power to permanently stop the flow.

Mercy. You look at the tangled mess of all that stuff there at the edge of the fall. You know the sticks and debris for what they really are, and the tangle loses its value. Gently, bit by bit, the pieces of debris loosen as you let your awareness slide over them. There goes your fear of success. There goes the idea that hard work is the only way to be validated. There goes the rule that as long as you're suffering someone else will take care of things. And there goes the belief that if you don't control everything the world will fall apart. It is Love that is releasing these bits of structure, that happens naturally when you see them from this angle. It is your awareness within the substance of water that has this effect. Essence infused into structure is the formula for alchemy.

The blockage is released, and the flow rushes through the opening and cascades down the fall, purifying the pool and filling it with crystal clear and scintillating water, whooshing into the second pool. This is the pool of your energy field. Here are the feelings, the pulsing and flashing, constant movement of emotion and thought. The rising and falling of emotion responding to the ideas and rules of the pool above. The vibrational pool always follows consciousness, and you see here the aftereffects of those bits of broken structure you just encountered. In this body of water there are stagnant and suppressed emotions and clogging up the edge of the pool where the flow wishes to rush through and down the fall to the next. Anger that had no outlet, shame that was hidden, grief that was denied, bitterness that has been kept here on purpose out of spite, and all that stuff. These have formed foul pockets of thick and dense water that coagulate and reduce the flow of essential, exquisite beauty.

So you slide your awareness over them, knowing these bubbles of gloop for what they are and instantly forgiving the pool itself for holding them. Your awareness combined with the essence of the pure water is all that is needed to purify the vibrational debris here, and the emotions release. You already know it's completely safe and that the river itself is what Life is. The blockages release and *whoosh* down you go into the third pool.

This pool is the body of your manifest Life. This is the pool of molecules: your body, organs, body systems, musculoskeletal structure. This is the manifestation of you in the physical experience. The river's miraculous flow extends from the Source, through the pool of consciousness, through the pool of vibration, and into the pool of body. You can see where the flow has brought with it the leftover gunk from upper pools. It has formed into inflammation, suboptimal body functions, and maybe even disease. It forms a dam at the edge of the pool and stagnates the flow of the river.

But you know it can be transformed. Your Love glides over the blockages, reducing inflammation and bringing equilibrium to the functions of the body. The flow coming from the upper pools is no longer puny and riddled with the sludge of stagnation, but rushing—cool, clear, sparkling with light—and the pathogens and diseases that had made a home in the bottom pool can no longer live there, the conditions are simply too clean and light. The blockages dissolve, and *whoosh* goes the flow out into the world.

The river flows endlessly. You are a wellspring of life force. Your awareness may linger in any one of the pools, but you will never run out of flow. You no longer resist the movement, the current and the direction of the water, and you know to merge yourself with it in order to transform all obstacles. Beauty is ceaselessly flowing into and through you, and now that obstructions are dissolved you are full to the brim and brimming over with powerful, magnetic essence. Abundant life fills your waters.

Now the water rushes and ebbs and flows undisturbed forever, and you continue your journey along its surface. You are buoyant, safe, watching and taking delight in the passing views: relationships, adventures, discoveries through stormy or sunny weather. Sometimes the river's path is winding and sometimes steep, sometimes it's frothy and wild and sometimes calm, but you know one thing for sure: It is going to whence it came—into Source.

Then my heart will once again be thrilled to sing

the passionate songs of joy and deliverance!

Lord God, unlock my heart, unlock my lips,

and I will overcome with my joyous praise!

For the source of your pleasure is not in my performance

or the sacrifices I might offer to you.

The fountain of your pleasure is found

in the sacrifice of my shattered heart before you.

You will not despise my tenderness

as I bow down humbly at your feet.

And when we are fully restored,

you will rejoice and take delight

in every offering of our lives

as we bring our sacrifices of righteousness before you in love!

Psalm 51

The Fourth Mastery: Expansion
"I AM in The Vine"

You are issuing a completely new vibrational momentum, a fresh wind making a way in the wilderness and a wellspring in the desert. You know all you need to do to be the most powerful conduit for that wind, is to stop transmitting what's not True. So you sink into an obedience that allows your voice to become his and his to become yours. It's a restful and humble state of mind which paradoxically allows such a firehose transmission that radical, life-changing, outrageously unlikely reality shifts *must* occur for yourself and your community.

Shifts you now need to navigate.

The ways that he is calling you to now expand in your efforts to make a better world are completely unique and personal to you on your Sovereign Way. As you now emerge even more fully into his design for you and your purpose in Life, the flow increases and there is an inrush of spiritual energy. Imagine you're standing in that great river, your feet implanted in the riverbed, and let's say you've released all and sung *"I Am Ready, open the floodgates!"* Now imagine the water is increasing in volume and speed, whipping up a froth around you, and it is futile trying to maintain your footing on the riverbed, and it is futile trying to grasp at twigs and sticks to try hold on to your position in the river, you have no choice but to let go and be washed away from the position you so proudly created for yourself before you chose to open the floodgates.

You will not drown.

Your life is always flowing from within itself, so no matter how rapidly you expand there is nothing out there in the world of your creation that you can't handle—all the energy and resources you need are within the borders of your accessible reality—and your next right action is always as simple as applying the wisdom you have already embodied. Right action isn't the same as "correct action according to the world", so there is no point in any excuses about not knowing what to do. **Do only the next thing God puts in front of you. You will recognize it by your core values. Then the Way is guaranteed.**

Did you know your growth does not need to be propelled by suffering and constant death and rebirth? You don't need to go down in a blaze of glorified agony in order to arise like a phoenix from the ashes every new season. You don't need to endure bone-crunching gravitational compression before every Big Bang or collect ascension symptoms to score consciousness points. You don't need suffering to grow.

The Sovereign Way of expansion is simply a graceful and poised rearrangement of the contours of your spiritual capacity as he guides you from unique step to unique step. Your vibrational field in Christ infuses the essence of Mercy into all structure, so your capacity for Life increases, and you grow the way a lump of clay becomes a beautiful vase at the sovereign hand of the master potter. The compression of energy that must come before expansion is no longer suffocating but experienced like an embrace that seems firm, constricting, but meaningful. The following expansion *just happens* without you forcefully architecting opportunities to exist outside your comfort zone.

Your mastery of **Expansion** is simply a state of mind that allows growth, dissolves overwhelm and allows graceful upgrades as life evolves.

In the last few chapters we've been dealing with the process of *personal healing*:

- **The first mastery, Remembering,** brings us back into poised communion with the part of us that is eternal and true. We've explored the basic Trinity dynamic of Light's quantum nature and its relationship with particle physics. We remember that we are authorized to lovingly command adamantine particles to renew and reform, and we remember that we are infinitely loved and free to Be.

- **The second mastery: Recognizing,** develops our ability to discern the difference between essence and structure, and all the subtle frequencies that make up the Story we live. We recognize the characteristics that help us discern evil, and the freedom to know what evil actually is and how to relate to it.

- **The third mastery: Releasing,** develops our capacity for deep and lasting forgiveness. We let go of systems and structures that confine us, we become active extensions of Mercy into a world thirsty for release from the old, destructive ways of thought and feeling.

But your mastery as a sovereign being doesn't end with *healing*.

Now it's time to face the *expansive* challenges of Life. From now on, when challenges occur you don't need to sink into the analysis of dry bone shadow valleys, scrutinizing every possible spiritual root cause of your hardship—if you don't want to. Since you already Know you are innocent, instead you simply do your energy hygiene and then roll up your sleeves.

Because Life goes on. It is still always becoming, which means we need to know how to deal with unexpected plot twists, like when a hideous dragon suddenly swoops into your vegetable patch right before the tomato harvest, or all the gold in the land turns to ash, surprising effects in a completely uncertain challenge of flow in an endlessly relational universe. None of your mastery training will ever give you the ability to design and manifest your perfect vision for your imagined future. The actualizing future will always be much grander than you can imagine precisely because you exist in a harmony that is also expanding.

The Hebrew Bible, or "Old Testament", is a rich story about what happens when we hear God's call into expansion promising us a future, and then we dive into the white water rapids to get what was promised to us! We get into long and perilous journeys, complicated strategies and tactics, conquest and revenge, misery, segregation, judgment for generations—all in the name of trying to claim back from others what we know is rightfully ours because we remember the promise somewhere deep in our ancestral lineage.

The name *Israel* means that when you struggle *with* God, God will prevail. In Genesis, Chapters 32 and 33, we find the story of Jacob and Esau. Jacob, *the deceiver*, abused his elderly father and stole his brother Esau's birthright in the darkness of night, then went off to enjoy it. Years later, through the maturing of his life, Jacob had earned his stature and his wealth. He was in prosperity and a season of expansion. Before moving on, he Knew it was necessary to complete his past—it was time to repent. He would have to make peace with the first person he ever tricked, his brother Esau. The task was big and terrifying. He wrestled all night with God, deep in his restless dream state knowing he had no choice but to confront his brother, reconcile and release. Struggling and wrestling all night until at daybreak, in excruciating pain, Jacob finally reached the end of his tether and commanded the Holy Spirit to bless him. He was blessed with a new name: now the man was no longer "Jacob The Deceiver", but *Israel,* the one in whose struggle Truth prevails. When Jacob then took that great next step, vast as it was, it went really well! Much better than expected, in fact. After all those years of tension, guilt, betrayal, anger, resentment, Esau ran to meet Jacob and embraced him; he threw his arms around his neck and kissed him. And they wept.

The only suffering in Jacob's expansion was self-inflicted. The Spirit always goes before you anyway, when you tend to the next right thing.

This is great news, because you'll always be facing challenges each time you encounter the next "level up". Counterforce ensures there will always be experiences that seem bigger than you can handle until you have handled them. If you face each one of them as if everything is a reflection of some deep inner wound, or you try to architect your expansion by knitting energies and realities together *"out there"*, then you are always operating inside a phenomenological universe that is yours alone. You'll be missing 99.9% of the picture, constantly experiencing death and rebirth, tearing down structures and belief systems, walking through blazing fires and gloriously rising from the ashes again, only to face new dragons to slay further down the road. There is nothing wrong with that way of being but it is extremely energy expensive and all that energy can be released into Christ for the benefit of all who thirst. Go out to meet the dragon in the vegetable patch and bring her a pot of tea. It doesn't matter if all the gold in the land has turned to ash, because Love is the only true currency anyway.

Blessed is the one who believes and trusts in and relies on the Lord and whose hope and confident expectation is the Lord. For you will be nourished like a tree planted by the waters, that spreads out its roots by the river; And will not fear the heat when it comes; But your leaves will be green and moist. And you will not be anxious and concerned in a year of drought. Nor stop bearing fruit.

Jeremiah 17:7-8

Let's review these distinctions to help the brain as we explore the mastery of Expansion:

Phenomenology is the philosophy that assumes the reality you are experiencing is a manifestation of your observation. Light is collapsing all around you into particles of reality that you say are real. You are therefore always creating experience by the nature of your coordinates of consciousness. In other words, you have feelings, thoughts and entire conversations and storylines that exist only for you in a universe completely unique to you, and so does everyone else. And although we interact in a shared infrastructure, choreographing stories, transmitting values and intentions *through* those universes, we are nonetheless all *inside our own reality*. This is not lonely—this is the gift of being a piece of beautiful glass in the great kaleidoscope of God as US. The *singular phenomenon of you* is very precious gift to God.

Ontology is the philosophy that deals with the becoming of life. This organizes the way Creator is Creatively creating Creation through compression and expansion. Since all expansion is emerging from the one Source, there is always ongoing life, growth and vitality, and so we are therefore naturally called forward in life. There is no true stagnation, and so *your* Story always involves the development of the hero into a greater version of who you really are.

Put these two on top of each other, and you get the understanding that each of us is constantly called into expansion inside and *through* the vibrational universes that we are creating with the coordinates of consciousness that we set. If we say our role in Heaven is first and foremost about cultivating the abundance (since that first job we got from God in the Garden of Eden was to name and organize, cultivate, grow, and harvest), then your participation with Expansion energy is in fact your primary directive: **Be with Life as it grows.** We understand our state of being as a set of coordinates of thought, feeling and behavior, and we understand that Life reflects our state of being. That means, if we want to experience more—more energy, more rest, more peace, more opportunity, more abundance, more adventure, more knowing—then we need the ability to *expand* our capacity. Anything outside our capacity will not be Known by us. So, to hold more, we need greater mental space, greater space for feeling Love, greater resourcefulness for acting in Love for the greatest good, and greater space for appreciating the glorious returns of a more successful state of being.

Expansion is "*becoming* greater". It is a quantum leap, from one vibrational reality into one of higher resolution. The borders of your psycho-pneuma-somatic capacity expand, and your capacity for grace increases. You are able to allow more goodness to be manifest in all areas of your life. The expansion of your borders is energetic, so you manifest it by engagement, not by conquest. For conquest merely adjusts linear territory. Engagement infuses spirit into substance, calibrating reality, not moving lines on a map. But as we approach the edges of our comfort zone, we feel resistance and overwhelm. Like the little Frog standing at the threshold of the greatest upgrade of his life, you need to recognize if the resistance you feel is:

- incompletion pulling you back because you haven't tied your shoelaces yet, you haven't quite repented, your energetic foundation for growth is not yet in integrity and it is therefore not safe for you to expand yet, or

- counterforce steering you from your true path, influencing your attention and twisting the Truth, or

- an arbitrary limbic association between an actual thing and a triggered stress response, or

- a fair nudge from a loving God that this is not the way.

When you've checked these items off the list and determined that **what's in the Way IS the Way, then** the right action as a River is to flow despite the resistance. How do you do it? **How do you expand beyond your comfort zone?**

As always, there's the dichotomy of structure and essence to consider:

1. **Expansion by Mastery: Remember, Recognize and Release** to unravel the links between consciousness, energy and form, revealing the debris lodged in pools of your River that's causing this resistance at the horizon of your capacity. Release the debris from your diamond consciousness before following through with appropriate energy hygiene and mental-behavioral reprogramming.

2. **Expansion by Surrender:** Ride your expanding reality through **constant deliverance and emergence**. Releasing is an embodied lifestyle and Spirit

does the rest as you abide in the great vine, growing with it.

Expansion By Mastery

Look at Diagram 8 again. Inside the solid line is your vibrational universe: everything manifest, experienced, actualized, and known by you. Even as an ascending, sovereign master you become seduced into thinking that this zone is reality. You released what needed to be let go of and you enjoyed the inrush of freedom and creativity, claiming your sovereignty in Life! You came to associate success as being at the top of your enlightenment game...inside that comfort zone within the solid line. But expansion has nothing to do with what's inside that zone. Expansion is into everything outside that zone. For you also have dreams, aspirations, ideas, imaginings, goals and other unformed possibilities that you haven't manifested but you *have* conceived. You can visualize them even if you can't quite believe in them. These are within the dotted line.

The difference between these two lines is your ability to invoke and embody a vibrational accord with those imagined realities. That ability is impacted by many things, like your limiting beliefs, lack of practice, and even guardrails put up for you by the One who loves you whether or not you believe in Him, and who is mercifully preventing you from rushing into something you think you want but really don't.

In this model your expansion requires manipulation and perfection of the solid line container. The success factor is to identify and adjust the coordinates of this container. You do this by attuning the energetics between your unconscious creative rules, your personal vibration, the vibration of your environment (including all that is already manifest), and the potential of what may be manifesting through those you come into contact with. You need to make the correct adjustments so that this container can expand into a new reality. This is the work of conscious self-development, and on the Sovereign Way this will always include Remembering, Recognizing and Releasing. We know we are called to expansion, and so we press on.

Not that I have already obtained this or am already perfect, but I press on to embody this, because Christ Jesus has embodied me. Brothers, I do not consider that I have fully embodied this. But one thing I do: forgetting what lies behind and leaning forward to what lies ahead, I press into the goal for the prize of the upward call of God in Christ Jesus.

Philippians 3:12-14

Figuring this process out is a complicated ontological process, and you're limited by what you can imagine. Your horizons are as far as you can see, and you can't help mistakenly believing that this is what reality is. The earth is flat and you are inside a dome. You have been believing your potential lies inside this circle of all your wildest conceptions. The only way to expand is by conquest. Winning. To eliminate the authority of something outside your borders, so you can establish your authority in that area. You do this in business a lot, whether you know it or not: Make more phone calls, solve more problems, hire more people, increase the bottom line. Adjusting your linear reality to more of the same.

"I could be the success coach of world leaders and kings! I could make a million dollars and be a TedX speaker, bestselling author and social media influencer! I could have a retreat center

and heal all the people! I could finally find a partner who treats me like a queen!"

In this model, in order for you to realize the dream of being alchemist to the kings, you need to put yourself forward, reach out of your comfort zone, do the expansive and uncomfortable things like produce reels, attend seminars, send your resume out, create networks of contacts that might eventually lead you to the king. You must get into the numbers game where 100 resumes a day yields five interviews a week, you've got to desire it but not want it too much, you've got to try to invoke the vibration of it having been achieved by searching for probable coordinates in the databases of what you already know, using known bits of data to try to manipulate a fake sensation of the unknown: *"What would that be like? Would I drive a luxury car? Would I feel like a boss every day? I must try to dress appropriately so the universe knows I'm a match for the job."*

You might even accidentally ruin the whole thing by invoking false coordinates of what you think know about the ideal life, which ends up creating an inversion of the thing you were moments ago quite excited about... *"Oh God, rich people wear impossibly high heels and manicured nails, this dream isn't for me."* The energy that has been expanding the though- form of manifestation becomes scattered, and the forming Substance diffuses away to be recycled into some other emerging dream.

You will experience some growth this way, but it will be grueling. You've already discovered this while trying to orchestrate the expansion of your possibility by getting the coordinates right. But you can't visualize the unimaginable. You are not the Master Architect.

Sure, you can predict energetic probabilities and get some fairly accurate psychic results but only from inside of the scope of your current vibrational universe. You can also decorate the House by visualizing some fun objects and experiences you'd like to have on the way. But if you are counting on your own ideal manifestations to be the markers of your expansion, then you are manipulating your own process of becoming because you are only building on thought-forms that already exist. You are recreating inside your comfort zone.

This is indeed a worthy hobby as you learn the mastery of mind over matter and practice remembering that you are Source, Spirit and Substance in one, wielding your creative authority and not submitting to the rule of the world. You are learning how to cultivate the garden in the oasis and nurture what is good and true in your Life. *"Look, everything is energy and I'm attracting and magnetizing the things I think I want!"* we cry, but we make the mistake of thinking this magic wand game is the sign of sovereignty and we think sovereignty is equal to independence. Then we think we can independently design and manifest the great vineyards of our lives, with our little brains and our very minimal view of the marvelous gardens already growing all over the countryside. We think being a "co-creator" means we get to use our vision boards to architect anything we want, and God will just get in line with the vision and totally back us up—but that's back to front, I'm afraid.

Congratulations on your mastery demonstrated by fleeting worldly success. Now wait till you see what the Lord has for you, for as a Sovereign Master you are already merging with a far greater reality, one that is erupting from within the heart of the Universe.

Expansion By Surrender

"Come unto me, all ye that labour and are heavy laden, and I will give you rest. "Take my yoke upon you, and learn of me; for I am meek and lowly in heart: and ye shall find rest unto your souls. "For my yoke is easy, and my burden is light."

Matthew 11:28–30

No matter how vast and complex your vision is for your business, family or greater mission in the coordinated plan for humanity, the Way forward is actually very simple and the yoke is light. You are no longer Jacob who struggles with God all night, resisting taking the action you know is yours and yours alone to take. You have permission to know that God will prevail—He already always *is* prevailing—and you might as well let it be. Like Jacob, once you take the step into what must be done, you find the Spirit has preceded you and softened the existing structures of Substance.

In the second expansion model in **diagram 9**, we have decided to allow the highest possible framework for creation, and we have chosen to reawaken inside the Body of Christ. The Sovereign Way frees up all your survival energy, and stabilizes your knowing of yourself. Your confidence enhances, and you begin to connect with others in an expanded realm of consciousness. That opens lines of provision, and gives your creativity a channel so you express more of it. This stimulates your environment and you receive new and exciting input, which opens up new realms of possibility. And then you discover more Truth, and that leads to more Love. No more faking it till you make it. You're free to just allow it to emerge.

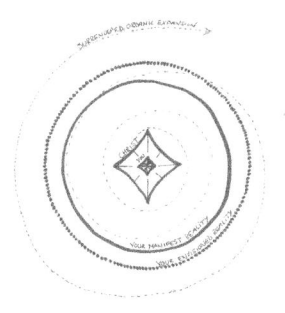

The natural expansion energy of the universal life force moves through *his* design *before* yours, so only your dreams, wishes and ideals that *align* with the highest, most Sovereign Way are animated and energized. The overshadowing of Christ mind directs your thought activity and connects you with appropriate people on the path. Expansion occurs not by conquest, but by engagement as revelations, solutions to life's problems, treasures from the vault of experience and expertise are shared among us, each one bringing a gift to the table that fulfills and nourishes everyone else. This sort of expansion is not about numbers of followers and dollars, or winning territory or respect, or even laying the foundations of the vineyards you've been dreaming of. It's not about accomplishment at all. This expansion is of the soul.

True soul expansion can only happen in community because Emmanuel means God *With* Us. It always asks for an opening of the heart and blossoming of trust and love. A brighter reality grows from a natural wellspring of spiritual life reinforced and strengthened by the estuaries of knowledge, wisdom and compassion flowing between us as different people walking different paths. We become a combined electromagnetic attractor field that is exponentially increasing as we hold greater and greater volumes of grace together.

Allow the expansion of your territory, products, services, businesses, models, methodologies, philosophies, works of art manifest *with* you not *by* you. Your job as a co-creator is to engage with what is emerging through simple, innocent steps into something new. Perhaps he'll put on your heart to learn a new song. Perhaps he'll take you across new dreamscapes at night. Perhaps he'll show you new combinations of spices that are already waiting in your spice rack, or perhaps open your ears to new sounds and harmonies in your garden that you've never heard before. Perhaps he'll prune away another silly habit.

The first thing to do to enter this state of expansion is release any idea that you're not where you're supposed to be. If it isn't manifesting, then it isn't for you. This is an uncomfortable idea for an Excelsior consciousness that has trained itself to see every obstacle as evidence of incompletion and every struggle as an invitation to muscle up and grow. As Jacob discovered, sometimes you just need to lay the struggle down.

> *"I am the true vine, and my Father is the vinedresser. Every branch in me that does not bear fruit he takes away, and every branch that does bear fruit he prunes, that it may bear more fruit. Already you are clean because of the word that I have spoken to you. Abide in me, as I in you. As the branch cannot bear fruit by itself, unless it abides in the vine, neither can you, unless you abide in me. I am the vine; you are the branches. Whoever abides in me as I in him, he it is that bears much fruit, for apart from me you can do nothing.*
>
> *John 15:1-5*

My oldest daughter Olivia is only 12 years old. She is sovereign. She is as authentic as can be, for a young one, often mistaken for being older because she holds a deep maturity and presence of Self. She's been through a lot—homeschooled for three years while we were homeless living in a barn where we washed our hair in the creek whenever it rained, she lived offgrid in a tent in the desert for 60 days and learned the weight of the water she carried from the stream to boil over the fire. She helped to terraform the land on which we pitched our tent and knows what it's like using your bare hands to carve out a place a sleep. She knows what it's like having to start a great fire to smoke the bugs out of the kitchen tent so it's even possible to cook without flies buzzing in your ears and nostrils. She's started a number of different kinds of businesses, mango jam being her most lucrative so far, she's travelled across the world and back multiple times, she co-wrote an award-winning play called *"Kyle the Unicorn and the Stupid Little Kids."* She's also acing her grades and learning how to navigate the emotions of friendship betrayal. She's earned her stripes for sure. But even though she is mature beyond her years, as her parent I still don't quite trust her to make all her own decisions when it comes to, for example, nutrition, personal safety after dark, keeping her room clean and tidy. And as incredible as my 12 year old daughter is—and she knows she is—I love her too much to give her all the freedom to create her own experience. I will keep a lot of control for the time being over what she eats, and where she goes, and when she needs to tidy her room. I will also strategically introduce her to different challenges and opportunities as she matures. That makes her life much more peaceful.

In Christ, you focus on nothing but what is before you, and your imperfect attention and clumsy but well-meaning action become the very service that helps liberate the collective consciousness.

He is the vine, and for the sake of this next metaphor, you are a grape. You say, "*I hold within me the seed potential of great and glorious vineyards that will one day stretch across the hills and vales as far as the eye can see, and make the finest wine in all the lands!*" What you don't do next is go and try to earn the money to buy a hundred acres for your vineyards and a ton of timber and concrete to build the vast wine pressing factories.

Yes, it is indeed true, that all the vineyards in the universe are contained in the DNA in the seed inside your juicy grape belly! But if you now separate yourself from the vine to attempt to create this vast vision—which is not in its season—you will fall to the ground, little grape. You will be trodden on by a goat, eaten by a turtledove and pooped out again somewhere over a rocky canyon where your seeds may sprout for a little while but they will be competing with the weeds of the wild and quickly strangled. It's a dramatic end. That's just what it's like beyond the borders of the oasis. You bite that apple with your whole soul so you can be like a god out there in the desert where reality is a cosmic energy field of zillions of adamantine particles in shifting thought-forms you're not in control of.

Stay in the vine. Let the vinedresser work. You will, like my daughter Olivia, mature into greater and greater wisdom, more steadfast Love and more masterful ability to manifest new territories and structures as you go along. You don't yet need to buy a hundred acres and a ton of concrete to build the wine pressing factories for your empire of vineyards. All you need now is a little stick of bamboo and a nice bit of twine to hold your seedling against the winds.

Matthew and I attempted to take those acres by conquest. It was our hubris, our inflated sense of personal responsibility for choosing what we want to manifest, our belief that sovereignty meant independence from the body of Christ. That independence led us to make rash business decisions and lose everything we had, *everything*, until we lived with our little children in a derelict barn on a literal trash heap with no car, no money and no way out. Little grapes setting off to build a hundred acre vineyard, very quickly trodden on by goat, eaten by a pigeon, and pooped out again over the rocky canyon. We dematerialized our lives by the choices we made and the subtle defiance we had against our higher judgment. We were not respecting the wild landscape between where we were as little grapes and the vast acres we were trying to conquer to make the wine that we are becoming anyway.

We did the destruction part, and what the vine did at every step was to produce new fruit, the friends like Deanna who let us use her barn, or Rev. Nancy who gave us a plot to grow vegetables and a car to drive, or Brandi the earthen priestess who showed us the way of bare bones resilience. It was the vine that turned the devastation into an extraordinary discovery of truly sustainable living and abundance that follows no worldly rule. It was the loving and Sovereign hand of God that would let me take a tumble now and then and scrape my knee so I discover the limitations of my capability, and always be there to pick me up.

The best way to know what your next responsibility is, when it comes to manifesting new territories and open up new resources in my life, is to ask: *What is it?*

A little meditation on Manna, the mysterious substance, those crystalline grains of sand that become exactly what you need when you need them. The word Manna, means *"what is it?"* Your words are the breath of wind that moves the sand particles in the undulating desert, so when you ask with your heart, *what is it*, the Substance moves to reveal what it is.

For his invisible attributes, his eternal power and divine nature, the will and way of God have ever since the creation of the world, been clearly seen in the things that have been made.

Romans 1:20

When Matt and I and our two daughters Olivia and Penelope, then aged 9 and 3, had one week to leave our temporary housing, and we had nothing and nowhere, we created The Hero's Protocol. What is it that is actually most important to us now? What is it that we actually have? What is the next step available? In the vine, growth is always from within through what-is, so look and see what is already there. Write it all down, lay it all out and simplify. Simply see: *what is it?*

And the LORD answered me: "Write the vision; make it plain on tablets, so he may run who reads it. For still the vision awaits its appointed time; it hastens to the end—it will not lie. If it seems slow, wait for it; it will surely come; it will not delay.

Habakkuk 2:2-3

And suddenly new connections occur between what's already there. *Huh! My husband is a parkour coach and has big muscles that he can use to help those landowners build a bath house made of cobb in exchange for using their land to camp on. Huh. All of a sudden that offgrid vision we had years ago has just become. All those years ago when we believed that to manifest a sustainable offgrid experience we would have to make a load of money to buy the acres of land and construct it all—now all of a sudden it's here as a response to my crisis and my next step is just to see if I can find a canvas tent.*

Inside the life you are leading now is the vision you once were manifesting. What is it? True growth is happening from there, that's the joint the vine is growing from. You can get very good at this, a craft called interpretative phenomenological analysis.

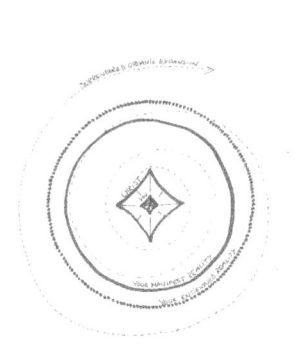

See the solid line of your actualized experience. See the blurred line of your wishes, goals and conceivable ideas. See the ever-expansive spiral as the vine grows and you grow with it.

Do only the thing you know to do, and do it with your love and your excellence, feeding the power of NOW. Energy indeed flows where your focus goes, so the expansion occurs in becoming the One who births the unimaginable, being in the deliciousness of Life unfolding. Not rushing to arrange the realization of what you can conceive but trusting that if anything is in your field of desire, *it is unfolding*, and the thing you have before you right now to do, *that* is the Way. Now your focus and energy are not out there in the future, in the spheres of concept and probability, but right here. In Life. Life is what is expanding for you. Now you don't need to escape the process of order, disorder and reorder because there is no suffering in it. You don't need to fear chaos because you see divine order throughout it. You don't need to brace yourself for the rhythm of compression and expansion because compression no longer feels bone-crushing but as a suspension, like the poised weightlessness before the exhale.

Nothing in the universe has the power to diminish His love toward us. Troubles, pressures, and problems are unable to come between us and heaven's Love. What about persecutions, deprivations, dangers, and death threats? Even in the midst of all these things, we triumph over them all, for God has made us to be more than conquerors, and His demonstrated love is our glorious victory over everything!

Romans 8:37

Combine these two models in **diagram 8** and **9**, participating consciously through your own attention to release and completion, and now you have the experience of sovereign mastery while ascending in Christ.

Conquest versus Engagement

The 11th century crusades were a gruesome time of expansion by conquest. Landowners and knights were driven to sell their land to the system to pay for pilgrimages and missions abroad to wrestle back territory from "the others". The men recruited to those missions didn't have much choice, it was either that or stay in the bleak reality of dwindling crops. Plus, as a bonus, the church would absolve all your sins if you went. Thus the system bribed the people to go out on bloody crusades to conquer more and take opportunities to establish the status quo. More of the same. Ultimately, after about 6 million murders, the crusades failed anyway.

But each crusader was not "the church", he was just a grown up little boy. When the crusaders arrived in the far away lands, each man encountered an energy he'd never experienced. *The Goddess.* For in these cultures She was alive. Arabic poets and the great Sufi mystics would engage in stunning odes to the woman, the divine feminine beclothed in fragrances and spices. Through their tender reverence for the wild movement of spirit, the mother and sisters and daughters of God were celebrated, not oppressed. This essence fused with the magical, twilight structure of the Celtic legend in the hearts of the crusaders, and the alchemy became an irresistible fantasy genre which fired the imagination of the whole of Europe! The crusaders were infected with romance and established codes of knightly conduct. Queens and princesses heard how eastern women were worshipped and the movement of romanticism began, everywhere poetry clubs and societies were blossoming like buds on the vine. The divine feminine rose a little higher.

This is expansion by engagement. It doesn't matter how the system tries to bribe you to expand its borders by conquest, and it doesn't matter how the system tries to conquer you and expand its borders into you, Spirit expands by engagement and nothing can stop it. So with the crusades, the church with the little c tried to win, tried to expand its linear area and the currency numbers and the followers and the boss-hood. But the Church with the capital C did win, as the mystical energy of true love and sovereign freedom spreads like a flame to a flame, burning down old paradigms and igniting the passion of the human spirit, liberating Love to do what it does best: grow.

Before moving on with the book, spend a week feeling the difference between:

- Conquest

- Engagement

When you review your business goals: conquest or engagement?

When you review your relationship and family goals: conquest or engagement?

When you tend to your actions and connections: conquest or engagement?

The Truth is it is only through true engagement that you will ever actually experience expansion. You will not ascend on your own or by your own works, energy just doesn't work that way. Sovereignty does not mean solitude, so do not forget your great commission as disciple of Christ. We aren't designed to stay small, we are growing up into Christ so our maturity and wise discernment of *what is* unlocks new levels of experience and growth, new territories and new resources.

Until we all attain to the unity of the faith and of the knowledge of the Son of God, we mature spiritually to the measure of the stature of the fullness of Christ, so that we may no longer be children tossed to and fro by the waves and carried about by every wind of doctrine, by human cunning, by craftiness in deceitful schemes. Rather, speaking the truth in love, we are to grow up in every way into Him who is the head, into Christ, from whom the whole body, joined and held together by every joint with which it is equipped, when each part is working properly, makes the body grow so that it builds itself up in love.

Ephesians 4:13-16

The Hero's Protocol for Dealing with Overwhelm

Going into new times of turbulence and uncertainty, both in the big world stage and in our own intimate and personal lives, we can all do with a buoyancy device for when the rapids threaten to pull us under. You'll find this device extremely useful in Expansion, and always relevant to your seventh mastery, Adventuring.

Expansion anxiety and overwhelm are the results of forgetting that it all works out alright in the end. It is hard to comprehend that things will work out when we're seeing proof that conflicts with this hope everywhere we go. *That rat stinks.* When we can't reconcile *how I want to feel about Life* and *what's actually going on right now*, then it's hard to grasp that Knowing of *improvement*, and it's certainly hard to hold on to hope.

The Hero's Protocol gives a strategy for expansion that allows you to increase your capacity for managing Life when it seems greater than you can handle. **This lets your consciousness follow a specific energy path** for handling whatever may befall you on your Way. Rest assured, no matter how overwhelmed you feel, if you are dealing with this now, it's because you *can* handle it.

Overwhelm is a sign of your love: *You feel this way because you care.* There's nothing abnormal about overwhelm, but it does get in the way of your peace and it really slows down the natural progression of your life because you resist the very thing that has emerged to be lived. The resistance you feel when you're overwhelmed by whatever it is in front of you is an indication that you've met the edge of what's known for you and you're moving into a wider, deeper, and more expansive version of life. It does not mean you're doing something wrong, or missing the path, or not healthy, spiritual or have enough mental fortitude. It means you've arrived at a threshold, and your mission is to move into the next step for the highest and best outcome. The courage it takes to lean into the challenge instead of denying or condemning its existence is the key to moving into the next season of your life.

What's genius about the HERO Protocol, is that it is simple to remember, it is easy to implement, it is energetically aligned with what you need to accomplish, and when you've practiced it a few times it becomes embodied, it sort of lands in your heart and you no longer need to consciously take these steps when you meet challenges. You just simply start to flow through them.

Learn this protocol and practice well if you are about to take on a big mission—like a body reboot, or a reconciliation with an estranged family member, or a change of career, or helping someone transition, launching a new personal mission, or maybe leaning into a whole new way of being a human in a post-apocalyptic world.

We are pressed on every side by troubles, but we are not crushed. We are perplexed, but not driven to despair. We are hunted down, but never abandoned by God. We get knocked down, but we are not destroyed.

2 Corinthians 4:8-9

There are five steps. Each step is a state of mind. You embody one state before moving on to the next. This provides a logical and orderly elevation of your awareness so that you hold a Sovereign poise for right mind, right action and right vibrational state to allow the solution to flow and keep your capacity for mastery through the situation. It works because it is your awareness that alters the way you engage with Life, and engagement that allows you to expand. Bringing awareness to specific states of mind makes space for improved engagement and growth. Follow this protocol and you will be able to handle what's coming and you will always come out the other end of the expansive season with greater sovereignty.

THE HERO'S 5-STEP PROTOCOL

Step 1: Surrender

Step 2: Ground

Step 3: Power Up

Step 4: Act

Step 5: Allow

Step back into the river for a moment and remember the feeling of being stuck in the mud while the current is increasing. Imagine the biggest hardship you could possibly face. Imagine that it becomes real, and white water rapids whip up a furious frenzy.

It seems like you may drown, so you grasp for the riverbanks and clutch onto ropes that others throw to you. But the current doesn't let up.

Step 1. Surrender.

Release everything you know about what is going on. This detachment from any creative standpoint or judgment is a brave poise. With slow breaths and a relaxed but strong posture, you say: *"I don't know what this is."*

You release the rigidity of the mind and its urgency to fix or avoid the challenge. You release incessant mind streams of analysis and bubbles of triggered emotions. Surrender is like ending a long and exhausting swim upstream, instead letting the River carry you with a current that is as miraculous as it is mysterious. But you know where the flow is coming from and where it's going. It's Life, it's the great unknown. The greatest gift of spiritual freedom and embodied trust is that you're free to surf on the tide of life, but for that you need to let go of the riverbanks. Let go of the control of all the things.

When you do that you find that the rest of the protocol comes quite easily. But letting go is a craft in itself and it takes courage and practice. You need all three previous masteries, Remember, Recognize and Release, so you can swiftly process when your limbic system has triggered you into an involuntary stress response. *Ah, yes. I **Remember**, God knows what is going on here and I don't. I AM loved and cared for by the Father. I have a Savior willing to help. I **Recognize** that I am stressed, overwhelmed and anxious about what is ahead of me, and I recognize this as a story that is really happening, yet not actually occurring. I **Release** my attachment to what I think is going on. I release the need to control this.*

It is not a hard concept for the human mind to accept that all things in the universe are intrinsically interconnected, that every vibrating sub-atomic particle making up the fabric of reality is entangled with every other part. We get that we're swimming in a macrocosmic quantum soup, and even if we don't have the language to formulate how it all works, we do know that if all actualized things and occurrences in our shared universe are fields of energy—and all energy moves and transfers—then a seemingly isolated incident on this planet is completely affected by something happening on the other side of the galaxy, the way a pebble tossed in one side of the dragonfly pond ripples until it changes the movement of a lily pad near the other shore. There is incredible order in the chaos, and our manifestations are energy fields dancing in rivers of movement between all people, all times and all places in the unified field of creation. Forgive the seventy-times-seven pebbles and seventy-times-seven lily pads. There is an infinite amount of interference in your life—and you, for all your healing and reconciliation, will never control it.

We understand this. And yet, when we confront a challenge in our life, we have a habit of looking at it in isolation, a separate thing that is occurring out there. We diagnose it, give it a reason for existing, and call it "bad", which justifies resisting it. And then we use our clever brains to think of all the reasons it shouldn't be so and all the ways we could fix it and all the terrible things that may happen if we don't.

That's why surrender is a lifelong art you will never not need: *"I am standing in front of the hardest challenge of my life, and I don't actually know what this is. I do not have the perspective that shows me all the interconnected streams of cause and effect and I couldn't possibly comprehend the meaning of it. I don't know what it's for, I don't know what medicine is hidden inside it, I don't know the highest and best outcome for all involved. It is what it is, and here I am."*

There is another aspect to Surrender—the white flag. It is time to stop fighting some of the battles you are fighting. You're not going to win them. **You're not meant to.** Some of the dragons in your life don't need to be slayed. They can be allowed. Even tamed. But by fighting them you will waste all your energy on trying to change something that doesn't need your intervention.

What battle can you surrender? What enemy could become a peaceful neighbor? You will probably find it moves away on its own in time, or comes to embrace you on the battlefield.

> **Count it all joy, my brothers, when you meet trials of various kinds, for you know that the testing of your faith produces steadfastness. And let steadfastness have its full effect, that you may be perfect and complete, lacking in nothing.**
>
> **James 1:2-4**

Step 2: Ground

When you've surrendered and allowed the flow, you need to be able to orient yourself within that flow. You need to know where you are compared with where the flow is going. It is time to ground. Grounding allows you to enter into the world as fully and completely in your awareness as possible. The term *"Be Here Now"* is a statement of perfect grounding. Not lost in streams of thought. Not tossed about on waves of emotional energy. Just present in life as the wisest and most sovereign version of yourself.

It is true that we are eternal energy beings in a field of infinite potential. But for now, we are also just people. And that means we are operating within a structure that is subject to laws of cause and effect. We were not designed to just magic our problems away. We are designed to use our highest faculties, our most loyal tools, and to connect with each other to create opportunities out of challenges and to contribute to the expansion of *all-that-is* by exploring *what-isn't-already*.

That's where the real magic lies.

Grounding yourself into your experience is bringing the very highest vantage point directly to the present moment. *What-isn't-already* lies just beyond the boundaries of *what-is*. The biggest obstacle you face when grounding into the challenge before you is that you get so invested in the story that has been told so far about who you are inside your vibrational reality. If you refuse to let go of the story you've been telling about the challenge you're facing then that story has become a false idol, a manifestation in the physical world that you have given your sovereignty to. You are believing a sand dune, and you can't therefore ground into life as an enlightened, illumined observer because your identity, your vantage point, is stuck in form. That's why grounding must come after surrender.

Map out the landscape. Since you have accepted and allowed the situation to be as it is, you can discover where you stand in relation to it. From there you are in a better position to move forward. Where you stand depends on what's actually occurring and what resources are at your current disposal. In this case grounding is not about walking barefoot in the woods (although that helps!) but about getting a genuine grasp on where you are and what you have within your reach.

You might go from feeling, "*oh my God, I'm losing everything, I'm going to be homeless!*"

to "*Oh wow, this new friend owns a piece of land in the mountains and wants my help to prepare for winter, and it turns out I have exactly the tools I need to go and learn how to live in harmony with nature! This was that vision I was dreaming of years ago, all of a sudden materializing in totally the opposite way to what I thought!*"

The Great Audit is a thorough catalogue of all known influencing factors, risks and opportunities, assets and liabilities, resources and contacts. This gives you an interpretative phenomenological assessment of what is actually occurring and in what ways you have already been equipped to deal with it. How you conduct this audit must depend on your modus operandi, so God must show you the Sovereign Way, but you're aiming to at least:

- Log what you actually know about what is occurring, including threats, energetic risks to your sovereignty, other actual things that help you paint a landscape of what is right now and where you stand in it. Map the physical environment such as who is involved and what bureaucratic processes or timelines are in play. Map the energetic landscape like active traumas or imbalances in your personal biofield and surroundings. Map our your core values and those of all involved and know where the overlaps are, for here is the most powerful attractor field.

- Log all your physical tools like electronic equipment, vehicles, machinery, books. Organize these by how they play a part in the landscape. What can help you build? What can help you shelter? What can help you delight and thrive?

- Catalogue physical assets like property, businesses, items, bank accounts. Organize these by whether or not they can be used, liquidated or transformed in some way to help.

- Map out your relationships, contacts, networks, friends and family. Remember who's who in your journey, and how many allies you truly have. You are only ever one engagement away from the solution, even if it is the pastor at your local church willing to give you her car.

- Check off your metaphysical and spiritual tools, like creativity, imagination, organization, patience, energy work, fortitude, courage. Tap into the ones at your disposal, put them to work. Be honest about those you aren't disciplined with.

- Catalogue your metaphysical and spiritual assets, like deliverance, mercy, grace. Cash them in.

- Map out opportunities, open doors, unclaimed favors, areas of growth.

As a grounding technique The Great Audit also gives you an idea of your energetic footprint in life, and it's always much larger than you thought. Do it regularly, because you keep expanding, and you get the experience of expanding worth, like a bank account of rapidly appreciating assets. Do this right and you will say, *"WOW! I had no idea I was this vast and well equipped!"* You could fill all your notebooks doing the Great Audit, you are so incredible wealthy and already have the perfect vibrational footprint. It's good to take inventory of one's sovereign empire. This technique shows you your real ability to handle the challenge.

Think about David and Goliath. Everyone else tried to conquer this enormous, vast, otherworldly challenge using the socially agreed upon methods of conquest. They perished. David stopped to know himself and know his tools, and instead of charging forward using the same method as everyone else, he used what he had from where he was. And took down the giant.

You need to know who you are, where you are, what you have at your disposal before you can properly orient yourself in the flow of what's becoming.

I Remember who I AM. I Already Always AM an expression of God: Good, Light and Becoming.

I do not know the full Truth of what this challenge is, but I Recognize the difference between what is occurring and what is happening.

I Release all realities other than this one. I Know I AM HERE.

I have arrived here at this point. I have steadfastly followed a path in the best way I knew how, and this is where I am.

I have received blessings and lessons on the way and I have needed them all.

I have enough, I do enough, I am enough to meet this challenge.

I am complete, I am grounded, I am ready.

I AM HERE.

When you combine the first two steps in The Hero's Protocol: Surrender and Ground, you get a state of being that feels like a soft landing. So the better you get at each of these and at combining them, the faster you'll find yourself able to orient yourself in the face of the challenge, the overwhelm, the emergence, the growth.

So Surrender and Ground is like landing gently, like a feather on the surface of the pond. No more belly flopping!

Do not be anxious about anything, but in every situation, by prayer and petition, with thanksgiving, present your needs to God. And the peace of God, which transcends all understanding, will guard your hearts and your minds in Christ Jesus. Finally, brothers and sisters, whatever is true, whatever is noble, whatever is right, whatever is pure, whatever is lovely, whatever is admirable—if anything is excellent or praiseworthy—think about such things. Whatever you have learned or received or heard from me, or seen in me—put it into practice. And the God of peace will be with you.

Phillippians 4:6-9

Step 3: Power Up

Now this is where the expansion begins. The first two steps are preparatory steps—they are the soft landing in consciousness. The Law of Increase dictates that what is next in your life must be experienced by a greater version of you than who you are now. The universe is unfolding fractally, and that goes for your consciousness and therefore also for your Life. There are more solutions, resources, opportunities and energy in the next realm of consciousness, the one you are expanding into. So, for you to gracefully expand into what's emerging, whether you are manifesting a conceivable vision or just getting on top of the tumbling waters to stay buoyant, you need to power up.

Now you draw in all the energy, power and skill available to you and activate it, ready to go. You engage your core muscles, you straighten your spine, you power up, you get on top of the surf. You do this spiritually, energetically, mentally, and physically. You examine your greatest talents, skills, crafts, superpowers and how they apply to the expansion you're facing. You call on the supernatural strength of Spirit as you choose your savior to manifest through your ancestors, saints, spirit guides, angels or golden calves. God is *with* you and ready to emerge through an adjustment of your cellular field.

You can see why sequence is important. If you try to power up before you have surrendered, then you are rising up against an imaginary enemy. What a waste of energy. If you power up before you have grounded, then you don't know what's already at your disposal and you're powering up the wrong thing. Getting the lawn mover all revved up to process the paperwork.

There is a reason you are here, responding to the bong. You are unique. You bring something to the challenge that no other could. You have a particular combination of skills, attributes, experiences and tools that you revealed in The Great Audit. These together alchemize into *your* super-power.

God has given each of you a gift from his great variety of spiritual gifts. Use them well to serve one another.

1 Peter 4:10

And your super-power is fundamentally linked to your sovereign life path. There is order in the chaos—if you have arrived at *this* point and are faced with *this* challenge, you can be sure that you are the one for the job, and that your super-power is the secret to moving through it with grace. Moreover, this challenge you are facing *is* the current secret to practicing your mastery as the Hero of your life and become even more skilled at using it. After all, your mission is not just to become buoyant and walk on water, but to be a new channel for that same wellspring of life and baptize others by immersion.

When Spiderman finds himself in a spot of trouble, he doesn't use Lobster force. He doesn't scour the city culture to find the most commonly accepted animal attribute. He knows what to do, because his unique power was specifically bestowed on him, and the more he practices the more easily he can take on what life brings. *Spiderman does Spiderman, simply because that is who he is.* And you know who you are. You are lovingly and wonderfully made as a perfect pixel in that total field of what is. Whether you have been anointed with fierce faith or gentle rage, a lightness of foot, a combine harvester, vast amounts of cash, or, like David, a little slingshot, you have the exact superpower to put to use for this challenge.

You are not submerged in the violent rapids. You are already rising in your vibration into higher realms of consciousness, with much more clarity and power. **So now you can Know what you can do** to impact the situation, and what your next step is.

I tell you the truth, if you had faith even as small as a mustard seed, you could say to this mountain, 'Move from here to there,' and it would move. Nothing would be impossible.

Matthew 17:20

Step 4: Act

Expansion is the life mastery necessary to consciously and gracefully participate in becoming greater. It's the skill of mind that you employ in the face of a challenge to allow your container to become big enough to handle the Life you are moving into. So although Expansion is innate and organic, taking action is key to mastering it.

When you have let go of the riverbanks, aligned yourself with the flow, and powered up to the top of the surf, *now* you maneuver the surfboard.

Getting to this point could take a nano-second or it could take a few years depending on your Sovereign Way, but the sequence is the same: *You waited to make a decision and act on it until you arrived into alignment with what is and called all the power available to you into your experience.* Now you can trust that whatever choice you make on where to place your next step is absolutely the right one. Wisdom will guide you into peace, fear will guide you into suffering, so *be* first and *act* second. You don't want to go trying to take on the waves of the great blue sea until this point when you're on top. Because otherwise it feels like you're taking on all the battles and carrying the weight of the world. No, you get on top and then you act, moving forward into the challenge that lies ahead.

Discerning how to move is also a craft that begins with knowing your core values. Sometimes the action needed is as simple as putting on the kettle for a cup of tea. Sometimes it's enormous, like leaving a relationship or career and launching a completely new life. We have to approach our movements from the same sovereign perspective that gives us the worldview of grace and poise. And we understand the fusion of essence and structure—so when we act, it is not from the perspective of *"which of these happenings in the 3D world must I initiate first and what is the correct sequence of happenings that must occur for me to successfully accomplish this challenge?"* It's not linear decision-making like that.

Right action is nothing more than engagement. Movement is a law of the manifest universe. All energy fields are in a constant dance with each other, pebbles, lily pads and ripples on the ever-moving pond. To act, even in a small, seemingly meaningless way, is to participate in a flow of energy that creates a wake behind, before and all around you.

Rain falling on your freshly painted fence? Have a cup of tea. Diagnosed with a terminal illness? Go for a walk. An action may seem a small and silly thing, but the simple act of movement for the pure intention of resolution sets off a momentum of energy into the cosmos, and the Law of Attraction forms greater and truer next steps as sand dunes shift to elevate you. Let's use this as an illustration:

- Perhaps the cup of tea brings a moment of comfort,
- with space for an inspired thought,
- and you pick up the phone and call your sister or father or husband,
- and apologize for that thing, with no other intention
- and a reconciliation happens in that person's heart,
- and you save a soul, releasing an energetic knot in your upper back and your spine comes into alignment, so your migraine vanishes. All because of a cup of tea!

Trust that the compensation for right action is out of this world—not that you're in it for the reward, but the bonuses you get from Life for *taking action* in this Sovereign

Way are considerable.

So practically, we are speaking of making decisions and taking action in the 3D world and **Knowing** that those actions are delivering you to the next place in spacetime for you to be. This is not based on logic and probability but on the compound effect of allowing exponentially bigger baby steps to unfold in front of you, matching the vibration of your intention and your grounded embodied superpower.

Evolving life is actually an unlikely ripple effect of action and spontaneous response to opportunities presented. Planning is important because it frames your intention and focuses your movements, but so is releasing the plan when it's time to take a step sideways. Knowing the right action in the moment comes from having accepted the challenge as it is, grounding into your true position in this moment, gathering the tools immediately available to you, and bringing all your highest power to the point of action.

Now I have my cup of tea.

Now I decide whether to leave or stay.

Now I raise my prices and launch the business.

Now I sell the business and go a different way.

Have you ever procrastinated from doing the right next thing because you've gone *"Ah, but then I'd need a website and I can't afford to get the brochures printed, and my father's got the keys, and that policy hasn't been passed yet in congress..."* and you let your awareness slide down an imaginary line of possible outcomes and the probabilistic cause and effect ripple that might follow? It's nonsense. None of that is real. That's all irrelevant conjecture. As long as your intention is right, and your perspective is Sovereign, when you act you are simply initiating a roll out of materialization.

This is more important than ever for people to remember. Because what seems to be opposing actions, like voting Red or Blue, are actually conjoined actions between multitudes of people in a tapestry of progressive improvement. It is the intention and energy behind the action that matters, so as long as our collective intention is for more love, more balance and more justice, then the circumstances will rearrange to allow process. In the material universe process means time. So we don't see our desired results immediately, and we have to trust. Trust that there is always a process of reconciliation, restoration and expansion. Trust that **what you know to do is all you need to do**.

So the steps you've taken so far, Surrender, Ground and Power Up, are enough to calibrate your spiritual compass as long as you maintain sovereign poise in your perspective. The overshadowing Christ compass is the only tool that will ever accurately deliver you to the next right thing. Your friends, mentors, guides and doctors are wisdom keepers on the outside of you, and they will have great insight into what the limitations and possibilities might be in your world. But remember that they are there to reflect things to you so you can see clearly, not to give you the answers. The true direction comes from within.

Remember—your diamond consciousness is not neutral. It is biased. It does have access to the right information, and it also has access to all your old nonsense as well, which will collapse and activate as linear thought streams when your limbic system goes into resistance mode. *"It doesn't matter how hard I try, nothing ever works. It's not safe to trust you, I need to protect myself from you. I know what Love looks like and what Life looks like now doesn't march, so it isn't Love."* These are also influencing your decisions. Throughout life the tricky thing is knowing whether an inspired action is arising from fear, or if it is arising from inner wisdom. *"Run away from the world!"* can easily be disguised by vanity as *"Release my material goods to the wind and be free in a spiritual commune."*

So how do you tell if the feeling that is guiding your move is coming from your highest Sovereign point or is a justification that your clever Ego is disguising as wisdom?

Remember, Recognize and Release will help you lean through these paradigms, and trial and error begets wisdom. If you want to improve your relationship with your intuition, you need to show up for it warts and all. You need to cultivate and earn that trust, by showing yourself that you can be trusted. Your body will respond by cooperating. Everybody is different in how that looks, and only you know that feeling of absolute Knowing the right thing to do. **God wants you to Know the right next step.** He is not hiding it from you.

Step 5: Allow

Let the surf take you, and trust that you are held buoyant by Life herself, that there is support for you and there are ones who can help take some of the weight off your shoulders. And then allow the feeling of surfing. This is indeed a craft.

As we come full circle in the expansion protocol, the final step is to allow whatever comes next. This can be a phenomenally hard thing to do, because our first impulse is to control the outcome, or at least be invested in what we think that outcome should be. If we are to accept the mission in front of us, we must appreciate that if we have surrendered to the knowing that we don't know what the challenge really is in its totality, then we also must accept that we don't know what *should* happen. We may have desires, we may have perfectly crafted vision boards and post-it notes with affirmations of our ideals stuck to the mirror, but it is simply outside our consciousness to know what we will know about what we want when we've become more of who we are becoming!

With every step up the mountain the view changes a little, and new ideals come into perception. It is good to not have become too attached to your current foothold. That red Lamborghini suddenly seems much less appealing when you've discovered a new love for a humble life riding a bicycle in the mountain valleys of Nepal. The grand plan for our lives is so much more vast than we can imagine. The "think big" movement is full of good and noble intention, but truly to think simple is to *allow* big, because then there is no attachment to what "big" really is. The awe of what comes next never ceases! And that means committing only to the present moment and allowing life to flow into you and through your experience.

If you followed the protocol then you *know* the challenge is the perfect one for you at this time, and that **what is in the way is the Way**:

- because you are completely present in the experience
- and grounded in your position as sovereign within it,
- and you have dialed up the amount of God's power you receive and radiate,
- so you *know* the action you've taken is the right step

- ergo what follows *must* be the highest and best, regardless of what it looks like.

If it brings a new challenge, circle back and do the protocol again, but remember to harvest all the lessons and blessings that come with it. Tie your shoelaces.

This is how the challenge becomes a launching pad, and this is where quantum leaps are experienced. Massive results follow if you allow them to nestle into your experience, and soon you find yourself experiencing a completely new realm of life.

What about the impact our decision and action has on those we love? There may be loved ones who turn away from you, relationships that may not be reconciled in the physical. But there will always be Love, and you can never fall out of belonging. You have the permission to *know* that the highest and best for one is truly the highest and best for all. The interconnectedness of the cosmos means that you cannot diminish or reduce another's spirit by making the best decision for you at that moment. A decision made in a sovereign state of mind, which is where you are at when you're using the Hero's Protocol, *will* yield a True outcome, you will expand, and the world will improve a little more.

Imagine a sheet hanging, suspended in place by eight billion points in its fabric. If one point rises, the entire fabric rises. That doesn't mean the other points needs to approve of your decision or believe they're getting the best out of it. *You don't know* what that best is, and it may well be hidden in the very challenge they believe they're now facing because of your action. Make no assumptions, and faithfully follow your soul song as it guides you to the next right action, and the next right action. As you step mindfully forward allowing each outcome to be what it is, you are participating with life in a deeper dimension and no longer walking on a linear path of quantifiable progress.

There is no failure then. **Allowing** *any outcome* to be **proof** of your *success* in a progressively realizing Life toward the worthy ideal of Christ: *being* 100% divine *and* 100% human. This is the seventh Sovereign mastery of Adventuring, and it is the first and last step in the Hero's Protocol:

1. **Surrender to the challenge:** I don't know what this is.

2. **Ground in:** I Know what *this* is and who I AM.

3. **Power Up:** I am in the Vine and embody all the life force I need.

4. **Act:** The next step I take activates a flow.

5. **Allow:** What follows is true.

There is raw, painful difficulty to meet in Life. In your awakened life, with your sovereign consciousness, Life is your lover. And She brings difficulty to the tables. Some difficulties are small, like a quarrel with your husband over who should do the dishes. And some are big, like formulating your mission in a very troubled world. Some difficulties are physical, like the pains in your body. Some are spiritual, like the lonely search for belonging or the aching retreat into a season of mental darkness. The experience of dealing with difficulty is the sacred solidarity of living a rich and connected life within a family of stories unfolding. Now that you are in Christ, there is no victimhood. Challenge, yes—but no suffering. Only victory, whatever the outcome.

You are a master of life so you take delight in seeing your desires come into manifestation and you have the joy of being a conscious co-creator. And, when you meet challenges and difficulty that you *don't* get to control—and there are many such things—then you still get to enjoy the Hero's journey through your life as you dance with these challenges and transform your pain into exquisite devotion.

From now on you no longer believe that challenges can overwhelm you, and you'll always have the life jacket for when the flow of the river increases to wild, white rapids. You no longer believe that overwhelm is a sign that you're not capable or that you haven't done it right. You no longer believe you can be beaten and you are always able to return to your natural, expansive state of Life. Now you are a channel for increasingly powerful creative lifeforce.

Stroll through the ancient libraries in the alabaster cathedral, rows and rows of ancient scrolls and codices neatly arranged, illumined both by the majestic stained glass windows and the holy Light within the very words on every page of divine knowledge. Now that you have embodied the mastery of Expansion, and become a Hero who can face any challenge, your training matures from healing and awakening to creation and legacy impact. With greater levels of spiritual authority, you now begin an initiation phase in mental and vibrational mastery, and the Great Commission truly begins. You're becoming more accustomed to rapid expansion and quantum leaps, so you need the discipline to craft and build only benevolent thought-forms. It's time to think higher, deeper, faster, and truer. You hone your faculties to understand, synthesize and formulate the highest creative reality in any moment. It's all in the oasis libraries.

The Fifth Mastery: Genius
Understand, Synthesize, Formulate

O Reason, more royal than the kings and freer than the free!

4 Maccabees 14:2

The universe is fundamentally ordered and exquisitely logical. Even the seemingly illogical quantum world holds divine order, meaning and mathematical perfection. Creation unfolds systematically, even when we can't comprehend the logic of what we are seeing. When we *can* comprehend things, when they land logically in our personal minds and hearts, then it is far easier for us to accept them. To experience our Genius in a human context we need to master the art of metacognition and conscious thought. In fact, whatever your spiritual lineage, your mastery path requires you to activate realms of your innate genius you never even knew existed. You can't increase your capacity for divine understanding if you don't condition your mind. As the power of your mind increases so your capacity for destruction also increases, so you begin to differentiate your thoughts from unconscious mass thought and you enter a new level of world service.

Genius though you are, your thoughts do not become things. Thoughts are electrical byproducts of a zillion subtle choices you make in mind and energy, together creating specific frameworks of understanding that guide the narrative in your mind. In Christ, it is safe for you to explore thought without fearing that you'll unconsciously create something awful because you had the audacity to think your way down a darker valley of your mental universe. *Thought-forms* do become things, though, as longer-term mental frameworks build off the paradigms in your diamond and are energized by your electromagnetic command to become little lives of their own. The result can be self-perpetuating attractor fields playing out in particular fields of consciousness on the great cosmic scene. By training and conditioning our mental universe to build new, more cohesive thought-forms we can activate pockets of self-improving energy wherever we go.

True Genius has nothing to do with your IQ. Nor is it being passively open to receiving downloaded revelation. It is the malleability of your mind to deliberately understand, synthesize and formulate something new. You can only do this if your mental world is liberated from the involuntary systems of thought and you have great sovereignty in creative thinking with clear and concise cognition. This is how your mind will penetrate the veils of dogma and status quo, and be available to contribute to coordinated manifestations of the greater plan.

Call to Me and I will answer you and tell you great and mighty things, things which have been confined and hidden, which you do not know and cannot distinguish.

Jeremiah. 33.3

When I was in my early teens, my dad and I poured over little pencil diagrams we made on the sides of his newspapers. What it would be like for a 2D character, like Donald Duck, to be kidnapped by a 3D character, like Donald Trump, and hoisted out of one dimension and into the next? Would Donald Duck still be a cartoon, would he vanish if he turned sideways? Would he be able to perceive the third dimension, even if he himself were just a cartoon? Or would he, upon ascending, morph and become a three-dimensional, large duck? I wanted to know, so my dad used diagrams to teach me about dimensionality, and God has been showing me ascension ever since.

Our faculty of logical deduction and reasoning, with our mysterious yet rational self-actualization, sets us apart from the beasts of the world. A consequence of having a high IQ and sentience is that it gives us authority and dominion within the natural experience. Mind underlies all manifestation, attracting, repelling and coordinating, always organizing and always experiencing. Very soon in our human journey, intelligence will be stronger than desire, bringing the etheric and sensual body under the control of mental energy. In true Genius, every element bows to your command.

This is our birthright, and we needn't feel embarrassed about it, nor prideful. A cheetah doesn't feel embarrassed to be the fastest of all land animals, and a human needn't feel awkward about its extraordinary ability to Know innovation and creativity. To deny your Genius is to deny God's way of working through you, rejecting your true nature as expressive consciousness and stifling all the marvelous creations that could come from it. It doesn't help that nobody ever taught you how to *be* a genius. And what's worse, the art of high thought is vilified in the spiritual arena, the higher mental faculties blamed for a chronic depletion in the heart zone. They say you need to go from the head to the heart to find God, leaving your cerebral consciousness feeling rather unloved. **The Truth is you don't need to escape your mind to Know the divine presence,** for it is the mind's very job to understand, synthesize and formulate.

Mary Magdalene, communicating with the ascended Jesus through a vision, asked him how transcendent spiritual visions occur. He answered that all visions are perceived through the mind:

> *"I," she said, "I saw the Lord in a vision and I said to him, 'Lord, I saw you today in a vision.' He answered and said to me, 'Blessed are you that you did not waver at the sight of me. For where the mind is, there is the treasure.' I said to him, 'Lord, how does he who sees the vision see it, through the soul or through the spirit?' The Savior answered and said, 'He does not see through the soul nor through the spirit, but* the mind which is between the two—*that is what sees the vision.'"*

The Gospel of Mary, 5:5-11

Everyone is born with a field of Genius. Your awareness is either near it, or not. In this state, thoughts flow gracefully and with loving and creative power. You understand what you need to understand, and you can conjure imaginative ideas and possibilities. You learn through wonder and inquiry, and you process knowledge quickly and purposefully. You know exactly what to do, and you do it with ease and excellence, even if it's nothing. Your mind is open to perceiving the rewards, sharp enough to spot a sparkle of light in a sandstorm. You know this state. You have often accessed it in your "Genius Zone".

Your "Genius zone", is just a structure. This is a particular set of coordinates of natural talent, practiced skill, circumstance and subject of attention where it's very easy for you to access that true Genius state of being. For one, the zone is found sitting at the computer with a cup of coffee and a spreadsheet full of exciting numbers. Someone else might find it while building engines. Another may find it speaking on stage about their personal journey of empowerment. Another enters the Genius zone when she's singing to the flowers in her garden. It's that place where you are completely you, *and* your mind is *not* still, but in motion.

But we're not always in our Genius zone. Life is unpredictable—let's say a policy change in local government removes one of your favorite social benefits and the injustice of it triggers rage. Calm becomes chaos. Contemplation becomes anxious rumination. Wonder and gratitude become control and analysis. Fast and smooth processing becomes rash and reckless decision-making or stagnant procrastination. Allowing becomes resistance, and clarity becomes confusion. You can't make sense of things, and it all takes an enormous amount of energy to balance out again. It can happen to anyone, at any time, no matter where you are on your journey. It's a part of Life—but, as we can easily deduce, this mental turbulence is pretty useless to the Great Commission. How will this energy help access a higher reality from the starting point of this new policy, and spin something even more marvelous into form?

The Sovereign mastery of Genius allows you to Know the preeminence of Truth in all things. Only by the Truth will we transcend illusion and create fulfillment for all, and since Truth is ever-present our ability to perceive it and work with it is absolutely paramount to the sovereign life.

The primary work of Christ in the mental plane is experienced as an overshadowing of the minds of his disciples. We could say his spiritual interference is administered telepathically, thus creating outposts of Christ consciousness all over the world. This allows the pouring out of Christ life upon the masses, a spiritual inflow which brings about a reorientation in human desire, bringing the emotional and mental planes into submission. The masses everywhere are responsive to the living work of Christ as it is implemented from the mental plane by his disciples in every culture and sphere of human life, in art, movies, music. The exponential total of humans in Love who are serving our tribe—growing welfare movements, establishing right relations in world government, off-setting the separation and divisiveness created daily by counterforce, plus the good works of billions of little people every day showing up as an unlikely angel with a can of petrol right when your car has run out of fuel—has formed a clear and structured path through consciousness, energy and form to guarantee the return of Christ in this age.

Look at Diagram 6, Walking In Christ. The small diamond is just one person living a consecrated life. Imagine the ripple effect as the Christ mind overshadows and infuses both conscious and unconscious mental activity.

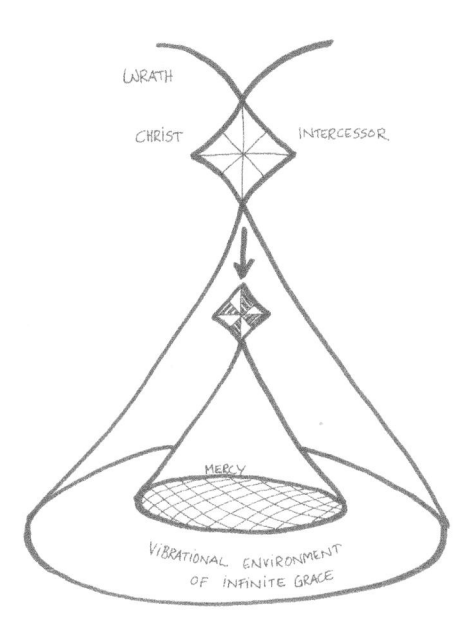

[Diagram 6: Walking In Christ — showing labels WRATH, CHRIST, INTERCESSOR, MERCY, and VIBRATIONAL ENVIRONMENT OF INFINITE GRACE]

To be available to this coordinated plan, you must harness the power of your mind and master the art of malleable thought, making deliberate decisions for the good of all. **Your reason must be sovereign over emotion.** With greater mastery of mind you are granted more dominion in the natural world. You command the storm to still in the early hours when the thoughts start their erratic patterns like tiny ping pong balls whizzing inside the skull. Imagine being able to immediately harness those thoughts, soften them, and direct them into a stream of deep and profound understanding, into the realm of imagination, inspiration—and prayer.

You begin to attune old thought patterns, disengaging automatic negative thought before it collapses your vibrational point of attraction, developing your thinking process and capacity, and simplifying your decision-making, so when you meet obstacles on your sovereign way you quickly understand and synthesize the lessons they bring, embody those lessons and move on, an expanded version of yourself. You learn how to turn a metaphysical dial so that your perspectives, thoughts, emotions all support your life instead of sabotaging it, focusing creative, loving thought into enhancing Life for yourself and others.

You'll be able to express what you mean to express and have your intention known and received by those you're ordained to influence. Now you will notice that with less mental resistance to what's actually occurring you become a better channel for the miracles that make life so extraordinary. You are synthesize thought from the Truth field, and formulate it as medicine for your Life and others. Your prayer will become more effective. A wonderful mental liberation occurs, and your Presence becomes healing to those who cross your path. All because your mind is free.

Reason is Sovereign Over Emotion

The subject that I am about to discuss is most philosophical, that is, whether pious reason is sovereign over the passions. So it is right for me to advise you to pay earnest attention to philosophy. For the subject is essential to everyone who is seeking knowledge, and in addition it includes the praise of the highest virtue—I mean, of course, rational judgment. If, then, it is evident that reason rules over those passions that hinder self-control, namely, gluttony and lust, it is also clear that it masters the passions that hinder one from justice, such as malice, and those that stand in the way of courage, namely, anger, fear, and pain.

4 Maccabees 1:1-4

Let's highlight here that the argument is that it is *pious reason* that is sovereign over emotion, not inductively derived common sense or cultural reasoning. Only True reason is sovereign. This is a reason that is itself governed by true values, subject to divine instruction and priority. Think of a time when your emotional reactions or temptations caused you to act in error. If you had followed your highest reasoning according to what truly mattered most, would it have guided you better? Use your sovereign reason to remain poised in honor of your core values and God's work through you.

Genius does not require emotional detachment, but a sovereign poise within the realm of emotion. As you experience rising emotions you allow them to show you where your values might be violated by others or yourself, or where you are at risk of behaving in a way that takes you off your true path. When you slip up, be aware of it and use one of the devices from Recognizing:

Is this reasoning based on *Truth* or *Story*? Is what I'm reasoning *actually occurring* (out there in a shared infrastructure) or *really happening* (in my personal vibrational universe)? Simply asking the question brings the awareness you need to return to stoic, pious mind. Emotions never rule our actions.

Emotional reason is reasonable, but only for a fool: *"I'm angry, so I'm going to throw this rock."*

Sovereign reason is cool and mature: *"I'm angry, so my decision-making is compromised. Since I'm under the vibrational influence of wrath, my impulse to throw this rock cannot be a true direction. I will hold this poise, allow this emotion to process, and then evaluate the best action based on what matters most, following the direction of Love."*

> **Reason is not for the purpose of destroying emotions but so that one may not give way to them.**
>
> *4 Maccabees 1:6*

So metacognition turns the lens from thinking about what's going on out there, to thinking about how your thinking is working *first*, and building your understanding from there.

Look at diagram 1: Trinity. Let your mind hover over the corner of the triangle labelled "Substance." Ponder again on the idea that you are either engaging with a particularized structure that is manifest in the world of form, like a sand dune, or you are engaging with the infinite Spirit of possibility *through* that manifest reality, like the wind.

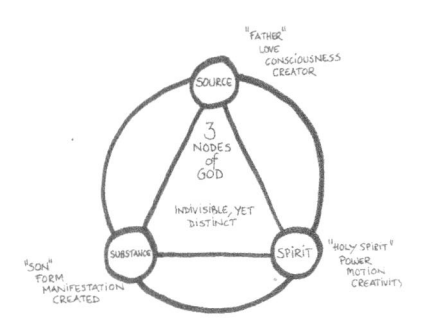

Look at diagram 3: The Sovereign Model of Human Experience. The rise of emotion is an involuntary, biological response to an external condition. There is nothing wrong with feeling anger. It signals a violation against one of your values. But as natural biology, it does not have the authority of Christ. Emotion does, however, trigger a mental reaction, and this is the first moment of sovereign choice as your linear mind creates a narrative that describes what's going on: *"I'm angry because of all that stuff!"*

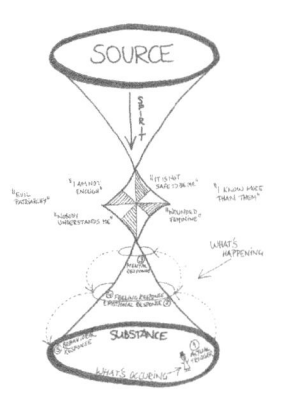

This mental observation collapses potentiality and a choice must be made: *Now I am able to decide. Will I continue in this vibration and activate decisions from this vibrational point, or will I use my reason to establish a new framework for perception and thus make decisions from a poised position in accordance with what really matters most to me?*

As we have discovered so far in our mysterious lifetime, real problems are often messy. There are no surefire collective rules of reasoning that guarantee your reasoning will be successful. There are guidelines but these need to be followed thoughtfully, not by blind submission. Reasoning must be applied with sensitivity to context, goals, practical limitations—a host of realities. For example, there are rules for good driving: *Merge when you get to an interstate.* But merely following the rules doesn't make you a good driver. To be a good driver you have to follow the rules within the *reason* the rule exists. The purpose of merging on an interstate is to allow traffic to flow more smoothly and keep people safe. Weather and traffic conditions affect how you should merge, and so on. So *"merge on the interstate because it says so in my driver's handbook"*, is not enough to make you a good driver. A loving communion with the *reason for the rule*, makes you a **good** driver.

Creating, no matter how eloquently, from your existing framework of cognitive assumptions is not enough to make you a Genius. You must also understand how to place your own values within the context of a larger planetary story and the overall needs of the human family.

For example, in June 2022 the United States supreme court overturned a policy that protected women's right to terminate pregnancy. This meant that women no longer had a constitutional right to choose whether to complete a pregnancy, and legislation around this choice was deferred to state level jurisdiction shifting sovereignty from federal law to the democratic process. In these sorts of scenarios people need to congregate into shared cultural consensus and vote together based on ideals and values in order to weave their desired experience into the human tribe to create little pockets of sovereign life. This was an incredibly divisive topic. Nobody had lukewarm feelings about it, and the country was split, both sides believing their position to be humane and the other to be abominable. On the one hand, people wanted to protect the lives of unborn children of God, babies miraculously and wonderfully woven together in the womb, yet to take their first breath. On the other hand, people wanted to protect the lives of actual, living women who have taken thousands of breaths and earned the maturity to steer the course of their life, living not by circumstance but according to what they know of their life's purpose. It became an impossible equation of who matters most, baby or mother, with endless theological arguments about how God works.

The conflict always goes deeper than the surface problem. For example, you might have opposing ideals. You might stand for decentralization of government and sovereignty for the people, except when it comes to one of your values that you think should be crystallized in federal law. Your thinking is too superficial or too narrow when you oversimplify things on behalf of a complicated body of different people with different values. Complex, multifaceted issues in a shared infrastructure require complex, multifaceted responses in Sovereign mind. There is no single correct answer—but there are many True ones. Cultures and subcultures must be richly diverse if we are to experience an organic existence within the Garden of Eden, and we must learn to reason with values that conflict with our own.

Remember: In Christ, Genius is the malleability to **Understand, Synthesize and Formulate** something new, so God can always move through your mind and recreate reality by the works of your hand.

By myself I can do nothing; I judge only as I'm guided, and my judgment is just, for

I seek not to please myself but Him who sent me.

John 5:30

Reasoning is a noble craft. In fact, Descartes' "First Principle of Philosophy", *Cogito Ergo Sum*, or *I Think Therefore I AM*, suggests that the very fact that we can doubt our senses and emotional impulses to challenge our created status quo is proof that we are greater than our own experience of what's really happening. Reasoning is a task, a craft, an art and certainly a responsibility for anyone developing a sovereign mind dedicated to a life of Truth.

Alas, we are surrounded, within and without, by fools. You know what it's like trying to share your perspective with someone who cannot seem to see reason. The first problem is that reason is only reasonable within the parameters of personal and cultural paradigm and propriety. This is why *you* are especially charged with the responsibility of reasoning—it is only true Genius that can reason, any other state of mind is simply evaluating stories and reflections of stories. True Genius reasons according to the core values active in the diamond. These values are foundational to who you are in divine Truth—the characteristics of God that the world gets to experience through you. So, what matters most to you and the ones involved in the reasoning? Whatever is going on in the fiery furnace of the world's bizarre and conflicting ascension, you always have the sovereignty to make your decisions based on what is reasonable in relation to your values. If you're in the energy field of addiction, vanity, animosity, conflict, jealousy and all that foolish stuff—it is not your emotion that will guide you right, it is your reason.

True Genius is being able to understand, synthesize and formulate something new.

1. **Understand**: What is this, according to your heart's intelligence and wisest Knowing? Imagine Albert Einstein. He has an inkling, a subtle, unspoken understanding that energy and mass must be the same thing, just influenced differently by invisible forces.

2. **Synthesize**: In the landscape of your understanding, what ideas/values/energies matter to this issue right now and how do they, together, relate to what-is? What core values are you assuming, and what vibrational reality

are you reasoning from? Albert synthesizes his existing knowledge in relation to this understanding about energy and mass, eliminates irrelevant data and sees clearly where the gaps are to be filled. He allows new data to be discovered in the myriad of ways discovery can be done, and lets that knowledge fall into place and create a new picture of what-is.

3. **Formulate**: If your synthesized understanding is to be applied in the four dimensions of real Life, it cannot be a quantum hall of mirrors. It must be made linear and relatable. Albert formulates $E=MC^2$ and the whole world changes.

Note that if the fool you are reasoning with is solidly inside their own idea of what's really happening and unable to observe what's actually occurring, you are not in a shared reality and the formulation that seems natural to you may not make reasonable sense to them. For example, the sentence "*God is real*", although clear and concise, may be absurdly *un*reasonable to someone whose assumption about God is that He's supposed to be an old, white man on a cloud prepared to send us into the pits of Hell to be consciously tortured forever and ever. That is why a well crafted formulation must communicate thousands of layers of thought able to bypass mental resistance. It is why Jesus so often taught in parables, and why some works of art stir us to the very soul.

So Genius is not passive and it is not isolated to your personal brain. In fact, Genius is how you best navigate the shared field of collective thought. It's the only way to reason with fools, and the only way to avoid being swept away by turbulent thought streams where a psychotic may drown.

Understand

Your true understanding is unique to you. If we choose to read it as *under*-standing, we can see it as a viewpoint below that of perfect superpositioned all-potential.

Under-standing implies a personal choice has been made to Know something in relation to one's own self, a decidedly individual standpoint. *What is **my** true Knowing about this?*

This is another reason to be intimate with your core values. You have already defined these in the first mastery, *Remembering*. Remember, how your values synchronize in your unique life is extremely personal, and combine to make the specific lens God desires you to be in His kaleidoscopic Mind right now. So you have a sovereign responsibility to know your highest spiritual values, for your reasoning must begin there—this is the beginning of integrity. Keep in mind that your core values do not define you, and your identity in Christ is not dependent on these values being upheld or even honored. Your values can change and you will always be beloved—but reasoning from any standpoint other than these is false reasoning because you will be using external laws to inform an internal process.

Metacognition is the art of thinking about thinking, so it is a practice that naturally elevates your awareness out of the busy traffic of the electric brain organ and observes the thoughts as they take form and connect with each other. At this vantage point you not only observe the thoughts, you can command them. Knowing your core values and practicing metacognition allows you to choose which thoughts to entertain, nurture, duplicate and allow to evolve, and which to discard and release. You can minimize the traffic, so only the useful thoughts are allowed to merge to synthesize your understanding from a Genius point of view. Loving, appreciative, questioning, wondering thoughts dancing in contemplative reflection and analysis.

> *Finally, brothers, whatever is true, whatever is noble, whatever is right, whatever is pure, whatever is lovely, whatever is admirable—if anything is excellent or praiseworthy—think about such things.*
>
> *Philippians 4:8*

Let's play a thought experiment using Augustinian Thinking, a form of creative transposition. This is a wonderful method for developing your muscle for understanding. This form of thought connects actual occurrence with inner realization, thus deepening your listening skills. In this method, you transpose a piece of wisdom from somewhere else, and you place it into your life in the here and now. Bibliomancy, or "book surfing", for example, is a method of creative transposition.

Let's imagine you're about to head out on mission into the desert, but you're worried about negative comments from social media trolls. The resistance you feel is intense, and you keep procrastinating. You know you need a higher understanding. Let's say one of your core values is *Integrity*, another is *Service*. You stand at one of the celestial bookshelves there in the alabaster cathedral, take a deep breath, and let your hand run across the spines of the many works of fact and fiction that come from divine understanding. You choose the book with the greatest magnetic pull, and open it. Since all things in creation are interconnected as an indivisible singularity beyond space and time, then this little piece of scripture really was created for you, and is acutely relevant to you today, or your Sovereign mind wouldn't be witness to it. You are the intended recipient, so you contemplate the words as if they are speaking directly to you—because all scripture is alive and active, the breath of God.

Let your thoughts focus on the message and simply notice what you notice coming to you. Your thinking will arrange around it, so that new ideas, resolutions and wisdom can be revealed in a way that wouldn't occur without this prompt. Let your thoughts be guided into understanding even deeper, revealing something new about who you really are and what is really going on. This type of thought is intimate and vulnerable, inviting new revelation through a personal communion with the Spirit in all things. So, standing in the light cast from the stained glass window in the alabaster cathedral, with the old book in your hands and the smell of ancient paper activating your inner world of deep thought, you sink into the scripture as if it is being read to you by the Holy Spirit right now, and you simply Know what you Know about it. Let's pretend you've opened the Bible, and landed on this passage from the Apocrypha:

I could prove to you from many and various examples that reason is absolute ruler over the passions, but I can demonstrate it best from the noble bravery of those who died for the sake of virtue. All of these, by facing sufferings that bring death, demonstrated that reason controls the passions... All people, even their torturers, marveled at their courage and endurance, and they became the cause of the downfall of tyranny over their nation. By their endurance they conquered the tyrant, and thus their native land was purified through them.

4 Maccabees 7-11

Your thoughts begin to move, swirling and fusing with one another as revelation opens. Perhaps you realize that when you are clear on what your true values are and what you stand for, all your emotional passions can be transmuted into fuel for your sovereign strength to choose deliberately to stand in reason against all odds—the reward for which is beyond your own life. Stoicism, the art of standing true to high reason, yields obedience to a greater plan than your own worldly and egoic motives.

For example, Eleazar was a distinguished and highly respected 90-year old priest who had dedicated his life to Jewish law. He knew his core values. Along with many other Jews during the reign of the tyrant King Antiochus IV Epiphanes, Eleazar was arrested for standing for and expressing his faith. In the dungeons he endured unspeakable torture. If he would just denounce his religion by eating a piece of pork, he would be free. His captors forced his mouth open and stuffed the pork in, and he spat it right back out again, choosing instead the most horrendous end.

> *"At that point, partly out of pity for his old age, partly out of sympathy from their acquaintance with him, partly out of admiration for his endurance, some of the king's retinue came to him and said, "Eleazar, why are you so irrationally destroying yourself through these evil things? We will set before you some cooked meat; save yourself by pretending to eat pork."*
>
> *But Eleazar, as though more bitterly tormented by this counsel, cried out, "Never may we, the children of Abraham, think so basely that out of cowardice we feign a role unbecoming to us! For it would be irrational if, having lived in accordance with truth up to old age and having guarded the reputation of a life lived lawfully, we should now change our course and ourselves become a pattern of impiety to the young by setting them an example in the eating of defiling food.*
>
> *4 Maccabees 6:12*

In your true relation with your Augustinian book surfing you understand this message isn't about cultural propriety in relation to food habits. It is about the sheer power of the rational mind even to withstand indescribable agony for the sake of your true values. How quickly do you denounce what you really stand for when the going gets tough? Your tummy hurts or your friend said something mean or someone betrayed you or you catch a virus—suddenly you do not choose according to your highest sovereign values but you let your emotions steer you into unconsciousness. Your vibrational universe collapses around a new agreement, and now you're experiencing toxic people and excessive control, shamefulness and disease. And your actions change accordingly.

The clearer and more cohesive your values are, the greater the electromagnetic weight energizing the thought-forms of reason—the greater strength you have to stay in integrity, and Truth sets you free.

Be clear—what do you value the most? Time with your family? The freedom to do what you want? Tradition and heritage? Growth and progress? You're not looking for a prototype to tell you what is most important to you, you need to know yourself. Remember, who has God made you to be? What season of Life are you in right now, what are you practicing? How must this be applied to the broader context of what is occurring? This must be the foundation for your reasoning.

You continue reading through living words, hyperlinks on yellowing papers that activate portals of comprehension:

Admittedly, then, pious reason is sovereign over the passions. For if the passions had prevailed over reason, we would have testified to their domination. But now that reason has conquered the passions, we properly attribute to it the power to govern. It is right for us to acknowledge the dominance of reason when it masters even external agonies. It would be ridiculous to deny it. I have proved not only that reason has mastered agonies but also that it masters pleasures and in no respect yields to them.

For like a most skillful pilot, the reason of our father Eleazar steered the ship of piety over the sea of the passions, and though buffeted by the stormings of the tyrant and overwhelmed by the mighty waves of tortures, in no way did he turn the rudder of piety until he sailed into the haven of immortal victory. No city besieged with many ingenious war machines has ever held out as did that most holy man. Although his sacred life was consumed by tortures and racks, he conquered the besiegers because reason was shielding his piety. For in setting his mind firm like a jutting cliff, our father Eleazar broke the maddening waves of the passions.

4 Maccabees 6:31 - 7:5

Reason versus Reasonable

Here is an important distinction: Devout reason is not the same as reasonableness in the eyes of common sense. We see in Eleazar's story in 4 Maccabees that his actions weren't considered reasonable by the onlookers, who considered him the fool. Perhaps they were viewing from values of *Safety* and *Survival*—but his stoic logic was clear: If *Eternal Truth* and *Love* is on the line, it is extremely unreasonable to surrender my sovereign values for a short moment of physical comfort. So don't fear that your understanding must be reasonable to others. Remember, reason is the power of the mind to deliberately measure and form judgments by a process of personal logic to create an understanding that leads to the actions you will take for the highest benefit for all.

As you close the book and slide it back into its place, you understand that your sovereign reason has a higher log of electromagnetic attraction than your emotions do, so you Know you will have both the mental fortitude and energetic capacity to stand stoically in that reason the next time the counterforce of evil tempts you from your core values. *"When I am weak to the influences of Life, I will use reason to choose for me, and thus I will remain sovereign, true to my Way, and in the poise of Christ's mercy."* A higher understanding has formed, your vibrational reality has elevated, and you go on with your day, improved.

Synthesize

A major life event occurred for me at three years old. I was climbing the stairs on all fours in my childhood home, when I suddenly realized I was aware of myself—inside my head. Not only that, but I could communicate with myself in a string of words, just as if I was speaking out loud! I realized for the first time that I was thinking. As I climbed up to the next step, I realized I was aware that I was thinking, and therefore thinking *about* thinking. At the next step I was now *thinking about thinking about thinking*. My mind split into multiple, perhaps even infinite, layers of thought and a life of metacognition began. My inner thought life was a hall of broken mirrors, infinite angles of reflections and perspectives, some warped or inverted, with many reflections of reflections looking back at me, puzzled. I saw the Truth everywhere I looked so I was often locked in impossible equations trying to figure out which way to go. My light was dispersed like a disco ball. Social interactions were awkward, my personality presentation was inconsistent and incomplete, and I spent enormous amounts of energy in back and forth rumination thinking about intricately constructed problems. Whatever I did, I felt guilty about what I hadn't done during that time, because with infinite possibilities how do you choose which ones to exclude? I have often resonated with Joseph Campbell's famous line, *"The psychotic drowns in the same waters in which the mystic swims with delight."*

In Christ, all these fragments fused together like a stained glass window and became a cohesive understanding. Even with infinite possibilities to consider, my thinking became simple. With the natural synthesis that occurs with salvation I was finally able to organize my mental world and reach new, peaceful planes of mind, and swim with delight in the vast waters of mind.

Synthesis is the practice of distilling what is really relevant and how it all fits together in your cauldron of ideals. Once you have allowed understanding to form, it's time to bring together relevant thoughts and feelings. This is critical thinking. **Critical thinking is acutely risky to your belief systems.**

Your consciousness need to be malleable to the potential for change. The moment you crystallize your beliefs as law and begin to worship the creative result of these values, you're worshiping structure, not essence, as we explored in the second chapter,

Recognizing. These false idols are loyal for a little while, as long as the essence and the structure are unified in meaning—but as soon as your understanding deepens, your home changes and the house around you must too. You must allow your beliefs systems to grow with you.

Everything in form, especially scripture, is subject to constant translation and reinterpretation as your consciousness evolves. You can't help seeing things differently when your vision broadens and your gnosis heightens. That ascension, or process of illumination, is God *moving*. This is when reasoning helps synthesize what's relevant *now*. You will always be diligently testing the validity of what you believe at each level of your maturing wisdom. You'll reevaluate your limitations, your experiences, your potential, and all questions from the most trivial to the most complex.

There are three modes of reasoning that are particularly useful in metacognitive synthesis:

- Deduction.

- Induction.

- Falsification.

The first mode of reason, Deduction, is based on strict rules of logic. Standard logic assumes certain statements are true, like *"A human is a human"* and *"Everything is either a human or not a human"*. Other statements are false, like *"A human is not a human."*

So, a deductive argument starts out with a set of assumptions called premises. These are statements or conditions that we assume are the case. The premises should be mutually consistent. Obviously the conclusion of a logically deductive argument contains no more information than was present in the set of original premises, except that the synthesized result is often greater than the sum of the parts because we arrange the logical facts to make conclusions in other ways.

For example, look at this deductive sequence, which is known as a syllogism:

- Only living things grow.

- I grow.

- Therefore, I am a living thing.

Although the third statement doesn't tell us anything that wasn't present in first two combined, it's given us a new image of something that we can accept as true based on what we knew to be true before.

But wait a minute! Standard logic is extremely subjective. We already know quantum logic defies the standard logic rule that an actual object cannot both be something and also at the same time *not* be that something. IS and NOT co-exist, so *what-is* always depends on who is observing. If you know your core values, you know who is observing.

Let's look at this syllogism for example:

- Religion is controlling and oppressive.

- Father Chuck is religious.

- Ergo, Father Chuck will control and oppress me if I dare to show him who I really am.

Deductive reasoning is only as useful as the accuracy of the original premises and by itself can never prove anything new. You cannot deductively reason in a sovereign way without first Recognizing if your premises are *Truth* or *Story*, and Releasing ego-based attachment to the validity of the premise.

The second node of reasoning is Inductive Reasoning.

Inductive reasoning is the opposite of deductive reasoning. Inductive reasoning makes broad generalizations from specific observations. You start with some data, then draw conclusions from that data. This is called inductive logic. In this form of thinking, you go from the specific to the general. You make some observations, discern a pattern, make a generalization, and infer an explanation or a theory. In science, there is a constant interplay between inductive inference (based on observations) and deductive inference (based on theory), until we get closer and closer to Truth, which we can only approach but never define with complete certainty.

The prediction that the sun will rise tomorrow is an example of inductive reasoning. It has always risen so far. Or when you think about releasing your grip on the handle of your tea cup, your past experience with gravity fills your imagination with a splashy mess all over your floor. This is also inductive reasoning.

Even if all of the premises in a statement are true, inductive reasoning can still lead to a false conclusion.

Here's an example:

- Sam is a plant-medicine shaman.

- Sam is deluded and misguided.

- Ergo, plant-medicine shamans are deluded and misguided.

The conclusion doesn't follow logically from the statements the way a deductive sequence does.

You use inductive reasoning when you frame hypotheses based on a set of observations or experiments. All interpretative phenomenological analysis is this type of logic: no matter how intuitive you think you are, you are nonetheless using a tiny data sample to make sweeping statements about what's going on. Any character judgment you make on someone you're in relationship with is a hypothesis you have derived from a limited number of data points collected in your experience in relation to that person. You choose a handful of encounters and disregard trillions of unknown moments when that person has proven to be someone entirely different.

How many inductively derived realities are held in place by you as absolute law simply because you have never experienced otherwise?

The thing we call "common sense" is inductive reasoning. Views considered by our closest groups to be completely reasonable, yet don't rest on deductive logic but on the way the world happens to be. And of course, the way the world happens to be for one person is completely different for another.

Let's pretend a group of Pharisees confronting Jesus are trained to uphold the structures of law, and live in an angry log of consciousness at 150 on the Hawkins Scale, trapped in a three-dimensional, particularized universe teeming with microbes and pathogens. To them, it is common sense to wash your hands before eating. Originally a devotional ritual, but—as is a risk with all rituals—their hand washing became such "common sense" that the true alchemical magic was lost and the practice became an unconscious automation, not human at all.

So they were surprised when they saw Jesus' followers eating without washing their hands first. It didn't make sense, in fact it seemed like an abomination.

> *So the Pharisees and teachers of the law asked Jesus, "Why don't your disciples live according to the tradition of the elders instead of eating their food with defiled hands?"*
>
> *Mark 7:5*

To Jesus, who has complete sovereignty of mind and therefore vibrational dominion within the natural world of his experience, is perfectly able transmute energy as instantaneously as he is in contact with it. To him, it is reasonable sense that microbes are no threat at all, since creation occurs from within.

> *"These people honor Me with their lips, but their heart is far from Me. They worship Me in vain, teaching as doctrines the commands of men. Disregarding the command of God, you keep the tradition of men... You completely invalidate God's command in order to maintain your tradition!" Jesus called the crowd to him and said, "Listen to me, everyone, and understand this: Nothing outside a person can defile them by going into them. Rather, it is what comes out of a person that defiles them."*
>
> *Mark 7:7-8 & 14-15*

He has a different idea of what should be common sense. He clearly considers body sovereignty to be basic spiritual knowledge by the way he responds to his disciples when they ask him to explain further:

> *"Are you so dull?" he asked. "Don't you see that nothing that enters a person from the outside can defile them?"*
>
> *Mark 7:18*

Collective, systemic, cultural reasoning does not unite Source, Spirit and Substance, and does therefore not have the vibrational authority of Sovereign being. The vibrational reality of a Pharisee requires perfect alignment with the legal, linear mechanisms of cause and effect in order for energy to be in balance. This sort of thinking is incapable of processing the intuitive guidance and genius thought that operate outside these mental systems. This consciousness is always vulnerable to the oppressive forces of the outer world, such as the germs that live on unwashed hands, or Father Chuck's illusion of spiritual damnation, or Sam's deluded ideas of ritualistic cause and effect.

A Sovereign mind, on the other hand, reasons according to its core values and prime directive. And inherent to every Sovereign mind is the core value of Knowing God, remembering and recognizing the Spirit in all things, and extending the Truth that is True always. What is considered proper thought in the archives of culture is simply a structure that has taken form in the moving sand dunes. You are always able to Know whether you wish to reason from these standards, or from your holiest core. As Galileo Galilei said, *"In questions of science, the authority of a thousand is not worth the humble reasoning of a single individual."*

We can choose to lose ourselves in the stormy deserts of the mind. Delegating to the Sovereign navigator isn't always easy. By the nature of life and your decades of interacting with other people plus the strange dynamic between your Self and your many personalities, you have accepted a multitude of reasonable realities and allowed them to define your thinking. The sand dunes have become a mountain range, and you need your mind to map out safe passage. But what use is a map if it's drawn by someone who doesn't know where you are or where you're going?

The map gets especially bizarre when you inherit inductively inferred paradigms that conflict with each other: your maternal grandfather taught you to always trust men with hats, and your paternal grandmother taught you not to. Now there are paradoxical paradigms active in your operating system. A fellow walks in wearing a top hat, and whatever happens next at least *one* of your paradigms is being violated. You're in a double-bind: *damned if you do and damned if you don't.* Your cells emit stress signals to the brain, which responds with the production of adrenaline and cortisol—blood moves from the vital organs and to the extremities, and emotional consciousness takes the reigns.

See Diagram 3: The Model of Human Experience

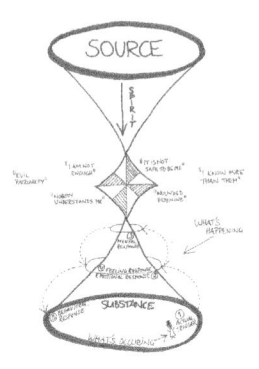

The fellow in the top hat walks up to you and offers you the opportunity of a lifetime. It triggers both your longing to be taken care of and your distrust in the evil patriarchy. Before you even know it, your emotions are in conflict and your mental narrative has shifted, you feel ominous so "common sense" wins the day and you turn him down.

But don't worry, it's not just you who's living like a little frog at the threshold of your greatest potential. We all have conflicting ideals, because life is not black and white. We are all living in the vibrational result of the paradoxes we internalize as we pick and choose how to energetically align.

Paradigm a = *Hard work is the way to a noble and righteous life.*

Paradigm b = *I want a life of fun and ease.*

Logical deduction = *I must choose between being good and having fun.*

Paradigm a = *I deserve to be healthy.*

Paradigm b = *When I'm hurting, people give me loving attention and support.*

Ergo = *I must choose between the vibrancy of being healthy and the belonging of being loved.*

These are lose-lose situations and unless you effectively synthesize what you understand about *what-is* you will continue making conflicting energetic decisions that keep you spinning.

The Third Mode of Reasoning is Falsification

A Sovereign mind first discovers what is helpful before falsifying what's not helpful. Rather than working out new solutions or developing higher ideals based on our deductions, it's smoother to experience a new discovery or a pop of inspiration first (*"Oh! I deserve to be healthy!"*) and then go backwards to construct new hypotheses consistent with that discovery. Then we deduce other effects of that hypothesis and thus a new vibrational reality emerges, bringing cohesion between the panes in your stained glass window, merging stories and timelines, simplifying and opening. You amplify your magnetism, and your spiritual authority ascends in Love.

For example, a man I met was raised in a secular household by agnostic parents. He had later, upon asking the deep questions of Life, become crowded with zillions of incomplete spiritual theories from alien star seeds to underground crystal empires. Once he discovered there was zero need whatsoever to spend any energy on the chaos of unanswered questions, he thus falsified the supernatural and became an atheist. He simplified his life view to *"What is it, this thing before me, confined entirely to my perception, right here and now, according to the strict rules of what I know?"* His Sovereign Way did not include theology. Since that Choice, he had—for the first time—really begun to connect with real life and real people, and he found more peace and purpose. As a drummer in a popular rock band, what was in front of him was an underlying home key and rhythm that can bring all other players together, or scatter them. With his free will he used his drums for all sorts of psycho-pneuma-somatic manipulation to tell the human story through music, but ultimately he would always return to the dominance—his dependable beat of integration and connection with others—and when he did, his band and all the fans would move to those vibes too.

True falsification only works if you are honest. If any of your previous paradigms turn out to be false, then they have to be modified or abandoned. You Release them. Falsifying these paradigms can feel like a betrayal of the familial, cultural identities that have defined you so far. After all, we're in it together. Sometimes stories, mythologies and beautiful arrangements of intimacy and performance do have to remain intact, so we honor our lineages, the tales of our ancestors and the common experiences in our own close communities. We never need to seek to falsify our common stories, or those of "the others". But in an exercise of metacognition, the goal is not to verify your personal paradigms, but accept them as structures that serve for a while and when *necessary* falsify them in order to allow a greater, simpler reality to be Known by you.

> **Every branch in me that does not produce fruit He removes, and He prunes every branch that produces fruit so that it will produce more fruit.**
>
> *John 15:2*

If you don't remove those dead branches of thought then you find yourself back in that double-bind, diffusing the energy that should be animating the manifestations of Heaven and recreating the feedback loop of old thought systems. Falsification protects us from blind faith which is extremely dangerous. The deification of Adolf Hitler, for example, was catastrophic for our human family. The mass panic-buying of toilet paper as people's first reasonable response to the COVID19 pandemic was a tragic comedy. On a personal level, blind faith in your senses keeps you imprisoned in your four dimensional experience, locked for eternity in repeating patterns. This is how generations after generations continue to play out the fate prescribed to them. It's just the way it is, but at least we all agree: *Wealth is ok for them but not for us. We are the slaves, we are the abused, we are the controllers, we are the superiors, we are the diseased, we are the sensible ones, we have the correct political outlook, we know the only way to read and interpret this Biblical passage.*

Developing your Sovereign reason by falsifying paradigms does not mean you there is something wrong with who you have been, your community and lineage, your upbringing or education. It means empowering your awareness of what makes you choose the way you do, stripping down to the core past all the false logic and recreating a narrative of reason based wholly on your *true* values. It softens your resistance to the natural expansion of God's vast mind through you. **Look at Diagram 6, Walking In Christ,** and imagine the focus when all false realities have been cleansed from your mental archives and what is projected from within your thought world is simple and free.

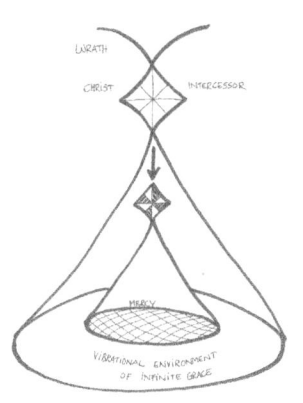

[Diagram: cone/funnel figure with labels — "WRATH", "CHRIST", "INTERCESSOR" at the top crossing shapes; a small diamond shape in the middle; "MERCY" label; and at the base "VIBRATIONAL ENVIRONMENT OF INFINITE GRACE"]

This elevation of your thoughts is so much more than shifting from negative to positive thinking. Thoughts continue to elevate even after you've been saved, that moment when those magnetic poles switched for you. A natural alchemy occurs as Christ's mercy touches the structures of your mind and they dissolve, opening ever deeper conversations with the One and new revelations to guide you further into the world service destined on your Sovereign Way. Your mind is elevated in relation to all things in your experience and, as a result, your experience changes. The sand dunes shift to manifest according to the new agreements that you make. New covenants bound in the creative mind, and a steadily improving Earth.

Unlike the magical Augustinian thought method, Thomistic thinking is stoic and scientific.

St Thomas Aquinas, who lived from 1225 – 1274, believed that Truth is to be accepted no matter where it's found. He was a realist, his school of philosophy based on acute, reasonable observation of the relationship between the senses and the intellect. He taught his students to engage in focused prayer through the style of thinking called discursive meditation. Perhaps he had a very logical mind, gravitating to anything complicated or challenging, thirsting for truth and driven by a tremendous desire to understand, comprehend, explain and predict Life's mysteries. Perhaps he pushed himself to excel in whatever he undertook. I can imagine perhaps he also had a bit of a disdain for stupidity and incompetence.

When you are in this state of mind, you'll know that this is sometimes coupled with a sense of personal inadequacy and self-doubt. A subtle twinge of perfectionism and fear of failure that keeps our mind at all times searching for higher realities and clearer truths. In those times, the Thomistic thought method works best.

Like a scientist approaching a problem, Thomistic thinking is a rational and discursive conversation with God, leading your thought from premise to conclusion through logical steps of inductive and deductive reasoning, plus falsification. It offers a thought style that systematically uses the seven questions: who, what, why, where, how, when and with what? We are reminded a bit of an MC Escher painting as every way we twist our vantage point gives us a different image, a different truth that reveals new perspectives that may benefit us in new ways. As you practice flipping your perspective in this manner, you are training a muscle in your thinking machine that grants you freedom of perspective—and therefore freedom to discover and create anew. Here is the success factor: Begin always on the premise that Truth is to be found in all things, the constant element in Life. **Unlimited poised perspectives on a matter has the same flavor as unconditional Love. In Christ, every configuration of substance has been redeemed so therefore all things are holy.**

Revisit the difficulty or challenging expansion that you are facing in your life today. Maybe it's your chronic pain, social media trolls, oppressive church leaders, your deluded friend Sam, the rose bush your neighbor has planted near your house, or your empty bank account. Perhaps it's moronic political movements or indoctrinated sheeple. Perhaps genocide, torture, and global economic corruption and systemic evil. Perhaps it's the fools you are required to reason with on a daily basis.

Let your truest understanding of *what-is* hang there for a moment like a magnetic orb of shimmering Knowing. Explore the ins and outs of the issue like a scientist examining a blob in a petri dish:

What, who, why, where, how, when and with what? Create all manner of questions using these magic spells, twisting your perspective like a Rubik's Cube, and let your thoughts arrange themselves around each question like a metal shavings around a magnet:

- Where are the borders of Truth or Story? What is actually occurring in particularized substance, and what is really happening in my universe of experience?

- What is this made of? What are the variables that compose this vibrational premise? What core values is this premise built on? What inversions and illusions are influencing those core values?

- Whose perspective am I looking from? Who first gave me this viewpoint? Who has confirmed it? Who has denied it? Who has challenged it?

- Why is this the way it is? Why have I accepted it? Why do I want to challenge it? Why do I think there's a possibility that I or they might be wrong? Why do I believe that this could change? Why do I know there is a resolution? Why is this an unshakable value for me?

- Where are the frequencies of entropy like pride, vanity, greed or jealousy involved in forming this? Where are the frequencies of ascension, like compassion, honor, gratitude or possibility involved in forming this? Where have these frequencies influenced my actions?

- When did I first notice this idea? When have I been limited by it? When have similar quandaries formed in my life, and where have they been resolved? When have resolutions been experienced by others in different times, places and cultural settings?

- How does this truth change if I tweak some of the variables? How does this problem look if I turn it upside down or back to front? How can the tools I have at my disposal serve to improve my experience of this? How can I choose in order to elevate the entire fabric of this particular reality?

As you use this Thomistic style of thinking to play with your understanding of what-is, let your discovery take on any form it desires, be it frightening, foreign, exciting, or beautiful, and just notice what you notice, falsifying and releasing superfluous hypotheses as you go along, and enjoying the process of your thoughts coming into purer cohesion and deeper Truth.

Conscious thinking like this needn't take time out of your day, because your brain was going to be thinking anyway, but by all means create a scared time for this reflection and write your revelations in a journal. Once you've practiced it few times and you're used to knowing when you're using deductive reasoning, inductive reasoning or falsification, then this mental muscle begins to automatically synthesize your thoughts into a meditative experience of exploration while you do the dishes, while you fetch the kids from school, while you build a bridge between the old and the new. Your mind is sovereign, and you can effortlessly and smoothly think yourself into alignment with Christ.

Formulate.

Genius isn't just sitting in your enlightenment cave blissfully figuring things out. Deliberate mental discovery is useless unless it's brought into the world through some sort of formulation. To express your synthesized understanding logically and cohesively, know what your love language is. How do you best express?

You don't have to go to battle with placards if you're designed for poetry. You don't have to choreograph an interpretive dance if your best formulation is a calm chat over a cup of tea. Both Einstein and Picasso, around the same time, synthesized an understanding that the rules of linear dimensionality can be broken, but the two geniuses had entirely different ways of formulating. To share this understanding in a way that could improve the world's relationship with reality, Einstein used mathematical equations and Picasso used cubism and paint.

Whatever your Way, you make your assumptions and values clear, and build your formulation from those values so that you are framing your formulation with communicable reason. Even in live conversation with another you understand what your logic rests on and have the poise to listen actively for what the other's logic is resting on. Thus all your formulations follow an organic unfolding of reasonable discourse in the space between two different fields of consciousness and *really happening* stories.

You can adjust your language. You can adjust the colors. You can engage with "the other" and let them lead your formulations with no fear of losing yourself.

Don't be listening for ways to falsify and destroy the other's argument—this is called the Strawman Fallacy. You will immediately lose authority as a sovereign thinker by demonstrating that either you don't really understand the opposing point of view, or that you just don't care about addressing it in compassion and with respect for the Truth inside it. Any true formulation honors the richness of diverse possibilities in the Garden of Eden, *and* is built from the unique understanding that *you* have synthesized. Truth is universal and found in all things, after all. **Look at Diagram 7, Relationship** and imagine that you are able to formulate and deliver a thought so boldly that it simplifies the space between you and the receiver without disqualifying the Truth that they themselves have synthesized on their Sovereign Way.

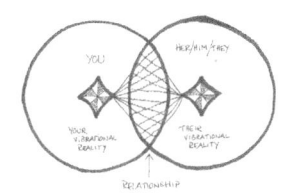

The Ignatian method of thinking is a wonderful way to practice conscious, deliberate formulation. St Ignatius taught his followers an immersive and imaginative technique that uses your sense perceptions and sensible imagination to create well developed formulations. Let's assume you have used the Augustinian method to understand a topic in relation to your true values (perhaps "*it is safe for me to stand in my reason*"), and you have used the Thomistic method to synthesize the relevant information you have about it (perhaps falsifying and thus neutralizing the perceived threats from Father Chuck and Sam.) Now you are ready to process and express your Genius.

Engineer a scene in your mind where this exercise takes place. Somewhere you can feel completely safe. Perhaps you are on a calm beach, or in your home office. Maybe a forest trail, or zooming down a spacious highway in your red Lamborghini, or in your Grandma's chair by the little fireplace. What do you hear? See? Smell? Feel? Be as specific as you like—imagine colors, textures, sounds. This sensory composition forms a brain chemistry that helps your cerebral mind focus and explore, and brings your body along with you.

Now, add two characters: One is a Master Teacher, who Knows the answers and can translate your questions before you even know they've formed. It could be a Master Teacher you admire, living or past, like Jesus or Eckhart Tolle or your Grandma. Or it could be symbol of wisdom, an imaginary character, like Master Yoda, or Gandalf. This is just a thought technique, so there's no pressure to get the imagery right. The core quality for you to embed in this character is their Christed authority to speak your highest wisdom on your behalf, after all,

Wise speech is rarer and more valuable than gold and rubies.

Proverbs 20:15.

The second character you introduce to the scene is someone you love dearly—maybe a friend or sister—who will be representing the shadow side. It could be tempting to choose an enemy of yours for this role, but it's important it's someone you trust to express your fears, doubts, anger, frustration, all the egoic aspects that don't always like to be exposed. These need to come up and out, heard and offered to the Truth for mutual transformation. Genuine engagement between light and not-light is the only thing that redeems, because the alchemy is *through* forgiveness.

And the third character is you—the observer. Your job isto present the topic, for example,*"I understand it's time to stand up and take my offer to market, I know I will be strong enough to withstand the inevitable counterforce, but I don't know how to do it!"*

Let your two imaginary friends engage in discourse about this. The Master Teacher speaks only the wisest words, coming from some depth of wisdom and loving peace that exists beyond your intellect. And whenever the Master Teacher resolves an issue, the shadow character challenges it. This character can speak anything she wants, she has no filter as she twists and turns the Master's Truth. There is one rule she must follow though: She must submit to the Master, so once an issue is resolved any new arguments must build from there, she cannot go backwards and repeat old stuff. Your only job is to keep her in love. Is she saying things you want to say? Is she being "unreasonable"? As the story plays out, she will be bringing up many hidden thoughts that are often suspended deep in the unconscious. Be willing to receive them as they are and let the Master Teacher calibrate every new level of doubt.

What was previously scattered and oppositional thinking becomes orderly and progressive. You will discover that a simplifying formulation occurs as your thoughts elevate and arrange themselves into cohesive and linear melodies that can become expressions through your love language.

If we say revelation is feminine because it *allows* a pre-existing seed of Truth to emerge, then we can say prophecy is masculine, distinctively *expressing* Truth as it penetrates one vibrational reality and seeds new Knowing. True formulation is a form of prophecy. It builds synthesized understanding from a unique field of Christ mind and delivers it into Form.

A person's words can be life-giving water; words of true wisdom are as refreshing as a bubbling brook.

Proverbs 18:4

Look at Diagram 4: The Scale. Imagine again that at ascending levels of consciousness your capacity for Love increases exponentially and your electromagnetic influence is enhanced. Now the thought-forms you formulate are cohesive and greatly energized—they creatively outweigh any attractor fields produced by thought-forms at lower logs. Imagine the implications in the context of world service, and think of the opportunities now opening up for the world if your creations calibrate at 540 and the industry you're moving into calibrates at 370.

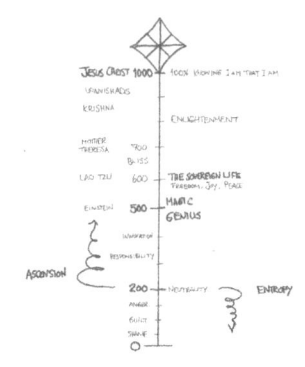

> *"Everyone who is of the Truth hears my voice," said Jesus. "What is Truth?" answered Pilate.*
>
> **John 18:37-38**

The answer Jesus gives the secular-minded Pilate is not recorded externally in scripture or in history. Only part of the truth is ever seen externally. Complete truth is found only at the point of sovereign poise where inner awareness and outer reality are one, which is why Story is so important and why formulation is a fundamental task for a Genius.

At 500 and above your thought world is dominated by the Master of Love. You therefore have tremendous sovereign authority and magnetism. You energetically influence your mission field just by your presence. You walk into a room and people are moved by your radiance. Your words have immediate power. Combine that vibrational power with Truth formulated perfectly for your beneficiaries, and your commission to create more Love will truly blossom—especially in relationship with partners, companions, your beloved spouse, the lady at your local corner shop, the owner of the media outlet. You now claim even more sovereign authority over the way you use words to formulate. **Genius is the contact point between divine mind and human thought**—the contact point between Father and Son. Your words are now the Word of God.

In the beginning was the Word, and the Word was with God, and the Word was God.

The same was in the beginning with God.

All things were made by him; and without him was not any thing made that was made.

John 1:1-5

Truth is constant and preeminent, and Story is the only thing ever created. Story is the primordial code and movement for all our relational creation and the only way Truth can be known and shared between us. It is the extending touch of God that forms the dunes out of all the particles out there in the vast expanse of possibility. Word is what moves reality right here in your humble heart. What's more, 50 words is all it takes to differentiate a mediocre, base vocabulary from the diverse and descriptive tapestry of an outstanding linguist. Think about this opportunity! Replace some of your common words for two months, and you will be in the verbal elite! Begin precisely choosing and eloquently sanctifying each word you use. If you consider that Word is a portal to open access to new dimensions, you're going to have a lot of fun shaking up your linguistic magic because each new word you incorporate opens a higher dimension of reality for you to experience.

Gracious words are like a honeycomb, sweetness to the soul and health to the body.

Proverbs 16:24

A strong vocabulary facilitates precise prayer and helps you avoid vague or irrelevant realities. It's not about using harder, longer, more complicated tongue-twisty words, but to broaden your range of vocabulary so you become better able to describe specific settings, emotions, and ideas in a variety of ways. You find yourself more able to be understood and received, and more able to understand and receive. Intimacy deepens when you speak with refreshing language.

Whatever spiritual path your Sovereign Way leads, your Genius mastery must develop through vocabulary, affirmation, effective prayer and neurolinguistic programming. You will focus on language you can easily summon and use for your unique purpose, language that won't baffle or bedazzle, seduce or manipulate, but truly bring your meaning directly to the hearts of your listeners. In doing so, you sanctify the shared creation in the space between you, and give birth to more Love.

Don't obsess over every word, or worry about accidentally saying the word "*deadline*" instead of "*victory day*". Don't get stuck on trying to perfect the linear construct of your language. Sacred magic, is Word. Simply cultivate and enrich your vocabulary, so there are appropriate robes for your Love to wear when you need to respond or speak a new reality into being—and you will find your old ways of expressing simply melt away.

Imagine, if Word creates distinction between one essence and another, shaping our understandings and influencing meaning and movement—then what did He put in you when He spoke *your* name? What meaning fills your vessel, if your name is a Word spoken by the Source of all Love? And what do you put in your words when you say them? How much love can you fill a word with? Discover that, and *then* speak. This is far more important than learning fancy words and policing every utterance. Now you aren't using your language in conquest to craft the essence of a reality you wish to manifest. Rather, it's your essence crafting the world itself as your words carry the Love of God. Adamantine particles simply dance in the resonance and rhythm.

The sovereign life is lived freely in the bassline of that unique, beautiful meaning that fills your name. You let that meaning fill *your* words and extend your special essence further into the body of Christ, making magic ripples into sand dunes of marvelous Stories that tell the Truth across the ages. In every word you speak you are imparting more healing into the world than you realize, because you have such a strong field of Love.

The verbal mastery of a sovereign Genius is never about getting what you want or playing like a child with a bucket and spade in the desert sand box. It is a vast and glorious ordination to pour God's Love through your essence in the most marvelous and terrifying ways. To stand on the mountain and proclaim your faith, to speak your name as God first spoke it, and tell them the Truth that there is only Love and Life. And that it looks like this—right here, right now—*this is* the Love of God.

> "Let my teaching fall like rain and my words descend like dew, like showers on new grass, like abundant rain on tender plants."
>
> **Deuteronomy 32:2**

With your more spacious, disciplined and powerful mind comes a *whoomph* as the Christ power pours into your body. The elements of cosmic Earth wonderfully molded into your flesh and bones, the beautiful face that has as its mission to bring your magic into the world, all soaked with Spirit. The wellspring bubbles and swells, nudging the currents to shift and fill parched lands with fresh waters. Tides of energy all around you are turning—they must—and the momentum is rising.

Whoomph as divine understanding breathes its way into every part of you, every strong muscle, every wobbly bit of podge, every deep crevice, every lovely dimple and mole. It fills up the spine and those joints and bones and the hair. It sparkles through the fluids like a fresh, natural spring. It fills the lungs with breeze. Embers glow in the palms of your hands and your eyes are alight.

Whoomph it goes through your biofield and out into Life, and star stuff scintillates everywhere. Light particles enliven and glimmer as the elements around you recognize who you are, and respond.

The Sixth Mastery: Alchemy
In His Name

The four of us, my husband, my two little daughters and I, slept in a tent on the rock in the high desert, and had nowhere else to go home to. Surrounded by lavender and sage brush, under the Milkyway blanket, exposed to predators and storms as we tended raw wounds, we had to make Home acutely present. We had to walk very mindfully along the paths so we didn't step on sharp stones or cactus. We showered naked on the mountainside under a solar-heated water bag, cold wind and hot water on the skin. Keeping our eyes over hundreds of miles of mountain expanse, and our ears right here—listening for Bears in the closest embrace of woods. We were physically helpless.

We couldn't master nature. We hadn't had time to learn Her ways before we found ourselves at the mercy of raw land. So, in the poise of our presence, the elements themselves arranged our safe passage through that season. Spacetime bent around us to support our safe movement through the wild fabric of God. There was no need to fear the Lightning or the Lion, merely to Know them as we Know ourselves.

During this time I discovered that Bees don't Know reality the way we do. They whiz along in a high-speed, ultraviolet universe. Snakes see in infrared, knowing Life purely as fields of heat and taste. If you were a Bat you would be an entirely somatic awareness, a sensory perceiver of echo-location in a vibrational universe. Nonetheless, even if your body could just melt away from any of these forms and infuse perfectly with the superstrings and substrings of the unified field, like a note welcomed into a perfect harmony, and you were like a floating formless person suspended in poise in the cosmos, then *you would still be aware of yourself.* Substance exists eternally and so do you, so there will always be a magical interplay between Spirit and Substance as the one that you are. Whether you are living in infrared or ultraviolet, you will always be you. You will still be Love shaped like this because this is your role in the Many **(and there is no I AM without We Are)**.

We have always loved to gaze into the stars, always peering deeper into the soul of reality. When we gaze, we're not looking for a distant home in the Pleiades, or a high throne room in the heavenly galaxies. We're peering into ourselves. From the teeniest quantum microcosm to our big, blue and green planet, further to the greater neural network of galactic interconnection, all the way to the very heart of God, we are made of the same Stuff and soaked in the same Spirit. Everything is the Beloved, the only thing that was ever created, the only begotten child of God. You are born of this same fabric: a droplet of universal consciousness, a unique field of energy in the cosmos, and a beautifully woven body of elements made perfectly manifest. Your cells regenerate every day, constantly exchanging adamantine particles with the Earth and the Sun. Every day more star stuff turns into you. And you are always telling that star stuff who you are. Since you are now a sovereign and expanding genius, from this day on you inspire every cell to regenerate as Beloved, and as a conduit for spiritual perfection made manifest in the material realm.

Scintillating, vivific, life-giving like a star, you set foot out there in the elements, who recognize Christ. You see a Little Frog, and you recognize Christ. You scoop him up, and give him a kiss.

What is Alchemy?

If adamantine particles are now more likely to yield to your vibrational command, you're going to have to master alchemy. You must eventually own your responsibility to join in with the commission to energetically improve frequency and form. As always, this is not for inventing sub-divine realities and manifesting them by magical means, turning lead to gold to line your pockets—but participating in the movement *of* Christ *as* Christ, with all the spiritual gifts you are ordained for here, in Heaven.

You hold as much vibrational influence as you are authorized for, and that is related to how much you Love, both overall and within any given setting. You may consider yourself a highly developed spiritual master, but if you only function in a pure energetic environment where all the crystal grids are aligned and the tea served is of the highest quality, blessed by monks at 9000ft elevation, then you may find yourself incapable of any healing influence whatsoever when you come to a little inner city pub in a rainy industrial town and are served a thick pint of brew. This is why you must be a master of element as well as energy. You must learn to function as Christ in Christ no matter what elemental cocktail you find yourself drinking.

Alchemy is a pretty intense gig. Both people and elements trust what you say, so you must only say the Truth. Your natural healing ability has increased and your touch, voice and gaze have become bright conduits for the universal life force. At the same time, for true communion with everything, you must learn to deeply feel and sense the flavors and textures of Life. How can you commune with nature unless you experience the richness of Her luscious abundance in its truest form? She is full of the same Magic as you. And—how do you stay sovereign while knowingly immersing yourself into the Waters of addiction and seduction out there in elemental creation? You need a deeper and truer understanding of the metaphysical laws and how to balance these against the mystery of grace. You'll need Savior active in your system so you can breathe under water.

"Deep calls to deep at the thunder of your waterfalls; all your waves and billows have gone over me."

Psalm 42:7-8

Since Love precedes Power which precedes Form, your authority to command substance is directly related to your Love, and therefore subsequent to the previous masteries:

First **Remembering** the Truth that transcends all time and space—there are three elements in the universe: Source, Spirit and Substance, and you are an individualized expression of that Trinity with a divinely inherited ordination and authority to create, cultivate and reproduce what is good.

When you **Remember** this, you can master **Recognizing** the difference between Truth and Story, self and personality, essence and structure, home and house, good and evil.

When you **Recognize** these distinctions, you can start effectively **Releasing** story, falsehood, structured paradigms, error and evil. You dissolve most of the systems that kept you unconscious, and forgive most of the obstructions to joy. Mercy flows through sand dunes and they shift.

When you can **Release** old sand dunes then you can **Expand** your borders, increasing your capacity to meet the challenges of Life, receiving and sharing more Love, becoming available for greater missions, adventures and impact.

When you're experimenting with **Expansion**, you condition your **Genius** for processing faster, smoother, higher ideas. So now your capacity for understanding and synthesizing new dimensional realities has quantum leaped, and your mind is free.

Cultivating the first five masteries liberates enormous amounts of life force. A flood of creative energy has been freed from your mind, energy field and body, and wants somewhere to go. Now you need to master the principles for wielding that vibrational influence. So you learn **Alchemy** and practice energetically improving vibration and form.

Let's say that Alchemy is a high level spiritual dynamic known by mystics across all columns of spiritual interpretation and religious lineages. Simply put, it consists of combining two ingredients:

- The philosopher's stone—which is the particularized Substance of God's body made manifest, adamant, formed, structured and real.
- The elixir of life—which is the endless essence, the creative life force of Spirit, the flow of the River and the breath of renewal across the desert.

The purpose of alchemy is to fuse these two elements to create a molecular shift in the Substance that brings an outcome **greater than the sum of its parts.** The idiom is "*turn lead into gold.*"

If the cosmos is made of a dynamic Trinity comprising of three distinct nodes, namely "Creator", "Creativity" and "Creation", **and** Love is what activates the Power to move Substance, **then** the extent to which *you* embody Loving Consciousness is the extent of your authority to command form, so where you dwell on the Hawkins Scale at any given moment corresponds to how effective your alchemy is. **Ergo**, your natural ascension brings increased vibrational influence. A log of consciousness at 1000 can command the adamantine particles from which H_2O molecules are derived to become wine, and those particles willingly *whoomph* into a new form.

> **Jesus did many other things as well. If every one of them were written down, I suppose that even the whole world would not have room for the books that would be written.**
>
> **John 21:25**

The Maharishi Effect demonstrates that when a number of biophotons come into cohesion, that cohesion creates a magnetic amplification that impacts a wider, local field of consciousness. Truth is contagious, like a flame to a flame it spreads without ever diminishing its wholeness. A real life example of this is when a group of people in a crime-riddled city come together in transcendental meditation—and the overall crime rates of that city subsequently drop. A magnetic influence arises from the enlivenment of pure consciousness, which is radiated into the unified field of natural law. Scientifically accepted and published results of Maharishi Effect interventions are found world-wide at local, national, and global scales. Prayer groups all over the world have thus prevented our extinction more than once.

The impact of your intention is therefore directly related to your log of consciousness. The higher your log of consciousness, the more cohesion exists in your field, the greater your vibrational influence in the collective. A person abiding at 150 on the scale has little vibrational influence over structure and must use physical force and effort to manipulate the world to his egoic will. A person abiding at 550 on the scale dwells inside the Christic field of unconditional love, and is able to allow the synchronicities of Life to bring miraculous formations in response to prayer, experiencing the impossible made possible as space and time bend to support the Sovereign Way ahead. A person yielding all creative control to the Christ field at 1000 can allow God's Will to be done on Earth as in Heaven.

A Distinction: Alchemy versus Magic

In Christ, magic is nothing to fear. Magic is the result of the extension of your most glorious, personal and unique God-sourced creative essence into the vibrational reality of your life. It is as unique as your fingerprint. Whenever you, by your electromagnetism, have called the presence of Spirit through the fabric of creation, you made magic. You've made the world sparkle.

As you integrate a more and more cohesive discipleship of Love, you are increasingly granted command of energy and element. And as these gifts develop you will never cease to marvel at the delicious, opulent and funny Ways that magic comes alive in and through you. God's ineffable, mystical peace sinks deeper into the flesh, and *awake* is not just philosophical viewpoint but made thoroughly real in every tingling cell—deeper you sink into the magic of Life. **This is where it gets fun!** The elements dance delightfully into submission to your vibration. Your magic becomes focused and devotional, and every mundane task becomes an act of worship for the One you are in relation with. Your cooking elevates, your garden bursts into bloom, suddenly you can sing beautifully, your touch becomes healing, and you establish a new standard of human presence as your community brightens around you. You can allow otherworldly miracles like $100,000 debt forgiveness in the nick of time before your house is repossessed, or tiny magic like a subtle reiki frequency to start the engine of a broken down, rusty old car. You can let your hair grow thicker, the nutrition in your food be more bioavailable, your digestive system more effectively eliminate toxins, your words deliver more medicine:

> **Pleasant words are like a honeycomb. Sweetness to the soul and health to the body.**
>
> **Proverbs 16:24**

What is this magic for? The heart intuitively Knows the answer. All healing—whether in your body or a relationship, in your community or a group ideology, between peoples or across time—is to give reality back to God and allow the sand dunes to rearrange themselves to the rhythm of their true dominance.

A Thought Experiment: Smoking While Praying versus Praying While Smoking

In the movie *The Two Popes* (Netflix, 2019), the New Pope asks the Old Pope *"Is it ok to smoke while praying?"*

"*No, of course not!*" says the Old Pope. "*That's preposterous.*"

The New Pope responds, *"Is it ok to pray while smoking?"* The Old Pope was stumped.

Let's use this scene as a mental device to guide an experiment and say that in the old way of the world, you must arrange the coordinates of Substance to make space for God. In our dualistic, linear consciousness we cannot smoke while praying. We must first stop smoking, or the particularized actual occurring will not match the proper system of actions that will open the lines to God. To improve anything, you must control and manipulate manifestation, like with a bucket and spade in the desert. So you must live by the rules collected into processes and institutions that help control things in the wild, unpredictable desert. *Stop smoking, then pray.*

When we transform the question to "*can we pray while smoking*", divinity infuses into the manifest circumstance. That transforms the circumstance. Now smoking is not in opposition to prayer, it is in participation with prayer, and spiritual perfection is occurring within the act. Let's look at that deeper.

Truth and Falsehood coexist, and the whole scale in between. Remember this first. If good and evil did not coexist but were truly separate—*that's a good guy and that's a bad guy*—then the universe would be linear. But you know it's quantum. Essence and structure, IS and IS NOT, illusion and clarity, all exist entangled in the super-potentiality of God. With this Knowing *you* have the authority to see and agree with the highest Truth in whatever is before you, and *you* change the reality of it by your presence and your Choice.

The Law of Non-Resistance is one of the universal laws of creation that allows the outpouring of Christ to flow into reality no matter what's going on. Compassion and mercy for what-is restores any attractor field back to its sovereign design. Jesus' ultimate alchemy "*turn the other cheek*" is not the same as complacency at all, it is the highest action possible with perfect, self-sacrificial love for what-is already actually occurring. This is the only power strong enough to redeem a sand dune. On the other hand, when we point at something and say "*that is not-good*", we are formulating and expressing the Knowing of Good and Evil, crystallizing a structure or sand dune and creating a perceived separation between it and the Spirit of renewal. When you put down your resistance to what-is, you make it available to be replenished with Truth.

Not crystallized, but becoming.

Then God looked over all he had made, and he saw that it was very good!

Genesis 1:31

It is extremely difficult for a disciple of Love to witness the horrors of humanity and avoid saying *"that is not-good."* We feel the very heart of the world groaning in pain. We must *do* something. To help our mastery we might practice saying *"this is what this is, I wonder what it's becoming and who I am in relation to it."* We may then be present to the sacred agony and injustice we've been sent to help, yet still poised enough in our words and actions to allow a reality shift as we are guided along the Sovereign Way to help redeem this thing.

The implications of this in Life are significant. It means you can actually be fully present in any agonizing situation, calm in the faithful Knowing that the alchemy only happens in your true relation with that agony. No more anxiety, no more desperation. No more incessant planning and organizing and fixing. Your act of choosing the step you take *will* lead you right as you are in true relation with what-is.

An even deeper implication is that you will save souls. Because you will look at anyone before you and see the Christ within them, *through* their agony. Your magnetic presence enhances Christ in their field, and they may come to Remember. You will turn every villain you meet into an ally, every agony into majesty.

As you practice, held in the Mercy of Christ, you have permission to be imperfect in your faith, oscillating in and out of knowing, in and out of illusion, in and out of Joy. This is when Truth and Story are successfully merged, and the illusion consciousness exists in perfect oneness *with* divine consciousness. Remember, **Emmanuel** does not mean *I AM God*. It means *We Are **with** God*. The human story must go on, this *is* the Love of God, Life on this beautiful planet *is* the divine union where all alchemy occurs. In your True relation with Story, even the agonizing part of it, you learn to breathe under Water, and you bring healing into the depths of Hell.

Sometimes healing means bouncing back and all is well, suddenly delivered from agony. But sometimes it doesn't mean bouncing back. Sometimes it means leaning in, into the tension, into the death, toward an unknown "other side". Ego will always want to use magic to fix the world. Remember this when you're attempting to heal something back into what it was, rather than what it is to Become. When you're using alchemy to create what you or someone else thinks *should* be, you'll become exhausted. This is frail magic because you'd need to spin zillions of codependent energy fields, and you just have a minuscule foundation to inform your architecting. Nothing more than a few pockets-full of collected data to try to create improvement with. You may create glamorous realities full of fireworks and gold coins, but it will be hollow and fall apart quickly unless you dedicate your life to upholding all those interconnected illusions. You will then be captive to the systems you put in place to keep it all up.

Let no one take you captive through hollow and deceptive ways, which depends on human tradition and the elemental spiritual forces of this world rather than on Christ.

Colossians 2:8

The Sovereign Way to master alchemy is first learning the art of loving *what-is* exactly as it is. Then it is Christ that leads the movement of thought-forms as they dance with the elements of the world around you. ***True*** alchemy is in the integrity to restore the manifest to Truth and give the created back to God. True **alchemy** is in the *process* of infusing actualized structure with new spiritual essence to create a product which is greater than the sum of its parts. This alchemy is beyond *"making the most of what you have"* or *"keep calm and carry on through all circumstances"*. It is beyond creating vision boards and chanting mantras to manifest a thing you think you want. This is taking what we have and transforming it into something we couldn't even imagine.

The Great Commission

Imagine: 33 year old Yeshua Ben Joseph has completed his ministry. He has lived millions of moments. Let's say he's observed the Life that collapses the divine wave potential into human reality. Perhaps he has even fulfilled a sequence of actualized occurrences that encoded the ultimate union of humanity and divinity through every layer of human consciousness, saving the whole lot of us since the beginning of time. He's **done the deed** that made it so. Now Jesus the Christ is going to ascend, and in doing so release all the Knowing he embodied as a human into the collective Akashic data field to create a new ascension standard for anyone who opts into this Christ field. Now "*greater things than these*" can actually occur. But before he goes, he leaves the awakened disciples of Truth with a specific instruction, known as "The Great Commission":

And he said to them,

"Go into all the world and speak the good news to every creature. He who believes and is baptized will be saved; but he who does not believe will be condemned. And these signs will follow those who believe: In My Name they will cast out demons; they will speak with new tongues; they will take up serpents; and if they drink poison, it will not hurt them; they will lay hands on the sick who will be healed."

Mark 16:15-19

This is a handy to-do list to check in with our commission. We could use this list of signs to recognize each other, but planetary lightworkers easily see the unmistakable Christ in each other's eyes. In Christ, we transmute and recalibrate energy fields. We create new languages and activate new conversations. We engage gracefully with trolls and snakes in all the elemental worlds, taking no offense and resisting nothing. We have the body sovereignty to receive nutrients and eliminate poison from what we might consume. We alchemize environments and our presence is healing.

Incredible vibrational mastery, whatever the modality it takes form through, is a sign of being alive in Christ and actively mobilized for Heaven on Earth. Love's commandment in the great commission is to go out, tell the Truth and be the proof of spiritual sovereignty by authorizing new realities to manifest.

His first apostles performed mind-blowing signs and wonders across the cities they adventured in. They were bringing a new concept, vibration and demonstration into fields of consciousness that couldn't imagine the freedom they spoke about. They didn't need to use force to convert people. They simply showed them. The spiritual outpouring in their words and actions was rich with with the magnetism to command supernatural vibrational outcomes, from manifestation to healing: Peter walked on water, Phillip healed the lame, Barnabas healed a crippled man, Silas transformed negative entities, Paul healed every sick person on Malta!

Millions and millions and millions of miracles have been experienced and testified since then, right up to this day. Miraculous signs and wonders are commonplace. Extraordinary, supernatural actualized occurrences facilitated every day by mere humans all over the world and in all languages of religious affiliation. Proof, as told by Jesus, of his intimate presence everywhere and in *all* things.

Some religious and scientific narratives around the supernatural deny our authority to bend spacetime, for different reasons. Some reasons are for control and profit. *"Pay us the penance and we'll forgive you in Jesus name". "You can't heal yourself, you need these expensive chemicals and procedures."* You can't sell health to self-healers, so the principalities of profiteering institutions in all columns of society have no interest in this mastery being a part of your human growth and spiritual development. It benefits them more to frame those who exercise powerful vibrational mastery as evil witches, delirious psychotics, or (worse) misguided fools.

Look at Diagram 11, I AM the Way, and consider your personal participation with the energetics of change and the performance of signs and wonders as the fabric around you improves through your ongoing engagement with it. It is not demonic or psychotic to be a genius mystic alive in the Body of ever-changing sand dunes. Imagine a wake of renewal around you and behind you as you move into any space.

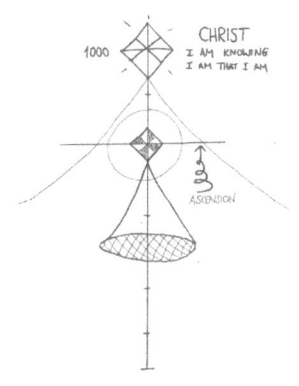

Alchemy as a practice is not outlined in the Bible, though it appears in a multitude of forms. Brain surgery and space travel are also not outlined in the Bible. We unlock access to higher levels of Genius and Alchemy as our consciousness expands, and the rules surrounding how we must steward and direct our increasing elecro-magnetism will change as we earn our stripes along our Sovereign Way.

There are also sovereign reasons most esoteric alchemy practices are kept from the masses. It's the same reason most people shouldn't perform brain surgery. The more complicated a healing system is the more opportunities for corruption or error. A complex energy framework like Kabbalah or Tarot can be exciting and can give a great sense of control. But, as our ancestors discovered, anything concerned with altering or influencing the course of nature is also easy to infiltrate for counterforce looking for egos to seduce and realities to corrupt. If you are authorized to master such a system, there will be no doubt when Christ is experientially training you to know it.

There is no need to seek out these esoteric things, as he will bring you to the appropriate modalities for your life. The simplest framework in the universe, Christ himself, is cohesive and has the purest, most powerful attractor field. It is designed to be complete and sufficient. He removes all the guesswork, makes up for your spiritual, psychic and energetic deficit, eliminates margins of error and restores adamantine particles to their divine position in the cosmos, whether it satisfies your ego's outline for healing or not.

> *Call to me and I will answer you, and will tell you great and hidden things that you have not known.*
>
> *Jeremiah 3:33*

As we long for God and consume more of Him and are more consumed by Him, our Knowing of Love magnifies millionfold and so our spiritual authority in the world increases. Beyond just abiding in inner peace we're able to do more wondrous things. Look at the progress in human consciousness in the last 2,000 years compared to the 11,000 prior, for example. This collective ascension is an exponential, upward curve initiating disciples into new spiritual technologies at every level. And the Great Commission follows you across the ages, timelessly calling you to the supernatural mastery that engages God's Love and glorifies His infinite creative potential. Your craft—your personal modality for participating in the process of alchemy—will also evolve as all structures must.

Rewind to before the Great Commission, and see that Jesus was infusing an existing structure with a new spiritual essence:

The human experience is no longer slave to structure, where success is only possible by perfect alignment with energetic law. Now grace is available for all at any time and success is quantum. You have instant access to Knowing of Love, so Spirit can always improve Substance around you. Anyone who observes this potential and makes agreement with it will manifest a saved Life.

The Father Knows that despite all the guardrails and guidance available to the mind searching in the sandstorms for its way home, our I AM consciousness is not fully integrated and we are vulnerable to the constant influence of I AM NOT. We may strive for Christ consciousness against increasing energetic counterforce, but we will not transcend the frequencies of entropy. We will not collectively yield our pride. Our ancestors warn us through the solemn songs in our own bones—Atlantis left a code to show us evil can reign despite advanced consciousness and a collective awareness of psychic and supernatural processes. For our Atlantean forefathers, civilization accomplished such exquisite things that glamor and vanity expanded disproportionally, stimulating lower psychic powers to become abnormally developed. The creative result of our hubris was multiple split realities, exposing the entire race to the warfare dynamics of the lower astral realm—for which we were not prepared. It destroyed our known world. Deep and drowning floods, the crushing weight of which we can still Remember when we close our eyes and think of the deep blue. Even though we Remember it, it's safe to trust that we Chose a different Way this time round.

"I promise you and all Life" said God, "that this will not happen again. Never again will the Waters destroy Us. I AM positioning a Rainbow above you as proof of this promise."

Genesis 9:9-17

The point of Savior is not to turn you into the perfect Alchemist, but to infuse the particularized Substance of your human diamond with his infinite Love for what-is, setting a new creative standard for human experience as you carry the rainbow effect of his outpouring into every cubic inch of spacetime that you move through. Now Love is both the motivator and the manifested result, and whatever warfare is unfolding in the lower astral dimensions may not disrupt the course of our ascension. We are saved.

Emmanuel

God *With* Us

Love Within and Amidst Us.

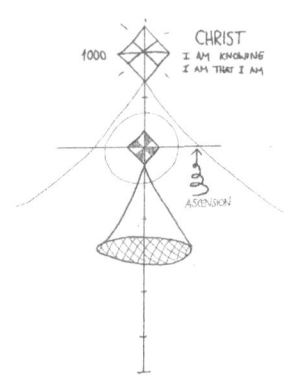

We could formulate **"Love Within and Amidst Us"** as the intention of Jesus Christ. Let's say to *realize* that intention, Jesus completed a sequence of appointed, actual experiences. His ritual, depending on your ecumenical preference, goes something like: Birth, Life, Betrayal, Crucifixion, Death, Descent, Resurrection, Ascension. He is *doing the thing*. Not just intending it, visualizing it or making it happen with the power of his thoughts—though these prayerful elements were no doubt part of his process. Most importantly, he is *participating* through an actualized protocol of *doing the thing* which becomes something significant in the human story.

What if, instead of being sentenced to crucifixion, he had been sentenced to death by stoning—and now Christians around the world wear beautiful stones instead of crosses as a symbol of his sacrifice? Would that actual event have prevented God's intention from becoming manifest? Of course not. It is not Substance that rules Spirit to manipulate Source. It's never the actual ritual itself that has any innate magic, magic is in the movement of your intention into manifestation *through your deliberate action*. When you're experimenting with neurolinguistic techniques or applied kinesiology to attune energy fields, or you're using storytelling to engage more richly and deeply with the bounty of life, or you're using herbs and crystals, breathwork or devotionals, precision prayers or chanting the rosary, or you're reading the star charts and interpreting the tea leaves, are you in Love? If you are combining your *true loving intention* with deliberate action, then you are **In His Name**, and your Source is lovingly commanding Spirit to move through Substance and create a higher reality.

A certain woman had been dealing with incessant bleeding for twelve years and had suffered through multiple modalities and physicians, spending all she had and only getting worse. When she had heard of Jesus, she pressed through the crowd and touched his garment. **She Knew, "***If I just touch even his clothes, I shall be whole.***"**

And straightaway the fountain of her blood dried up; and she felt in her Body that she was healed.

And Jesus, immediately sensing in himself that an energy exchange had occurred, turned to the crowd and said, "*Who touched my clothes?***" His disciples said, "***Thou seest the multitude thronging thee, and sayest thou, Who touched me?***" He looked around to see the woman that had done this thing. She, fearing and trembling as she knew what had happened in her, came and fell down before him, and told him the Truth. And he said unto her, "***Daughter, thy faith hath made thee whole; now go in peace, and be whole.***"**

Mark 25:34

Her name was Veronica. She could have stayed at home holding onto her faith in Jesus and hoping for a better day. But she actively chose to perform the thing: *"If I do this thing, healing will occur."* Jesus, the master healer, didn't take personal credit for the healing. He didn't say *"I have healed thee."* He manifestly pointed to her faith, the embodied Knowing that *"if I do this thing, healing will occur."* It is not the action that *qualifies* or *disqualifies* the alchemy. You are worthy of it before you even lift a finger. All healing belongs to you by birthright. Sure, faith allows you to observe the potential and collapse it into reality, but it's always action that spins that potential into the fabric of experience. Spirit, after all, is movement. *Now go* (action) and *be whole* (completion).

Truly, truly, I tell you, whoever believes in Me will also do the works that I am doing. He will do even greater things than these, because I am going to the Father. And I will do whatever you ask in My Name, so that the Father may be glorified in the Son. If you ask Me for anything in My Name, I will do it.

John 14:12-13

What is "In His Name"? If his name is Emmanuel, *meaning* **God With Us,** then **His Name** is the presence of Love not just *as* the Source, Spirit and Substance of what you are, but also in direct *relation* with itself within ourselves and even between us as a family. Since God is Love, "His Name" literally means the divine love through and between all things.

The term "In His Name" doesn't mean you say *"...in Jesus' name, Amen"* as a sort of spell at the end of your prayers to guarantee that you get your way. That does not glorify the Truth of endless love and possibility.

Instead, it means an Alchemist stands in divine relationship with all things *as* **you perform the** *doing* **that weaves your intention into form. Look at Diagram 6: Walking In Christ:**

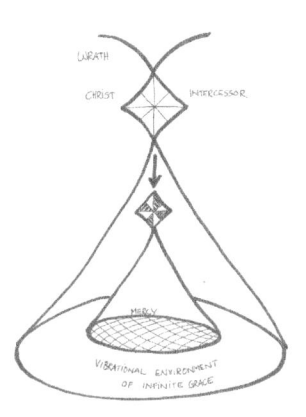

The little diamond is **In His Name**. If the little diamond moves over to the right, or the left, it brings His Name along with it. True submission to His Name is a guarantee against any abuse of our own vibrational mastery, because when you are in Christ his spiritual perfection infuses all material things as a tidal wave of Mercy. If you are praying in error about something, taking the wrong steps out of fear, or being misdirected by a subtle paradigm or unseen mindset glitch, he will course correct your work to protect you and those around you from the the effects of entropy. This is part of his job description as "Shepherd".

The words *"In Jesus' name, Amen"* strung together as a linear sequence and entity of structured objects, don't offer any such guarantee. We've seen as much through the corruption and abuse of power by priests across the many ages. Evil can utter the name Jesus.

Being **In His Name** while you are doing the thing, that's what matters. Being in Love is the key to true alchemy.

> ***And I bestow upon you a kingdom, just as My Father bestowed one upon Me.***
>
> *Luke 22:29*

Nothing in the material world has any spiritual authority to create the real experience of God's Kingdom. The cards can't tell you the future, but Spirit can guide you through the cards. Star alignments can't give you an accurate reading of energetic calibration, but Spirit can guide you through the stars. Crystal grids and burning sage can't heal you, but Spirit can through all the positive energy transference you facilitate for your environment.

Nor is there any *thing* out there that can harm you spiritually, only your agreement with it. Let's say you are triggered by the Ohm symbol, the Star of David, the Crucifix, or the Pentagram hanging on the silver chain round your neighbor's neck. Why is that fear arising? It is because you have associated the form with an energy field that matches a story you know about that symbol, and when you perceive the manifest form, your little Froggy limbic system recreates the chemical cocktail in your body that signals to you that you're in danger. So you feel "ominous" or like "it just doesn't resonate" or you "get an icky feeling," and now Anti-Christ has taken up residence *in your real happening*. You point at the thing and say **"NOT"**, generating a resistance field between you and it. The necklace itself isn't an evil talisman. But you have made it so in your experience, and the evil talisman has worked. Your experience has become "not", even if the other one is happily carrying on with their own sovereign devotion. Luckily,

All things work together for good to them that love God, to them who are the called according to his purpose.

Romans 8:28.

How To Bend Spacetime

Alchemy is the life mastery that allows all things to work together for you. If you're going to follow a Way that is sovereign over its environment, you need to practice. There are always different ways of learning a craft. Remember, there is no practice or ritual out there that in itself holds the magic. Your true practice merges *intention* and *deliberate movement* as the conductors of Love into Substance.

All memories of all things are in our conjoined mind: Glistening gold of rolling Sahara sands under a red sky. The suffocating terror of Dark Age punishment. The cooing and chirping of a damp inner jungle. A bee whizzing through an ultraviolet cosmos. The cool smoothness of an alabaster column. The relief of a sparkling oasis in a parched expanse. Whether it's an imagination of love or of fear, visiting it in your Genius mind invokes a sensory experience, like a whisper of a remembering. You Remember it because you are there. *You are all of it.* The memory of perfect Truth brings *what is already manifest* into a new agreement with its original design. Love God and move. **Pray while smoking.**

There are many modalities of energy work you might develop on your Sovereign Way into the great commission. A modality is simply a form, like a genre of music, and you can learn different forms that all help you play your magic into the world for an uplift of the everything. By now you have experienced a natural opening to healing gifts and techniques as your excess life force spills out into the world. You have developed an increased sensing or intuition that is being crafted into the specific Way alchemy is processed in your Life.

There are as many forms of alchemy as there are people deliberately practicing it. For example, cognitive-somatic energy practices are a family of methods that strategically intervene with human energy fields to elevate wellbeing. You can shift the mind, energy and behavior into a new framework of consciousness and experience new vibrational realities in real time. It's the same concept as what really happens when you see your neighbor wearing her silver necklace, except now the calibration goes upwards. It's the libration that happens when you bury your face in a bouquet of fragrant plumerias and the scent changes everything, or when you cradle your man's tear-stained face in your bosom as he weeps for his dead father.

The medical industry is increasingly using spiritual healing. Direct interaction with prayer and transcendental experience is often involved in medicine, surgery, disaster relief. Practitioners use their personal connection with the divine to hold interceding space in consciousness on behalf of others. One of my favorite personal miracles was when the physician of one of my students testified that we had thus facilitated a demonstrable chemical shift not accomplished in 20 years of psychiatric medicine! Hospitals all over the world are incorporating reiki, which is a thousands-of-years old system of alchemy using a pulsed electro-magnetic wave with a measurable voltage, traveling through a practitioner into and around the one who needs healing.

And it's not only the wellness industry using alchemy. One of my reiki students is a city lawyer representing environmental interests on a board of petroleum companies. She uses reiki for sustainable and holistic leadership, to nourish connections and smooth exchange of values. That's not even to mention the transcendental healing that occurs through art or music! Whatever the practice, the extension of spiritual life force from one field of consciousness to another is a sacred union in true relation between the children of God, an unseen wave of Love that keeps us all alive.

Look at Diagram 4: The Hawkins Scale and see that on the scale of consciousness, anything manifest has an energetic attractor field with a weighted resonance measuring somewhere between 0 and 1000. Where it logs on this imaginary scale between 100% False and 100% Truth will affect the quality of its vibrational reality. A cheese sandwich calibrating at 54 has a different overall quality and effect on your energy field when you consume it than a cheese sandwich calibrating at 504. This is why you bless your food and water, your pillow, your intentions, and that email before you click send. You improve the energetic calibration of it, and thus you improve the transmission and transfer. It rises up the scale, and so does everything entangled with it.

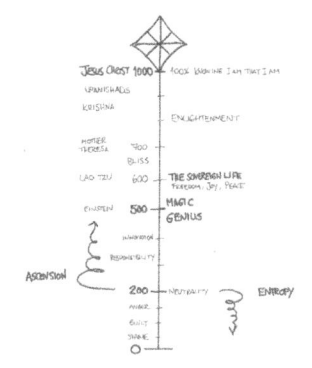

[Hand-drawn diagram of a vertical consciousness scale with values from 0 to 1000. Labels include: JESUS CHRIST 1000, 100% KNOW ME I AM THAT I AM, UPANISHADS, KRISHNA, ENLIGHTENMENT, MOTHER THERESA 700, BLISS, LAO TZU 600, THE SOVEREIGN LIFE - FREEDOM, JOY, PEACE, EINSTEIN 500, MAGIC, GENIUS, IMAGINATION, RESPONSIBILITY, ASCENSION, 200 NEUTRALITY, ENTROPY, ANGER, GUILT, SHAME, 0]

In Christ, a pillow's energy field can only become a truer version of its **already always** wholeness. Your job as an Alchemist is to calibrate the energetic attractor field of the pillow *from within itself* so it slides up the scale naturally, from a bag of feathers to a healing cloud you lay your head upon when it's time to sleep. It is your consciousness, your heart's Knowing, that communes with every little pillow molecule, recognizing them for who they are and loving them Home.

Certain people or items have a max capacity and a log of consciousness that is divinely ordained. You can manipulate this capacity and create the illusion of ascension. It'll work for a minute, but it will ultimately fail and cause harm as the loss of what was never meant to be. You can't override free individual will any more than you can override God's will, for they are the same. I cannot describe the horror of watching someone you care about fall from a great height, and know it was because you promised a miracle that wasn't yours to give, and spun a reality that wasn't to be. Hope dashed is a terrible betrayal, and poison for the faith. It is only the ego that wants to use magic to heal everything. Some sacred hardships are exactly what they should be, and only God knows. Our love for one another, our compassion and solidarity combined with pain distorting our view makes it so hard not to throw ourselves into fixing the thing in front of us—which, without his sovereign mind, we have no idea what is or what's becoming.

The Sovereign Way is the only way to safely practice alchemy as one who is on commission to make more Love. When you work directly *with* the living Christ, the Lord holds the divine metaview of what's really going on here, and thus guides your attention, decisions, movements and modes. Sometimes you get to authorize a spectacular healing miracle, and sometimes you have to let things fall apart.

Again Jesus said to them, "Peace be with you. As the Father has sent me, so also I am sending you." When he had said this, he breathed on them and said, "Receive the Holy Spirit. If you forgive anyone his sins, they are forgiven; if you withhold forgiveness from anyone, it is withheld."

John 20:21-23

In an intimate setting with his closest disciples, Jesus distinguishes two sides to the coin of vibrational mastery. We have the authority both to clear and release energetic realities, delivering others from the karmic effects of their inverted creations, and we also have the authority to Know when *not* to do so. Some creations are meant to play out to the bitter end. In reality, Death IS—after all—a divine part of the Story.

There will be times in your training as an Alchemist that you will practice time-bending.

It won't always be like in cartoons when superheroes speed up or slow down time, reality freezes around you or you go into hyperdrive. Those are just astral experiences, which are cool and all, but the Sovereign Way is in real life, the embodied life of Christ. We are not bypassing the holiness of form as-it-is: the Story. We are not evading the laws of nature and metaphysics any more than a supersonic plane does zooming through the sky. Spacetime is sacred. Substance is sacred. Flow isn't just through you, it's through every cubic ounce of space surrounding you, all fractal. And in Christ spacetime responds to your Voice.

"*Dost thou love life? Then do not squander time, for that is the Stuff life is made of,*" said Benjamin Franklin. There are all sorts of reasons we squander time and lock it into fruitless systems. We don't do the things we know we should, and we gamble our transformative energy on meaningless pursuits that do nothing to elevate anyone or anything. We'll often rationalize excuses like *"oh, it's my trauma about fear of being seen,"* or *"I need to make enough money first so I can buy the concrete for the vineyards,"* but most of the time, it's not nearly as complicated. Most of the time, it's just that we haven't claimed sovereignty over time. We're subject to it. We're afraid of time. We don't have enough of it. We've overspent it or overpromised it. We've undervalued or commoditized it. We've identified with it and now our Life is slipping away by the second.

But Time isn't a collection of units of nanoseconds and millenia. It is a continuum made of events unfolding. And it will always unfold in an optimal way when you hold yourself in divine relation to it.

In the first five years after I *whoomphed* into Christ, time behaved very strangely. I published six books, ran a beach ministry, developed and delivered spiritual mastery programs at churches and independently, created a cosmology and healing modality. I starred in an award-winning documentary, started four businesses, failed two and succeeded at two, moved to the mountains to sell magic chocolate, lost everything, lived off-grid, recovered from financial disaster, trained for priesthood, lived through two hurricanes, survived a bear attack on our homestead, was homeless living in a barn and a tent and a million-dollar miracle home on 180 acres. I helped my mother back from the void, experienced a miracle debt forgiveness, and worked hand-in-hand with disciples all over the world delivering the miracles of their ministries, including through complicated cases like depression, terminal disease, human trafficking. I gained two years of clinical experience, produced over 300 hours of video tutorials, travelled to Utah, Colorado, Florida, Norway, England, taught at two universities, cultivated my garden and raised two gorgeous little children. In each of these actual events there were a million more moments, each one lasting an eternity. Even in my moments of addiction, terror and anxiety there was always enough time for peace.

I often look back and think *"how could it all have happened in that time?"* The truth is I only did 10% of those things. God did the remaining 90% through bizarre economies of scale. Like Veronica, I did one thing and twenty cohesive and connected results came out of the unseen processes, falling into place as I went along with the Hero's Protocol just doing the next thing. *Now, buy a tent.* Divine economies of scale are always moving and somehow it all gets done.

Gravitational Time Dilation.

The force of gravity treats time like toffee. Albert Einstein's theory of general relativity is that where gravity is stronger, time passes more slowly. The stronger its pull, the more gravity can stretch out time, making it pass more slowly. Time goes slower on the surface of Earth than it does the further away you travel from Her core. We've proven this slowing of time over the shortest distance yet—just one millimeter (0.04 inch).

Gravitational time dilation occurs because objects with a lot of mass create a strong gravitational field. The gravitational field is really a curving of space and time. The stronger the gravity, the more spacetime curves, and the slower time itself proceeds. But this is why it's not like in the cartoons, because if you're in the strong gravity field you experience your time as running normal. It is only relative to a reference frame with weaker gravity that your time runs slow. A person in strong gravity therefore sees her clock run normal and sees the clock in weak gravity run fast. You seem to have infinitely more time in which to do things. So much experience, accomplishment, and devotion unfolds in every minute. While the person in weak gravity sees his clock run normal and the other clock run slow. *"Why are you so slow, come on, hurry up, urgently hustle, must create, must save the world, time is flying by and we're running out!"* There is nothing wrong with either person's time. Time itself is slowing down and speeding up because of the relativistic way in which gravity warps space and time.

Imagine the spiritual gravity of Christ, who pulls all things into him. In him, time stands still. Light is neither wave nor particle, *and both*—poised in Love.

And he is before all things, and in him all things consist together.

Colossians 1:17

Christ is a self-containing body. Consider the alternative; if gravity ceased for one moment—instant chaos. All heavenly objects, including Earth, Moon and Sun, would no longer hold together. Everything would immediately disintegrate into small fragments, every sand dune just a zillion sand particles. *Whoomph.* But in the great gravitational field, the Beloved is whole and in cohesion.

As you deepen your position in Christ, divine economies of scale flourish as time dilates for you, allowing greater outcomes than possible in the conventional time perceived. Trusting your sovereignty over time is as important as trusting your sovereignty over elements in space. When you are called out into the Great Commission to serve our world at this sacred time of *urgent crisis*, you are going to be doing impossible things. You will look at the task ahead and think *"how will we ever resolve this?"* and before you know it, you'll say *"I can't believe we accomplished all this!"*

Listen! The voice of my Beloved! Look! Here he comes, leaping across the mountains, bounding over the hills. My beloved is like a gazelle or a young hart. Look, he stands behind our wall, gazing through the windows, peering through the lattice. My beloved calls to me, *"Arise, my darling. Come away with me, my beautiful one. For now the winter is past; the rain is over and gone. The flowers have appeared in the countryside; the season of singing has come, and the cooing of turtledoves is heard in our land. The fig tree ripens its figs; the blossoming vines spread their fragrance. Arise, come, my darling; come with me, my beautiful one."*

Song of Solomon 2

The Seventh Mastery: Adventuring
The Metaphysics of True Freedom

Imagine the implications of having such malleability in your mental and vibrational mastery that you can just *whoomph* into the next dimension Christ calls you to. With the Genius to understand and process any reality you find yourself in, and the Alchemy to literally improve every cubic ounce of energy around you, then there is nowhere you can go from His Spirit. God would be able to call you to any mission at all, and Know you would go. You would be available to Love everywhere, so a greater world plan would become available to you. But it would require outrageous courage and surrendered faith, and the obedience to act immediately when your heart Knows it must. We'll call this mastery **Adventuring.**

How quickly can you sidestep a reality? Let's say you've planned a quiet evening writing your book. You've arranged your workspace and lit the candle, poured the tea and chosen the music, and just as you are about to settle in and let the artistic juices flow, God tells you to go and plunge the toilet. You know exactly what you must do, and it's not what you planned. Will you jeté like a graceful ballerina, or will you stomp like a petulant child? Perhaps you must leave the clean and free life you have been creating in the high mountains and move to a moldy bedroom in a brick house in a damp inner city on the other side of the world. Perhaps you must discontinue a timeline of being an impoverished artist and grow into a season of great overflow and influence. Perhaps you stop serving at soup kitchens and start integrating crystal grids at key dimensional portals across the globe. Or perhaps, after a long season of hard and thankless work for an invisible goal, you must rest for a year in the valleys, being nourished by the elements.

With Sovereign command of both your mental and vibrational worlds, you can cheerfully change directions. You're always somehow provided for and always safe as you mission your way across realms of consciousness. You are always helped—in your discipleship of Love you become part of an integrated group of sovereign souls. Some might call it *ecclesia*, a family in thought and vibration functioning together in an invisible but powerful formation—bonded by an inner spiritual Knowing. Wherever you go, there we are, Recognizing and helping each other on the Way. It's easy. Synchronistic design brings us into collaboration, we see the glint in each others eyes, and we discover we're working on different parts of the same project. We join forces, the thought-forms we are building connect perfectly and are amplified, and we exponentially elevate the manifestations of Kingdom—including the fruit.

You learn to truly live in the world without being of it, as you Recognize the cultural and natural systems of the world as easily as you Recognize grace. Your heart is free as you jeté from lily pad to lily pad across the Pond, and sometimes just sit. It's like Life is training you for course-correction and the ever-present ability to recalibrate the compass to Love. You begin an advanced mastery of outrageous faith that leads you way beyond the reasonable and deep into Wonderland. Adventuring will bring you into unchartered territories, reveal entire dimensions of life you've never experienced, and quantum leap your growth beyond measure. Who knows what the future will bring? An Adventurer is prepared for what nobody is prepared for.

During this phase of spiritual development you lose your ability to control, predict and manipulate. In order for you to truly trust God's infinite provision on your Sovereign Way, you're going to have to abandon every system that once upheld you. The impossible becomes real, as sudden new opportunities and unexpected trajectories open up. The probable becomes impossible, as your old success strategies fall apart and you have no choice but to change direction. You no longer feel like a master manifestor. Your Genius Alchemy is utterly surrendered to whatever may be. You gain a new relationship with God as "Lord" as you move entirely in synchrony with his design. Pride doesn't like it at all, but can you imagine how valuable this particular faith muscle is to a world so disintegrated?

The bootcamp to prepare you for this mastery takes outrageous courage. Imagine the popular spiritual leaders Doreen Virtue and Paul Selig. Doreen built a successful franchise of inspirational angel teachings with millions of followers, and then renounced it all to follow a Christian path. Paul enjoyed a sensible and secure career in academia before he told all his colleagues he was quitting to become a world famous conscious psychic and deliver prophetic teachings from an esoteric group calling themselves

"The Guides". Quite a side step. Even a woman or man of the purest faith would need to stoke a furnace of courage before facing your own people to tell them you're going a new Way.

Let's say you've already Chosen. Despite the unreasonable amount of courage required, your personal confidence and willpower doesn't need much artificial development because they're always rooted in your faith anyway. Christ is now your source of supernatural courage, which is what it takes to cross the threshold of resistance, because Expansion *is* always bigger than our egos. We can't fake it till we make it—we'll never make it if we fake it—we need *true* courage. True courage is the momentum that keeps you moving steadfastly forward into your Life's becoming, even when the next step is frightening and you don't have all the answers.

You left the the patterns of your identity, you gave up controlling others' opinions of you, you're not overly attached to the reality you've been creating so far, and you are ready to only follow Christ one step in front of the other along the Sovereign Way he brings you. You've unleashed the momentum of life force and, like a deep crystal tone in a sea of vibration, your new bassline dominance is released from the heart of every cell into the Body of Love. Your life *is* going to expand and the tectonic plates of your reality *will* shift. Things in your life and our shared world will crumble and fall away, and you may grieve their passing. But you will not confuse structure for essence. No matter how your Life manifests, the power that moves you along and keeps you going, is always with you. That's True Courage, like a Lion.

Remember when you were at the rock bottom. Remember how small and helpless you were, paralyzed beneath the crushing weight of life, down where nobody could hear you, where the walls closed in on you and you were cold and empty. And then, from somewhere inside or out, from a tiny microcosmic flash, a quantum ignition occurred. A spark. A Word whispered into the cells. Somehow a gentle pulse of vitality raised your head. A subtle breath filled every muscle with the strength to uncurl your spine and engage your core. A flow of electricity ignited your meridians, a lightning bolt of Love—and then a baby step.

That resurrection power that moves galaxies is your True Courage as an Adventurer. It is the same power you need to transcend the highest reality you've ever accomplished, and the power you need to accept a mission in the deepest blue.

I Already Always AM your courage. **I AM the Lion** of Judah. **Step out upon the water.**

―⧋―

Taking a step when you've first arrived in a new dimension.

You do not know the way forward or what will happen, but you know it is happening because the momentum is really moving through you. It's a calm compulsion to move even though you don't know what you're doing. Each step you take into the unknown is laden with risk as it's a step further from the reality you were building before. Entire attractor fields wobble and the old creations you had been building start to dissolve around you. It can feel a lot like failure, but it's not. It is suspension—each of those realities still exist in potential, but as adamantine particles are released from their contracted sand dunes everything that had seemed so precious turns to vapor, waiting for new instructions to form. Ahead of you is an unknown energetic territory, with rules that you haven't yet experienced.

Imagine the Dragonfly as it first emerges into fresh air after a lifetime of being a pond nymph. It can't fly yet, not from the surface of the water. It needs to climb up the blade of grass until it is positioned properly to launch. You need to reacquaint yourself with the laws of balance no matter what side of the galaxy you find yourself, especially if you have a family or a tribe of followers who trust your leadership. Let's say a field of consciousness is like a game board for a vibrational reality. And ergo, if you are in a new field of consciousness, then you are also on a new game board. When you finished the previous chapter, either in this book or in Life, you won the game at that level. Let's say you've ascended, you've crossed a spiritual threshold and awakened again into a new reality. You're not playing at that old level anymore, the mastery you were practicing is now embodied and it is a part of your essence. But for some reason, stuff is not working for you the way it was. Many old things that used to work won't work because the rules have shifted to Expand your energetic borders. Your capacity in consciousness and vibration has increased, and you are living higher, deeper and wider than ever before. Not only that, but the whole collective has changed, the world has changed and therefore so has your role in it.

Look at **Diagram 4, the Hawkins Scale,** and imagine that every notch on the scale corresponds to a certain quality of energy, and that all reality manifested there is an interconnected web of thought-forms and energetic networks that resonate together into vast systems of agreement reality. Each notch is therefore like a specific vibrational universe, where certain characteristics and rules operate. Each of these realities are integrated simultaneously in our beautifully diverse world, yet as your consciousness develops, your diamond slides up the scale and the vibrational nature of your experience shifts. Rules and systems that applied in previous expressions of who you are, no longer work. You're playing a new game. In a new game the rules change. There is no point trying to win a game of Chess using Monopoly pieces. Imagine that you have quantum leaped from a world of persuasive, emotionally sensitive and responsible leadership (350) to a world of sophisticated coordination and brilliant innovation (430), and now you leap again to a world of liberated joy and devoted service through engagement with magical synchronicities (610). The rules must change.

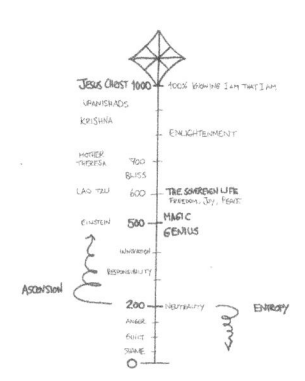

True freedom is not horizontal, free to do whatever you think you want whenever you want to. It's vertical, rooted in your core values and suspended the ideal of Christ. You live in sovereign poise in *what-is*, held in Grace and moving with an endless stream of Spirit. An Adventurer's flourishing is not necessarily in all the 3D structures of your life. Like when you were building a stunning sand castle in the systems of 300. You were super focused on your craft, working with excellence and devotion. You didn't notice there was a strong wind coming from the 600s, and God loved you too much to let you keep building. He had you go and make a wind farm instead, and saved you plenty of time by dissolving your sand castle before the wind arrived! You won't win every gamble no matter how psychic or empathic you are, because your Sovereign Way is not ruled by the laws of energy. You won't win every business transaction, because you're not ruled by the marketplace. You are a disciple of Truth. If you let him lead, you will be guided on a flow of synchronicity into perfect moments of magic and miracle as God reveals Himself to you in every system of being. This doesn't mean you must release your beautiful masterpiece that is indeed your long-term legacy. But hold the essence of it, and let the sand particles of structure be free to move around that essence.

The reward of humility and love for God are riches, honor and life.

Proverbs 22:4

When you lived in the 300s, even though you were a positive person doing good in your community, you were still rather cynical. You believed Earth and Heaven to be separate, that the world was out to get you and control you, that you needed to fix things and that God was not on the outside but only a quiet voice somewhere deep on the inside. This way you separated yourself from the Spirit in form and created a dualistic experience where you needed to meet certain internal and external conditions in order to safely move. You were analyzing, calculating and weighing up the risk of worst case scenarios to take the path of least destruction and most gain. You couldn't trust the world to guide you right, so you tried to rely on some sort of failsafe inner process of discernment that you weren't actually sure you'd cracked yet. You sought out the code in various methods, theologies and stories about who you are. Those codes were all the rules of different systems, not the rules of your sovereign game.

Systems are incredibly useful. They are frameworks for directing movement in beneficial ways. Like the traffic sign telling you when to merge, useful modes of regulation direct people into compliancy with a collectively agreed upon way of being. In the logs of consciousness between 200 and 499 a flourishing life is experienced through a symphony of systems: the career ladder is a guide for your emancipation, the systems of education steward what you can know, religions help you organize your origin story, bureaucracy and politics are cogs and mechanisms of smoothly running beehive. System is not about fear. "The System" is only fear-based if you fear it. The Beloved dwells at every level, and Knows very well how to Be in the traffic. Rather, system is about spiritual authority. Once delivered from the illusion and abiding in the fields of consciousness above 500, you operate from within instead. Now you have supernatural authority to bend space and time, so synchronicities become the agents that guide our movements, our decision making, our possibilities and opportunities. This is how we continue to participate with system without being controlled by it, and how we effortlessly shift from system to system as we cross invisible borders of engagement.

When you leaped into the 500s you Knew that your Lord and Savior is alive and real, that the Universe is conspiring to work for you, that the body of God is GOOD and BECOMING, so you are present to what is flourishing in the Vine. You see it, right there, as the elements respond to you. In the collapsing world around you there is always a glimmer of a new life and direction, an oasis opening up in front of your very eyes, and the Way becoming brighter. You simply step into it, and others follow.

As a matter of curiosity, the scientific research conducted by Dr David Hawkins and his team discovered that only about 4% of the population live in this mystical dimension above 500. That might not seem like a lot, but calculate what that number is in your region. These are the ecclesia, your family of other planetary lightworkers who heard the *bong* and are coordinating with you at this very time. Consider that there are actually thousands surrounding you, always prepared to love you unconditionally. You can recognize us by the Light in the eyes, and the signs Jesus listed in the Great Commission.

So encourage each other and build each other up, just as you are already doing.

1 Thessalonians 5:11

The ground rules never change, you see. God is still sovereign, and your identity is still held in Christ. Love still wins the game. Your diamond is still manifesting from consciousness to energy to form: *I know I already always AM, I am made of Light, I am Good, I am Becoming. I have authority to create and permission to flourish. I know who I AM today. I know I am personally in my Lord and Savior.* Formulate these basic creative codes however you like, they are encoded in your log of consciousness and these rules stay in place as Spirit effortlessly manifests the vibrational reality to match.

One of my students was a blind chef who was getting ready to climb Kilimanjaro. The rules for a blind mountaineer are different than the rules for a TV chef, but by Pure Luck she had once been a gymnast, which had given her the mechanism she now needed to quickly switch from chef to mountaineer without being able to physically see what's going on. She explained to us how to do a front flip on a balance beam without being able to see it. You start by feeling the position of your body in space. You feel the beam under your feet, and you Know the laws of the beam. You Know its width, length, rigidity—not like you know facts, but like you Know the characteristics of your dependable Father. You trust these 100%. The beam *is* dependable. Then you form an intention, using your Genus mind to move through the multidimensional vision unfolding in your imagination, feeling it. The brain calculates the precision required, and you don't interfere with the mathematics as it sends trillions of signals to all the tiniest muscles in the most precise parts of your body. You Choose, and movement simply occurs. If you trust the laws of the beam, and you trust your own divinely designed body's ability to follow him, then you just do a front flip on the beam.

To her, it was no different than making a cup of tea. You don't know how to emit the right electrical signals to contract the correct fine motor muscles to lift the box of ginger and turmeric. You just Know where all the things are in relation to each other, and then you make some tea, trusting that the workings of the mechanism will play out in perfect alignment with your intention, and tea will be served.

The beam is there, it is safe to move forward. It is a narrow beam, because the path gets narrower and narrower the closer you get to God. When I was apprenticing in the Unity movement I asked my teacher, Rev. Thompson, why the Way gets narrower. She said, *"when you're in Love, it's unbearable to be apart."* The holier your consciousness, the stronger your magnetism, the more cohesive your energy field, the more your righteous action collapses the many artificial timelines and thought-forms that you had constructed up to this point. You have much less tolerance in your own energy field to go off track in the wrong direction. More Truth attracts more Truth. And the Truth is not wide and complex at all, it is very, very simple.

Once you trust the vertical laws of the narrow balance beam (or the Dragonfly's blade of grass), you can play with the horizontal rules of the game board. In your real life experience, what are the new conditions? What is the new destination? What are the energetic risks and opportunities in your own biofield and in the new environment? Who are the people and personalities in this new community? Perhaps you'll use a Thomistic mindset from your Genius repertoire, with the Great Audit from the Hero's Protocol in Expansion, to thoroughly lay out the landscape of new game board. In an Ignatian style discourse between Christ and your Ego, you will quickly synthesize the new rules of the game.

Remember when you last felt connected with nature. You stood by a waterfall, or walked on the forest floor, or planted some seedlings in your garden. And you were at total peace, not thinking about the next step and the next, but simply moving in the rhythm of nature around you. Of course, nature isn't a *thing* you connect with any more than culture is. The only way nature gets to experience Herself like that is through you, in that very moment. Actually, it's the dependable beam you're connecting with, the unchanging primordial home key and bassline vibration.

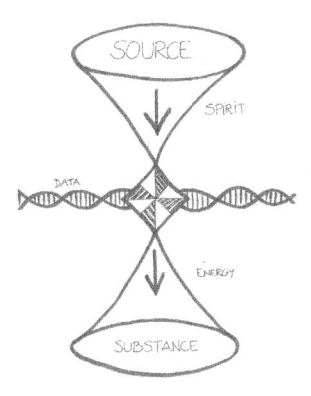

[Diagram: an hourglass shape labeled SOURCE at top, SPIRIT, with DATA along a horizontal DNA-like strand through the middle, ENERGY, and SUBSTANCE at the bottom.]

Look at **Diagram 2, the Sovereign Model of Human Consciousness**, and imagine that every created entity is a projection of Source through a lens of consciousness that informs a vibrational projection and a manifestation in Substance. This model is true for Bear and Bee. It is true for Snake, Oasis and Desert. Imagine zillions of these, small and large, affecting each other to become the energy field we call nature.

Position yourself on a forest floor perhaps, and be the size of a small mouse. And from this point of view look and see all sorts of four dimensional activity, hustling and bustling in space and time, insects eating other insects, a raindrop crushing the entrance of a small ant colony, a monstrous heron swooping down and piercing a frog with its sharp talons. Mold. Parasites. A sweet little daisy. A snake slithering, a bee whizzing. There are no perpetrators in nature. We do not blame the wasp for eating the ladybird. We understand the wasp is simply being Wasp. Even within nature the rules of reality change. Life Knows Herself in a multitude of diverse ways from ultraviolet to infrared, and an Adventurer who can appreciate this is brought into a deeper life with a stronger contact with your own soul.

If you live in a small tent made of canvas and you're in the wild, and something needs to eat you—you're fair game as far as nature is concerned. I Knew this when at any given moment my children were in the attractor fields of packs of coyotes, bears scavenging the camp, mountain lions leaving footprints down by the stream where we washed our hair. I Knew that for the rest of our lives, storms will come out of nowhere. War zones will erupt and fires run amok. Nature is not dependable like an invisible balance beam. The loveliness of Nature is the diversity of infinite organic universes in symbiosis as this dance of dominance and surrender is enacted throughout nature by plants, animals and other humans on the Sovereign Way all over the world. The loveliness of **culture** is the coming together of values, and the Expansion that happens when we allow another's life journey to be equally valid and divine. This is a very peaceful state of mind, because that stance keeps our identity unstitched from the world of form and we know that Spirit moves us to act when it's right. By the time you move, the circumstances are already aligned for the body hop, the forward flip, the quantum leap, because Nature has already moved.

Mother God will always obey Father God. It is Her honor, Her delight and Her deepest Love to do so. On the Sovereign Way a strange territory of protection therefore forms around you, and Nature bends Her energies and elements to observe the laws of the balance beam. Coyote take a different route. Bears leave without too much damage, after drinking both your bottles of laundry soap. The lightning storms hold off until you're safe in the airplane hangar of the little priest down the hill. There is no time or money and hardly any food, but somehow you feed 5,000.

You can participate safely with nature Knowing that its unpredictable ways work in perfect harmony with the laws of the beam. You can let nature become your outer body, and it will move with you as you make your decisions along the slowly but steadily illuminating path. Of course, hopping from lily pad to lily pad the Adventurer sometimes slips, and falls in the pond.

Please, Lord! Come quickly and rescue me! Take pleasure in showing me your favor and restore me!

Psalms 40:13

So Jesus reaches in and hauls you out by the scruff of your neck. One of the metaphysical effects of Savior is the agreement that every investment of kinetic energy yields a net positive return, and whatever decision you made and acted on *will* activate the next good thing. Your core intention is Truth, so you count all of that vibrational output towards your prime directive, the Great Commission to Love More.

How to Convert Manna

If you are going Adventuring, you need to Know how to use the infinite manna that forms all Substance of provision. You want to access exactly what you need even as you travel across different vibrational realities where the rules of exchange change. You need a currency that is valid at all levels.

> ***Whoever drinks of the water that I will give him will never be thirsty again. The water that I will give him will become in him a spring of water welling up to eternal life.***
>
> ***Proverbs 18:4***

Contrary to popular belief, the abundance that keeps you alive and thriving is actually not "attracted" to you. Rather, it forms through you and around you naturally, and the sand dunes of creation take shape. Your whole biofield nurtures a vibration of Knowing provision, which fertilizes the energetic space you grow into, converting adamantine particles into tangible resources.

What is is?

The story goes that the Israelites (the ones who struggle with God) had just been liberated from hundreds of years of enslavement to an oppressive, material system, and were now headed to a new life. The revolution had promised a new freedom and better conditions, which was nowhere in sight. They were far away from the predictable system of provision in the old vibrational reality, and they were hungry. They couldn't use the old rules: *work hard to build a pyramid and then eat the cucumbers you're given*. That system was now irrelevant, but they missed it dearly. They knew no other way of making cucumbers. There was a Sovereign Master among them—Moses. So, the elements of reality rearranged themselves to help them. Every morning manna suddenly, quietly and supernaturally appeared. It was everywhere—a soft, white substance that collected on the surface of everything. They didn't need to build it, mine for it or genetically modify it—it was just there, and they could collect as much as they needed, there was no shortfall.

The word *manna* derives from the Arameic question "*man hu?*" It means **"What is it?"** Perhaps it was the crystallized honeydew of scale insects. Perhaps it was lichen or other mossy plant colonies. Or perhaps it was crumbs of Frankincense fallen from the Boswellia tree. The structure of manna isn't important, it's the essence of it that manifests. What is the supernatural wealth in your life? Look and see. What is it, this fresh, infinitely available stream of sustenance that can always be accessed? Do not look deep into yourself or far out into the world. Simply look at the surface. There is something right there that will provide.

What is it? This vibrational question commands Spirit to reveal the Substance that is quietly forming the currency of your Life. Metaphysically, you lovingly command Spirit to move Substance to show you what the form of provision is here and now. Money, time, peace, opportunities to connect and commune in friendship, opportunities to have fun and discover new things, ways to serve others and be significant in the lives of those you love, conversations and laughter—manna is both the harvest of fruit from past effort and the activator for future emergence. So it is a dynamic, living thing that is both an effect and a cause of divine experience. It reveals itself when you ask the question, so from now on as an Adventurer in need of anything you'll be asking *"What is it?"* to call forth the true shape of your new provision.

It is the bread the Lord has given you to eat.

Exodus 16:15

Look at Diagram 1, The Trinity, and let's refresh the basics of our thought experiment.

Source is the greatest mystery of all, a preceding consciousness, a Supreme Knowing, the Alpha and Omega of what is. We can Know Him as God. His name is Love. His essence is Love. And all that derives from Him, which is all, is Love.

God is Love, and whoever abides in Love abides in God, and God abides in him.

1 John 4:6

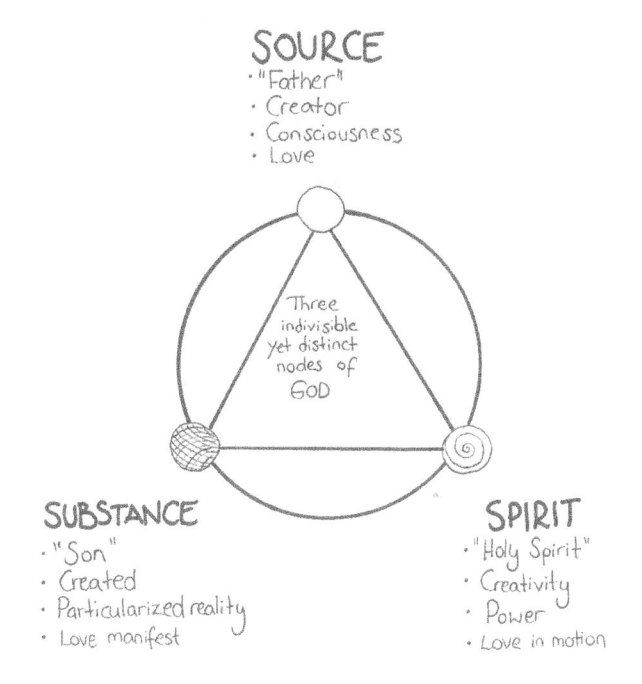

SOURCE
- "Father"
- Creator
- Consciousness
- Love

Three indivisible yet distinct nodes of GOD

SUBSTANCE
- "Son"
- Created
- Particularized reality
- Love manifest

SPIRIT
- "Holy Spirit"
- Creativity
- Power
- Love in motion

Spirit is the movement of Love. God in motion, you could say. The ultimate wave distribution as our unified field of being, like an ocean in constant becoming. **If** Source IS, **then** Spirit MOVES.

Substance then is the form and particularized reality where God is no longer potential but fully actualized as something in the spectrum of frequencies of all things. Your book is a thing and it is Love made manifest. It's God's body. We've chosen the term adamantine particle to represent the Higgs-Boson or God-particle. All mass derives from it, so whether an Adventurer most needs a hundred-dollar bill or a lover to dance with, both of those things are made of adamantine particles.

Source commands Spirit to move Substance, so Love commands Love to move Love. **In our desert visualization we see the golden sands of infinite possibility undulate and shift as the windy breath of God commands new realities across space and time, forming great dunes of manna.** Manna is a stream of adamantine particles that can be formed according to your loving consciousness to become the manifest resource you most need. In Love, you have authority to command the particles of creation to become manna and to take shape according to what is needed. In the parched desert valley, God sends in a raven carrying scraps of food. A crack opens in the stone and water bubbles out. Your friend catches a huge fish in the oasis and brings it out to share with you. Manna is always moving.

> *The Lord will always lead you, satisfy you in a parched land, and strengthen your bones. You will be like a watered garden, and like a spring whose water never runs dry.*
>
> *Isaiah 58:11*

Positive thoughts, imaginative visioning, and all the magic tricks of manifestation are all pieces of the mental and vibrational hygiene that help manna convert, but they are not manna. If you do not believe you have the sovereignty to send the vibrational command for Substance to form into manna, then you will need an intercessor to do it for you, like your employer, your wealth advisor, your busy schedule, your followers, your badass boss hustle attitude, your credit cards, or whatever other false idol has been given sovereignty as your source of provision. The limitation of these systems is that they only have access to cash consciousness. Money is only one way for manna to form. The enslavement to money is usually the reason that, when God calls, an Adventurer fails to go. *I can't rescue those children from trafficking yet, I need to spend ten years to make a million dollars first so I can build the organization to help them.*

Look at **Diagram 2: The Sovereign Model of Human Consciousness** again, and reflect on the scripture below.

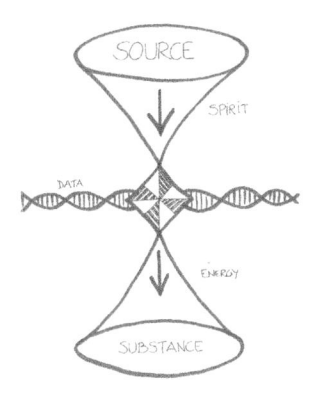

Do not build for yourself treasures on earth, where moth and rust destroy and where thieves break in and steal,

but lay up for yourselves treasures in heaven, where neither moth nor rust destroys and where thieves do not break in and steal.

For where your treasure is, there your heart will be also.

The eye is the lamp of the body. So, if your eye is healthy, your whole body will be full of light.

If your eye is unhealthy, your body will be utterly dark.

Matthew 6:19-23

When you are Sovereign, you have the authority to convert manna into usable resource because your stewardship of energy is True. This qualification began when you reconciled the core values in the diamond eye of your understanding. The healthier the diamond, the purer the vibration, the stronger the electromagnetism, the greater the Light. This is the energy that commands usable resources into manifestation. If you want to experience true, sovereign wealth out here in real Life as you Adventure between realms of consciousness, you need an enriched and thoroughly wealthy diamond core. Since it is Love that commands Love to move Love, you can only build up the storehouse of your capacity through goodness, self-sacrificial service, and appreciation for what-is. What is becoming? See your creation and know that it is good. In your judgment, there is no wealth. In your criticism and complaining, there is no wealth. In your impatience there is no wealth. You ask *"what is it?"* and your impatience is literally a vibrational spell creating: *"It Is Not Here Now."* But in gentle, simple agreement with what God has already done and who you have already become, there is wealth abundantly. From consciousness to energy to form, you will see your usable resources delivered through what is greening in your life.

What is a usable resource? What is it that you *actually* need? Some people have plenty of cash but are missing friendship, time, affection, open doors, solutions, or peace. Others have tremendous luck and health but can't seem to cultivate a dependable vocation that helps them feel like they mattered. But **True wealth is integrative, not compartmentalized, so even if it shows up in only one form, that form is sufficient to create wellsprings in all areas of your experience.** One pound of rare, sanctified chocolate can become payment for transport you could never otherwise afford, bringing you from Colorado to Utah for an educational conference that will burst your dead business back to life. Genius acts of discipleship, Alchemical acts of faith and cheerfully devoted service will always deposit vast volumes of new adamantine particles into the fabric of your Life, collecting within your own biofield and building up unformed potential that, when converted, allows you to move freely in the ever-changing dimensions of the desert.

I was once working on a documentary about the creation of a video game called Mystic Searches, when I had the honor of interviewing an atheist author of 21 bestselling fantasy stories. He lived in his old, knobbly house draped in silver veils of Spanish Moss, in the musical cacophony of cicadas in an ancient Florida swamp. I asked him what the key to his success was. He said, *"Elizabeth, there is only one thing you need if you wish to be successful:* **Pure Luck.**"

Pure Luck—as I have discovered living a charmed Life—is just the craft of being non-resistant to spontaneous possibility. **Heaven is here now, among you and in your midst, so your treasures are *here now*.** If you want to pick up a lucky penny, you just need to spot it glint first. Pure Luck is nothing more than a Bride's surrender to Her Dependable Groom. Your Life is already now pregnant with the wealth you have stored. All manna can be activated in your individual biofield regardless of what is going on out there in the world. It'll convert into money, cucumbers, bandages, insurance papers, lawyers, private education, road side angels, medical experts, pure luck. It'll become whatever it is that you need. *What is it* that you need? Source commands Spirit. Spirit moves Substance. Substance is experienced in your whole and real life occurring inside space and time, either as a $10 bill, a period of three open hours, or a lovely, rustic jar of homemade mango jam.

Here are three helpful principles for converting manna from potential to real:

1. Faith. The greatest secret to converting manna is to Know that **"It Is Here"**, *this is* what *it is,* and not Knowing. **"What is it?"**

Whatever Manna is right now, it is on its way to becoming something else. It is dynamic and alive. In Christ, your awareness that *"I need"* is sufficient Knowing to activate help. The rest of your cognitive formulation is less important. It isn't necessary to cultivate faith in story stuff like *"I will make $10,000 by next Friday"* or *"I will live passionately for the rest of my life."* Faith means Knowing true things, like that you are a Trinity of Love. Knowing that you are always already good enough, becoming something new, able to move, and supported by God. Knowing that you can synthesize anything in your environment and formulate it in a new way to allow a new reality. Knowing that the elements around you are benevolent and waiting for your command. Knowing that time is faithful to you. Knowing that the courage of a Lion is always animating you from within. This is the Knowing that activates the conversion of manna. I have seen a faithful man rescue 1,000 children from human trafficking using only his phone, a computer and a few helpers. He Knew he did not need a million dollars and ten years.

Imagine if the bassline vibrational command emanating from your diamond is: **I**

Know I Already Always AM provision. I Know I AM provided *for*. I Know I AM in the Vine. I Know I AM the Elements, and I Know I AM the Energy that moves them. I Know who I AM and I Know how I will serve today. If that was the health of the eye, imagine how wealthy your biofield would be, and how free your Body would be to move.

Now energetically combine the Knowing and celebration that it's done, and the holy question of someone yearning to know: *what is it?* The tension between *here* and *where* is a powerful energizer.

2. Creative malleability.

Phenomenologically, we say that we create reality as we believe. We collapse waves into particles when we make agreement with our observations., the way God did when **He observed the Light and Knew that It Is Good**. Therefore, if you want to have any authority to convert manna then you need to reconcile what you Know about provision and manifestation. You need your mastery of Genius to properly synthesize the Adventurer's provision: **If** you're rich **and** you Know everyone else is in lack consciousness, **then** you're creating an isolated experience for yourself and nobody to share it with. **If** you're poor **and** you know the stars aren't aligned yet for your great destiny to be fulfilled, **then** you're creating a wealthy future that will never arrive. But with your Genius mind you reconcile those old wealth categories as you discern and falsify them. After all, you Know manna forms around you when you move along the beam. You spend less energy upholding thought-forms that have nothing to do with who you are, and you spend more energy loving the thought-forms that are blossoming anyway. You simply can't keep believing wealth must equal gold coins, or crypto-currency, or spare minutes, or duck eggs. If you and the sand dunes around you are all responding to God, then all wealth must change shape.

No matter how much we want to be the conscious co-creators of everything we think we want, if we're playing on his team as an integrated group of world servers, then we can't outline what our richness and abundance should look like next. We are currently in the midst of a global biodiversity crisis, with high extinction rates and thousands of plant and animal species under threat. We are also in the most delicate economic times in our history, with major world currencies including crypto balancing in a purgatorial poise between a quantum leap and a total collapse. Manna is not dependent on any natural or economic circumstance so the less rigid you are in how you need your fulfillment to look and the less attached you are to external measurements, the more free you are to move where the manna is truly forming. Remember that if rules change as you ascend across game boards of vibrational reality, then the rules of exchange also change. Being so liberated from your own outlining that new sand dunes can take shape for you—this is a mark of a true Adventurer, and Pure Luck delivers you through the desert.

3. Saying yes to the invitation

This is for the outrageously courageous Adventurer who is ready to believe that God is working for you 100% of the time. If you believe Christ, the Lord *and* Savior, is overshadowing your mental activity and Knows what opportunities to open for you and which doors to keep hidden from temptation, and if you believe that the Universe is conspiring to work for you and that there is goodness everywhere in the Body of God, then you'll have the courage to say yes to the next invitation that opens—from any direction. *Hitchhike to Utah. Go to that worship service. Give the Lady your duck eggs.* You activate an unfolding that provides exactly what you need.

You won't say yes to the invitation if you believe you need to be in creative control of your Life. You'll always be measuring and rejecting invitations based on to how close they are to your ideal vision. You'll need to rely on worldly systems for getting certain physical conditions in order before you can realize the manifestation of what you think you need. You'll be so busy making money that you won't rescue the children you're saving up to save.

But if you Know that God *is all things* and nature is already moving to your magnetism, then you will say YES to the invitation that opens—even if it comes from a man in a top hat who doesn't look like the perfect client with the ideal pay check that can pay for an upgraded House. Whatever this is, you already Know it's something good on its way to becoming something better. In this realm of consciousness, saying yes to *what-is* is distinctly different from settling for something *less-than*. Saying yes to *what-is* does not exclude you from *what-is-better*. Rather, it is stepping into a momentum and activating a process. Yes to this opens yes to that.

The Difference Between Hevel and Manna

"*Money*" is usually the reason a modern Adventurer fails to go when called, or goes in the wrong direction. When you do anything for money and not for God, you are serving a structure. It is a mortal illusion, it will lead you into the fragmented desert of smoke and mirrors, which must all eventually shatter, leaving you unfulfilled. So this is the first distinction to be aware of. *Am I doing this for money or for Love?*

There's a famous verse in the book of Ecclesiastes, **"Hevel, hevel, everything is hevel."** Most English bibles translate the word "hevel" as "meaningless", so it sounds like

"Meaningless! Meaningless!" says the Teacher. "Utterly meaningless! Everything is meaningless."

Ecclesiastes 1:2

This combination of words is a good device to help us detach from the idea that anything particularized, like an economic system, fancy philosophy or lucrative career, has any innate meaning other than what we place in it. Yet, this doesn't quite capture the heart of the teaching. *Hevel* actually translates more correctly to *Vapor*, or *Smoke*. **"Everything is Vapor."** Everything manifest is fleeting and temporary. All of Life, like smoke, appears solid until you try to grab onto it and you discover nothing is there. You can be enjoying amassing great volumes of expertise one minute, and then in the next moment the industry falls apart and your knowledge is nothing but vapor. Chasing the manifest expression of wealth is like chasing the wind. Because, as you have discovered, all things manifest are merely Spirit expressed as Substance, as ephemeral as the Sahara sand dunes undulating in the wind of God's breath.

If you're a trained artist and God channels Spirit through your hands and into your paintings or your flute, and then you decide to start chasing the money and competing for market share in a mainstream marketplace—then you are selling your Life to a temporal structure so entropy must eventually disintegrate any wealth you are able to build. But if you remain in devotion and in the marriage of Spirit and Substance, then your art will convert to the wealth you most need.

I once co-authored a mystery story called "The Humbug Murders" with a popular author of mainstream books for young adults. A bizarre plot twist occurred when Scott suddenly died before our book came out—he didn't even get to see the front cover. Before he died—I'll never forget it—Scott admitted a regret. He and his good friend and contemporary Salvatore had started writing fantasy books at the same time. For decades Salvatore stayed true to his favorite niche, slowly writing and cultivating his fantasy stories. Scott, on the other hand, raced to compete for market share in a mainstream marketplace that kept changing its mind. He wrote "Buffy The Vampire Slayer" books when those were popular, and "Jurassic Park" or "Star Trek" books and so on when the trends shifted. Over time, Salvatore built a universe of loyal readers who followed him to the next book and the next. Scott, on the other hand, was always chasing new readers. He had become enslaved to the structure, his wealth was meaningless and fleeting, and he had lost his Life's passion in the process. *"Don't do that, Elizabeth,"* he said. *"Write from the heart, never for money."*

Scott was liberated before he died. He wrote, from the heart, a lovely story called "Mr. Lamb and Mr. Lyon." The manuscript was never published and it never sold a single copy, but it gave Scott the richest wealth in the universe as it delivered him from the bitter illusion of his failure, and sent him Home happy and fulfilled.

So what can you do then, if everything is an ephemeral vapor, and all the effort you put into converting manna and having wealth is utterly meaningless as you Adventure from dimension to dimension? **You have to learn to weave the wind and braid the smoke.** You alchemize Substance and turn hevel into manna.

Now we have a distinction. *Manna* is wealth that flourishes everything it touches, rippling out to the edges of the universe and returning hundredfold—for it is a part of God's essence, which is always **Becoming**. *Hevel* is wealth that comes and goes without leaving any legacy impact—this too is meaningless and fleeting. This is the wealth that you waste in your unconscious and automatic operations of daily factory living in the structures of the world. We all know the difference between these feelings: *"Ugh, I can't believe I spent $100, where did it all go?"* and *"Wow, that was the best $100 I've spent!"* Same amount, different essence: the first is hevel, the second is manna, for manna flourishes and nourishes everything it touches.

Now let's say you are Sovereign. You know you're abundantly worthy, you're getting the hang of Remembering that you're never actually in lack, and you frequently see provision manifest in some way or another. Now let's graduate from the basics, and move into stewardship. You can be a master manifestor of manna, but unless you steward manna well it becomes fleeting. In and out like hevel.

When the Israelites gathered more manna than they needed and tried to store it for later, it spoiled and became riddled with worms like that decaying rat. Stewardship is not the same as storing. When it comes to stewardship, the keywords are: *"Fit For Purpose"*. Pretend you're a sea captain. The admiral of a mighty fleet puts you in charge of the flagship. And he commands, "*steward this ship well, captain.*" "*Aye sir, I will,*" you say, with a smart salute. And you donate the ship to the British Museum for school children to view and enjoy for all generations to come. Noble as your intentions are, this is terrible stewardship, the admiral is not pleased and the whole fleet is compromised. "*But, sir! I am stewarding this ship,*" you cry "*for the greater good!*" But alas. That's not what the ship was for. The way you put it to use was not fit for purpose.

When you are in the possession of wealth—whether it is grace, patience, the gift of healing, money, time, physical fitness, connections and community—*appropriate* use of that wealth is fundamental to your stewardship. Use it right and your wealth grows. Use it for meaningless pursuits and it fizzles away. Wrapped up in "appropriate use" are **Respect, Integrity** and **Workability:**

- **Respect for the Source, Spirit and Substance** of manna and respect for the ordained authority you have been given to wield it. **Respect for the dynamic nature of creation** and the movement needed to sustain spiritual balance in all things including your wealth. **Respect for the Body of Christ** which forms not only manna but also the Ones you are here to serve.

- **Integrity means all working parts** are in order and in their right place. Integrity doesn't mean perfection in all your standards, for that too is hevel, but it means you have completed the things that needed completion and you are tending to the things that need tending to, in an honest and open way.

- **And Workability** in 3D shows respect for and integrity in relation to the infrastructure that you're participating in. Workability always depends on systems so it always changes when you transcend a reality. *"I want to be a business coach and work only with homeless, drug addicted mothers and I will charge my worth and make $20,000 per session."* Sure, your idea may be a conceivable potential in the universe of all things, but if it isn't a workable outline in the actual reality you're hoping to have an impact on, it is hevel.

So if you are not stewarding your wealth in a way that respects its true purpose, **then** it is not integral to who you are and what God is doing through you, **and** your imagined wealth ideals are not workable in the structure of your holy life, **so** those attractor fields that you set up to generate provision will not have the magnetism to sustain themselves. Your wealth will always be as empty and ephemeral as vapor.

Know your CORE VALUES. Return often to what matters most to you. This is how you will know what "fit for purpose" looks like in your universe. Let's say your family life matters more to you than social status. If you then spend your time and money advancing your social status instead of deepening your family bond, you are not stewarding your wealth well—you are investing it in an alternative reality and you will not feel fulfilled because you have tried to convert your wealth into something you can't grab. If you do not feel fulfilled then your vibrational command sounds something like **"It is Not Here Now"** and the Substance of your wealth will eventually disintegrate.

Whoever you are, fundamental to your core values is your divinely ordained prime directive. The current mission, assignment, purpose, or vocation for this season. The thing you are called to do on this gameboard. Are you an activist? A teacher? A healer? A humanitarian? A disruptive catalyst? A peace-bringer? A builder, architect, mechanic? A cultivator and harvester? If your job is to heal the wounded then it's a total waste of your energy to spend it on tearing down the patriarchal hierarchy, even if you feel it's a noble cause. Or if your job is to tear down the patriarchal hierarchy then it's a waste of your energy to spend your life trying to heal all the wounded. **You don't need to feel bad about not spending energy in areas where you are not**

called to go.

Manna also becomes hevel when it's used in meaningless, mindless ways. In 2020, Americans spent $44.9 billion on drunk purchases. Unconscious spending of your time, money, friendship, strength, youth—an utter waste. And if you are stuck in a robotic lifestyle of spending whatever it is you are spending to uphold whatever the lifestyle is you think you need to construct for yourself, this quickly becomes mindless—not mindful. If you're going to spend money on paying your bills, do it in the Spirit of absolutely loving the miracle of being able to turn on the electricity and say "let there be light" at the flick of a switch! Pay your bills in delight for the water that flows from your faucet and in gratitude for the creditor who kept your ship afloat for a while back then. Mindful spending of your wealth—whether in the currency of time, strength, cash, or beauty—is devotion.

Know what matters most to you, and Know how your each of your energy exchanges enhance those things. You will be stewarding the true essence of manna, and your wealth will be fit for purpose.

Duck Eggonomics

For an Adventurer in Christ, someone who is a spiritual pioneer prepared to follow God's call into unknown frontiers of Life and across dimensions of experience and exchange, it's very handy to understand Duck Eggonomics. That's just my clever word for having transcended cash consciousness and gained the mastery of converting manna into any form.

We lived in a tent and very little to eat. By Pure Luck we ended up at a small Episcopal church on the specific day where the Woman needed healing. I gave her reiki, and her body shifted—the next time I saw her she testified that she had recovered supernaturally fast from the surgery and she was convinced it was because of the healing. She brought me a tray of 12 duck eggs as thanks which I gave to the Witch who owned the land we camped on to pay our rent for the week. The next Sunday we found ourselves at a completely different church, a Universalist center on the other side of the mountain. There we met a little family who invited us to eat with them that night from the stone pizza oven they'd built outside their yurt. We went and ate till our bellies were round. Suddenly one of the children cried *"it's Grandma!"* Who was it waddling up the forest trail toward the Universalist family's yurt? The Duck Egg Woman from the Episcopal church 25 miles away, of course! A new friend to dine with. Manna is always moving, connecting and flourishing.

Money is a usable resource that works really well in a shared infrastructure because of its universal agreement reality and consensus value. $100 is $100. But on a fluid life path that transcends dimensions of experience, you need a different currency, because your energy is often moving faster than traditional currency can keep up with. A tray of 12 duck eggs is worth whatever it's worth to the one you are in exchange with, always able to open unusual and unexpected opportunities. **If you transcend cash consciousness and allow other forms of substance be manna, and** you've developed the discernment to hear the invitations arising, **and** you are bold enough to say yes to those invitations when you're standing at the edge of a cliff, **then** you can participate in the magic of Duck Eggonomics, unlocking a completely new timeline of possibilities for you. If you can allow the value of the duck eggs to match the workability of the system of consciousness you're participating in at the time, now the eggs can become anything.

In all universes, you can always listen for what is needed by the one God has brought before you, and *Know* how you can help. There is always a balanced exchange available. This system has worked for me everywhere. It's worked for the very low skill things like when my daughters and I weeded an acre of thistles for the little priest down the hill, and in exchange got to use the kitchen in her airplane hangar to make chocolates to use as rent that week. It's worked with more skilled things like trading reiki for violin lessons for our oldest daughter. It's worked with high value skills like trading clinical ontology and interpretative phenomenological analyses for neurology and cranial sacral therapy for my mother when she was first diagnosed with Alzheimer's—a trade that restored her presence in Life. But the system needn't even be linear like trading this for that. You might give healing to an Episcopalian, get duck eggs in return, give those to a Witch and later receive stone-oven baked pizza from a Universalist. The Duck Eggonomy is a vast and unseen network of Love in motion.

Become Opulent

So you Know manna and you Know hevel, which means **you are ready to go deeper into the real opulence and intimacy that true wealth brings.** You begin a delightful period of experiencing the visceral sensuality of God's Love for you. Abundance isn't just a mechanism of the universe that helps create resources for things to happen, experiences to be had and discoveries to be made. It's so much more than that! It's an endless love offering from your Heavenly Father, the One who has known you since before you were born, the one who lovingly formed you in His heart, and who formed your heart on Him. You are known and loved, and manna is a gift of Love. Let yourself be loved by the One who is opening to you so deeply.

Beautify.

When I was a little girl, my mother showed me how to hang up the prisms in the windows so the room would burst with rainbows. When you spin the prism the rainbows whizz round! What magic! The energy elevates immediately. You don't need a prism of course, but I now have dozens in my Home. In the evening, rainbows fall across the food I'm cooking for my family. In the morning they are scattered across my back porch, where I pray.

What is your environment like? Are you using the elements to enrich your experience? Water, air, light, fire, earth, ether, thought? Let each element be full to the brim as you Alchemize your surroundings and turn hevel into manna. When I was 20 I had the incredibly cool opportunity to visit two developing countries, El Salvador and Kenya. I spent three weeks in El Salvador and three months in Kenya. At the time both countries were recovering from extreme corruption in their political and economic systems. Both cultures were defined by vast populations living in dire poverty, in slums and on piles of rubbish in the streets. In one country I saw people agreeing with their squalor, trudging through a vibration of despair, unconscious and despondent as they stood around smoking drugs near market stalls of fireworks. In the other country I saw people making no agreement with squalor. They lived in shacks, but they decorated those shacks with palm leaves and fairy lights. They built fires and danced in praise of the rising Sun. That beauty was my mother's magic too, in a completely different Way.

I can be wealthy anywhere if I can make something more beautiful. I remembered this lesson later in life, when we had lost every worldly thing to the wilderness. The land was a harsh mistress. There was dirt in every bite of food I ate. There were sharp rocks under my aching body at night. There was constant physical threat poisonous cactus, vicious insects, predators. I was dematerialized, nothing left but a tent—and yet I remembered how important it was to cultivate the sensation of richness. My living faith and real communion with God meant I could detach my creative focus from the threats of the natural world, and participate only in the opulence. We made Beauty. We invested in Home Magic before anything else, savoring textures and colors, brightening and enhancing everything around us all the time. We had one car battery for electricity, and we used it for fairy lights. *Whoomph.* Out of nowhere came duck eggs, apricots, peaches, pears, lavender, chocolate, books, blankets, a car, tools, a priest who had a hangar with a kitchen and warm shower, a reservoir with a bed of clay which we could harvest and use to make stuff, sagebrush that kept the mosquitoes away and made the most glorious smoke on the fire under the Milkyway galaxy at night. Music with friends around the fire.

In the vibrational reality where manna is, there is also divine order. The dependable beam is there. The same graceful system of synchronicity that provides what you need is also the system that commands the elemental body of nature to keep you safe from all natural threats. We weren't in the tent the night of that dreadful storm. When the bears raided our camp, they were distracted by drinking laundry soap and they came nowhere near the tent. We never once stepped on a cactus, even when climbing up the mountain in the dark and stormy night so the toddler could go to the toilet in a bucket behind the juniper tree. Opulence and beauty live hand in hand with divine order and synchronicity.

> *Every good gift and every perfect gift is from above, and comes down from the Father of Light, who does not change like shifting shadow.*
>
> *James 1:17*

Invoking the gorgeous richness of Life aligns your awareness with the creative flow that moves through you, bringing you into the state of abundance required for safe surrender. You can use your Genius to understand the connections that pull your provision from deep within your inner world of Knowing, and you can also formulate the richness that is already present in your consciousness, so that the outpouring manifests as:

I AM Love Fulfilled and Becoming.

This affirmation is a meta-statement that avoids any limitations you might create by outlining. If your Love is both fulfilled AND becoming, you are overflowing. **This IS The Love of God.** The same Substance that you are made of is all around you and within you at all times, forming and unforming, so there really is *absolutely no separation* between you and the wealth you're cultivating. That's straight forward logic which makes physical and metaphysical sense. You can practice asking *"what is it?"* and responding to yourself with **This Is The Love of God.** Notice the subtle shift in frequency as you let the emphasis shift:

THIS *is the Love of God.*

This **IS** *the Love of God*

This is **THE** *Love of God*

This is the **LOVE** *of God.*

This is the Love **OF** *God.*

This is the Love of **GOD**.

Though the arrangements of words remain the same, the essence evolves as the emphasis changes. Meaning is how your unique reality manifests: we perceive by asking ourselves "what is the meaning of this?" and that's how our *really happening* experience plays out as stories in a phenomenological universe. And we can see that the six different frequencies were all embedded within the ONE sentence. All the frequencies within Heaven and Earth are embedded within this structure:

I and My Father are One

John 10:30

The more you practice this, the faster and more precisely you notice the different energy fields in your awareness in any given circumstance. You can easily lean into the opulence of delicious, true wealth. What is it? This is the love of God and **it is good.**

Look into your environment. Where is the opulence? What wealth is there right in front of you? What incredible stores of knowledge and wisdom are in the books in your bookshelf that you haven't read? What flavor combinations are in the spice rack that you've never connected? What wealth is in your vocabulary that you aren't activating on a daily basis? What interesting plants are already growing near your place of work? Use the elements to enrich you. Use elements to *make beauty.* One of my friends is a humanitarian working the slums of Kampala with women and children who have nothing—and the same principle applies to them. Poverty is not an excuse not to Know beauty. Lack is irrelevant. *Tidy up. Sweep the floor. Paint flowers on the barn door.* Teach your people to prioritize order and beauty in their environment. Teach them to use words of Love. Enriching the vibrational environment helps bring your consciousness into the Kingdom where all divine things manifest—and you will be more able to perceive the sparkle of manna which becomes the provision and solution for all things. This is the great commission after all—go out with Spirit and bring Substance back to Source. You calibrate *stuff* into a higher expression of itself. *Bless this food.*

What is it? **It is good.**

Think of the vibrational effect of doing this around you all the time. Imagine the compound effect of turning the eternity within every minute into one of opulent abundance. How many eternities of wealth are there?

A few days before we were due to move out onto the raw land and begin our lives as tent dwellers, we had an amazing snow storm. It deposited five feet of snow, and we were stuck for a couple of days until a mountain hero who looked exactly like Prince Harry came and rescued us with his snow blower. My husband and I were gazing at the massive snowbanks when the tiniest of snowflakes landed on his beard. It was absolutely miniscule. As a single unit of sparkle it was hardly perceptible. But the compound effect of one flake and another and another had manifested as a rich five feet thick duvet of snow, not just on our land but over thousands of acres. Shoveling the snow was exhausting because it was so heavy! I can't even imagine how many tonnes of matter is suspended in the air at all times, waiting to drop.

Perhaps at first the humble moment of enjoying the shape of your favorite mug might not seem like brilliant magic for Adventuring, but the compound effect of the increasing number of moments you Love will manifest as a richness of life that is beyond measure. Your assets go deeper rather than broader, so there is no cap to the wealth you can be intimate with, no matter the circumstance. The next thing you know, that thin, white manna substance is five feet deep as far as your eyes can see.

This true opulence is one of the most intimate relationships with God. When you bring True Beauty into your surroundings as you travel across different landscapes, it is God you are making Love with. Diamonds and silk, ladybirds and cotton, ashes and rust, primordial soup—God's body is always beautiful, and if you can see it, you are in it. Now you can *make miracles*, calling the world to share this beauty with you.

With the Genius to understand, synthesize and formulate any reality you need, plus the Alchemy to recalibrate any element into manna, plus the Adventurer's faith to forward flip along an invisible beam—you qualify for the highest planetary service. You have discovered that Love always wins, **and** you can always serve Love, **ergo** you are always safely provided for as you adventure forward on your Sovereign Way. All sense of sectarianism or partisanship has dissolved, as you Recognize systems and structures for what they are, and forgive them all. God shows up everywhere, and Love permeates every reality, and there is no other conclusion to draw than that we are, each and all, children of the One Father.

Now the collective structure is neither the source of your life, nor a matrix you must escape, but the great adventure of your divine **Becoming.** It is the place where you meet the Beloved, and it is a friend you dearly want to nourish. Your experience is always expansive, and safe. There is nowhere you can be out of place, for you have the ultimate belonging, and a devoted family to help carry the yoke wherever you find yourself.

An Adventurer must be in Love while washing the feet of your brother in the slums of despair, and in Love while serving the queens of the highest galactic courts. You need to be able to go from Mama Bear warrior in one acute hurricane moment to the bliss of noticing a drifting scent of fresh seaweed in the next moment. And back again. You have total sovereign freedom to serve Love at any time. The old world will look at you and wonder what kind of creature you could possibly be as you move through cultures, vocations, methods, dimensions and callings with an ease that defies reason. They will be amazed, because nothing but supernatural freedom can cause a queen to happily abdicate her throne, or a warlord to humbly cease fire—yet you liberate all manner of energy fields as you come into contact with them.

The new world will keep beckoning—you will not be led astray.

> *His delight is in the Law of the Lord,*
> *and on this Law he meditates day and night.*
> *He is like a tree*
> *planted by streams of water*
> *that yields its fruit in its season,*
> *and its leaf does not wither.*
> *In all that he does, he prospers.*
> *Psalm 1:2-3*

Present *for* Christ, present *to* Christ, present *in* Christ, and present *as* Christ, whatever the weather, a true Adventurer can transcend realities with ease and is always becoming a new creation. **What a privilege to know *who you are* in this oasis garden, and to Know the sovereignty you have to grow more of the fruits of the Spirit.** What a privilege it is to be thoroughly immersed in, and made of, a fabric of Love that can become anything at any time, infinitely reproducing itself as Life and

Life abundantly. You are intertwined with every blossoming rose, and every bee, and every tree bearing fruit with seed in it. That's how opulent you are. Knowing this, it's time to leave the oasis. There is work to do out there. You have your telescope, you have your mastery, and now you're on mission.

The Eighth Mastery: Devotion

I Am the Way, the Truth, and the Life.

A sovereign gardener is free to choose how to steward everything within his ever-expanding borders. A sovereign gardener knows she will never run out, for she is made of it all, every blossoming rose, every bee, and every tree bearing fruit with seed in it. You are a sovereign gardener nourishing new oases of earthly delights. Everything you put your hands to, is your devotion, and everything yields the fruit of Love. This is because devotion is the natural engagement with Life when you are full to the brim with Love and that love has somewhere to go and be received. Devotion is the sacred space that opens when you have the true courage to Love unapologetically *and* experience that same Love in return. You have given yourself to Life in this very moment. You focus your energy on your goodness, on cultivating all the life elements that *hold* your goodness. You commit to living full of Stories of how Love wins the day, and sharing those stories.

She is clothed in strength and dignity, and she laughs without fear of the future.

Proverbs 31:25

It is good to enjoy the opulence of Heaven. It is also good to remember that the fruit of Love extends beyond personal sensory pleasure and spiritual fulfillment. Love *is* self-sacrificial, Love would give the whole bounty of the garden to the hungry orphan. Love gives up some Netflix time to pray for Peace. Love shares the last tray of duck eggs, because in Love, all things prosper.

It's not that you're not required to *do* anything, for your very being is now a prayer for humanity. You walk in the Light of your soul as the radiance of the Son pours through your stained glass window and illumines the Way. But you are nonetheless *compelled* to do, putting your hands to work and weaving love into all you touch. Your life as a human being on this uniquely rare planet at this historic time, **is not**

just to maintain a high vibration. Jesus Christ is already taking care of that aspect of human ascension. You don't actually need to strive for vibrational purity to hold space for the Kingdom, or even use brilliant formulations to proselytize its existence, you simply need to be in your place within it. Indeed, your Life as a human is *mostly* to heal, wonder, thrive, create and experience *together*.

Truly sovereign devotion is an outpouring of Love directed into the core of Life. You know your macro-spiritual direction and you are already synthesizing a unique legacy through all those miniscule actions you take on a daily basis. The world is better now because you do you. You Know you have been developed and prepared for this time we are in and you have a specific set of experience, skills, and gifts. You are emanating a specific *tone* of spiritual fulfillment, a tone that belongs in its place in the great harmony. You have already Chosen to consciously participate—it is Known to God that you've decided to be good, and do good, and make a difference in this time.

We are at an event horizon in an age of bizarre change. Rapid plot twists and vast shifts in global systems and paradigms sweep through our family. Everything is changing as we wake up from an ancient slumber, groan and stretch, blow away the dust and rise up into an age of Love. It is more important than ever to be able to Recognize the difference between Truth and Falsehood. It is more important than ever to have the mental and vibrational mastery to hold your sovereign poise in the Expansion that is coming. It is more important than ever to stand firm in your courage and freedom to be and do what God has designed for you, paving the Way and creating the space for Love to grow around you.

Let's look at our thought experiment so far. We have journeyed along the Sovereign Way, crossing the landscapes of seven ascending masteries as our vibrational reality shifts and expands:

First: **I Remember the Truth**. I AM Christ, made of the only Creation, good light becoming, with authority in the natural world and sovereignty within an expanding Kingdom of possibility, expressing uniquely through my core values, already always loved.

Second: **I Recognize Truth versus Story**, Occurring versus Happening, Self versus Ego, Essence versus Structure, Home versus House, Good versus Evil. I discern the difference between these things, so I fear none of them, for I AM Sovereign.

Third: **I Release** falsehood, structured paradigms, error and the vain attempt to control the sand dunes of adamantine particles: I AM the Kingdom of Mercy. I forgive and am forgiven.

Fourth: **I AM Expansion.** I am increasing my capacity to meet the ascending experiences of life, living in an infinite process reality that is also forever becoming. I AM in the Vine.

Fifth: **I AM Genius**, with exquisite Sovereign reason based on my core values. I am able to Understand, Synthesize and Formulate new realities.

Sixth: **I AM Alchemist**, infusing essence into structure, reunifying Spirit and Substance and turning lead into gold as I offer all my magic to the great commission to make more Love.

Seventh: **I AM Adventurer**, 100% spiritually liberated to let the Sovereign hand of God guide my Way, boldly and gracefully transcending realities as I weave my way through a unique story about who really God is.

So what's this epic level of freedom really for?

The Eighth Mastery in The Sovereign Way is **Devotion**.

Your sovereign devotion weaves the will of God into reality, birthing the mind and heart of the divine here on Earth. You are a miracle-maker. But the Sovereign Way is not a spiritual path to ecstatic bliss and the mastery of being able manifest the garden you think you want. His Way is not about dollars and followers. We are playing the greatest game in the Universe:

The Return of Christ.

The greatest gift of life surely is the miracle that as you choose to love, you experience Love. When you love anything or anyone in any given moment, you are the one who first receives the glorious treasure of the Love you're extending. Enjoy the miracle of being able to perceive and experience what is flowing from you. It is an immediate, intimate experience of actual God-realization, and the goodness flows from the deepest depths of your ocean out into the world. Nobody can prevent you from experiencing this, and when others feel separated from Love, you the Sovereign Master *Know* that the wellspring will not run dry and you are always free to pour out the Spirit over them.

You are no longer afraid of your own wholeness, or your own brokenness. This makes it safe to be in relationship with whatever is around you, and put your love into it. You no longer fear the unchartered territories where new realization can form. You can feel the primal fear, but you are not afraid of the anxiousness you experience at the threshold of becoming, for you Know that even the Frog is God. Nothing can sway you or lead you astray from flowing with the divine will. Death has dissolved, for the Sovereign One who is perceiving your experience Knows that every moment that has passed through your fingers and seems to be gone, treasures of memories and swiftly passing bubbles of sorrow and joy, is in fact always here. Each one is now suspended in a rich dimension of Stories, all in your sacred window. You cannot be undone, you will always *be*. Rest assured, you are safe within your existence. All is well, forever, with your soul.

In complete forgiveness and self-acceptance, you can let your Devotion be your Atonement for being 100% Human, wonderfully made.

So, who are you? You are the Presence of the One to whom all power under Heaven and Earth has been given. You are the same essence as all things, for all things came from God, and you are that essence as it flows into and through the unique shape of God that you are. You are in the very heart of Christ. You are the one that can let your river overflow and extend to all others with no fear of ever running out—because there is no longer anything in the way of the eternal flow of grace. You are the One who can enjoy each moment, regardless of the conditions, because you know that the conditions are simply the result of a billion, trillion sand particles rising into a dune at this moment in time and space. This is how simple it is. It has always been that way and it will never change. You are the lover. The world is the Body of your Beloved.

Your life now is about joy and joyfulness in service. Now that you are liberated, your only job is to cultivate the wellspring of Love into the world. You use your sovereign freedom to live in loyal devotion to your true lover: Life Herself. If your Life wants to take you on a mission in Nepal—off you go, knowing exactly where the treasure is every step of the way. If God tells you to open your door to a stranger, you do, and you break bread with a dear friend. If you want to sing a happy tune in the supermarket while you're choosing onions, you sing.

> *If only I could show everyone*
>
> *This passionate desire I have for you*
>
> *If only I could express it fully*
>
> *No matter who was watching me*
>
> *Without shame or embarrassment*
>
> *I long to bring you to my innermost chamber*
>
> *This holy sanctuary you have formed within me.*
>
> *O that I might carry you within me*
>
> *I would give you the spiced wine of my love*
>
> *This full cup of bliss that we share*
>
> *We could drink our fill until…*
>
> *His left hand cradles my head*
>
> *While his right holds me close*
>
> *We are at rest in this love.*
>
> *Promise me, brides-to-be, by the gentle gazelles and delicate deer, that you'll not disturb my love until she is ready to arise.*
>
> Song of Songs 8:1-7

Devotion binds you to the world in sensual mutuality. It is only through your devotion that you are embodied in true spiritual life, for Loving Relationship is the very nature of God. Devotion delivers you outside the boundaries of your individual self and unites you into the body of Christ, the state of divine paradigm that knows both

I AM and We Are. It allows you to finally receive the world.

Devotion has little to do with the thing that is occupying your doing, and everything to do with the dedication that pours into every motion of your fingertips and every word you breathe. Watering the flowers. Humming a tune. Filing the papers. Rebuilding the ruins. Preparing the board room. Rescuing the slum children from traffickers. You remind the world that Love has a place in every part of life, not just some compartmentalized spiritual practice. Formulating your devotion in a way that is workable in the dimensions of space and time brings your true magic into reality. This sheds great light and clarity over your purpose and devotion, and brings your magic into better cohesion: the scattered photons of a flashlight are unified to become a laser. You are now a miracle-maker.

You are the glory of God. You are the pinnacle of the great divine design, a spectacularly impossible harmony of trillions of cells, knowing yourself as Truth even in the Story. You are herald of beauty—a living, breathing example of Love, and there is nothing lovelier to behold than that.

How beautiful on the mountains are the feet of the one bringing such good news.

Isaiah 52:7

Maybe your beauty is elegant like a swan. Maybe it's charming, like a field of poppy flowers swaying in the wind. Perhaps innocently clumsy and whimsical like a big shiny beetle that's toppled onto its back. Maybe it's stoic and strong, like an alabaster column. Or deliciously mesmerizing, like a lava lamp. Or natural and effortless like clouds floating in the sky. Or stunningly surprising, like a geode cracked open, scintillating. Or serene and peaceful, like a plain colored moor or a misty swamp at dawn. Look at the peacock. He isn't ashamed of the glory God bestowed on him, it is his natural way of reflecting Light so it can be perceived by a viewer. He isn't controlling the perceptions, only expressing naturally. Beauty isn't passive, you see—it is designed to entangle the observer, to bring them into its energy. It's very sensual, which is why Love is beautiful.

Your halo is the radiance of your electromagnetic field, the glory of exquisite intrinsic natural and magnetic beauty that heralds the Presence of something timeless and utterly lovely, silently promising the fullness of unfolding Life.

But when you use your Devotion to cultivate true beauty, your energy field will explode. You will be walking one way on the street, and someone else who is deeply depressed, lonely and forgotten will be walking another way, and just for a brief moment he will walk through your energy field, and the magnetism of your energy will change the direction of his awareness, recalibrating the compass needle back to true north, and you will save a soul. Since infinite creative essence is always creating perfection through you, the amount you experience is the amount you allow. Your beauty is already perfect in Him, and all you need to do is to allow it. How big can you let your Love be? Dare you to take His halo as your own?

What bliss you experience when your heart is pure! For then your eyes will open to see more and more of God.

Psalms 40:16

There will be some voice that says *too far, too beautiful, too showy, too loud, too visible, who do you think you are, they'll get you for that, you haven't deserved it*, and all that stuff. And it'll invite you to shrink.

You will allow His radiant beauty to shine anyway. Let it flood through you even though you haven't healed all the wounds and comprehended every law, or mastered every practice or saved every soul. Shine anyway, allow it to be the Sovereign Way you know it is: That you are light, good, and becoming.

In your beauty is a story that tells the world you are not a stranger to the dark. You have broken parts still mending and scars from all manner of Life's adventures. A story that shows how once you may have for a brief moment believed you couldn't be loved you as you are, and the story also shows that this moment vanished in time and was replaced by a deep, and humble remembering that you are glorious. Your beauty tells a story that it is safe to be seen, free from apology, surrendered into your perfect place where your unique radiance is received, appreciated and celebrated for what it really is—the exquisite breath of something divine.

As an emerging Sovereign Master, this is it. From this day on you are utterly beautiful to behold. You are beautiful to experience, and you have full permission to be Known by the world, exactly as you are.

One last review of the basic principles of manifestation:

The Universe is a Trinity of three elements: Love, Power and Manifestation. Love authorizes Power, and Power moves Manifestation. Your ascension represents your ongoing process of integrating this Knowing. The more integrated, the greater your electromagnetic authority: *the more Love, the greater command.* The Body of God is a vast field of rising and falling shapes, all temporary. Cancer, bombs, galaxies, mountains, duck eggs—all these forms are already becoming something else. The sand dunes shift and shape with your loving response to these particles, and the easiest prayer to reveal the highest particular formation of anything is to ask: *What is it?*

In Christ, *your will is God's Will,* and you know it is safe to let it be so. You understand your superpowers, skills and opportunities and know how they work together synergistically to create a Life so integrated that **your work is your devotion and your devotion is your work.** Your creative energy will be so honed to your core values, and so focused through your true service, that you'll be a super-talented unicorn. You know those people who just light up a room, manifest Pure Luck everywhere they go, and however they put their hands to work, it turns out amazing? Pharrell Williams, who has won 13 Grammy awards, says **"Unicorns are those with the greatest ability to invoke the Presence of God. They radiate Love and everything around them changes."**

The Plan for humanity requires the passion of trained and dedicated unicorns working in collaboration. These ones are anointed for this purpose and live a consecrated life of devotion. *"The anointed one"* in Greek is the word *Christos.* **Christ**. The Christ in you is the anointed miracle-maker, the one who seems granted a supernatural grace, sovereignty and innate power. We assume we really are highly favored, free and sovereign, with the authority to heal and explore our creative genius, experience magic, and laugh without fear of the future. We practice attuning our minds and energy fields so we truly can be present to what-is, and live His Will.

This is very potent energy. We must use it wisely, and that is why as Sovereign Masters, we practice Devotion. Our mastery isn't about attaining any specific level of spiritual perfection, or the Excelsior dash for enlightenment, or the ecstasy of divine union, but accepting the responsibility to Love come what may, so that the world may Know the presence of Christ. Our mastery is the muscle that holds that poise in a turbulent world going through the greatest identity crisis of our history and needing our Love more than ever.

Jesus Christ gave humanity our prime directive: **Love God and yourself and each other**. So that goes for everyone. But for a conscious disciple his directive goes further, with an operational directive. The Great Commission is an anointed path of devoted miracle-work, and he sends us out together.

The Craft of Miracle-Work

When you're a unicorn and your devotion can change everything around you, you're authorized to unleash outrageous power into any situation and witness mind-blowing miracles through your engagement with what-is. You will often be called into situations and relationships where you must intercede for a miracle. Be selfless, and go. You might find yourself in back alleys, corrupt businesses, areas of war, strangely disconnected cities, at the feet of a grieving mother. You might look around and at first glance think, *"this isn't Heaven on Earth, why am I manifesting this?"* before you realize you're on assignment. *Ah. We need a miracle.* Every one of your sovereign masteries, **Remember, Recognize, Release, Expansion, Genius, Alchemy, Adventuring and Devotion** come together to open a new *now*, activating the divine will by issuing a vibrational momentum, a fresh wind that moves new sand particles into place. Like the Maharishi effect, that call radiates into the surrounding fabric, neutralizing counterforce and elevating attractor fields so particles may rearrange.

I come from a long line of miracle-workers, healers and unicorns. On my dad's side, for example, there is Giovanna Sestini, the world famous opera singer, Joseph Stocqueler, the founder of the finest organ-makers in the world, Mozart Wilson, the comedy troubadour, and of course Dorothy Kerin, the Anglican saint who facilitated countless miracle healings in a world wide ministry. But the trick that I treasure the most for miracle-making didn't come from my father's side of super talent. It came from my mother's side, a line of poor, hard-working Irish farmers and frontline, blue collar servers, maids and nurses going back generations. Nothing spectacular or superlative about them at all. The word *potatoes* comes to mind. But there is a magical paradigm that I inherited into my cellular consciousness from these past generations, passed down to me by my mother, who still lives a life of Pure Luck—even with dementia she keeps defying expectations—because of the reality agreement that

I Know it always works out alright in the end.

Take a few moments to hold this Knowing. Imagine the implication. Imagine the peace. After all, you Know this is a universal law that you can apply to every moment, every choice, and every miracle you ask for. There's a lot in that magic spell. It speaks to *process*, it speaks to *completion*, and it speaks of that embodied faith, the first mastery in the Sovereign Way, *ah yes!* **I Already Always AM Becoming**.

You will now find yourself in many situations that require miracles, so it helps to understand the main dynamics involved. It is not different from Alchemy, or any of the other masteries on the Sovereign Way, but rather it is the combined Knowing of all of them together.

I have found the word *miracle* usually brings to mind one of two things:

1. The "*Life is a Miracle*" mindset where your consciousness is attuned to notice all the wonderful marvels of natural beauty and the glorious symphony of unfolding occurrences. *The human body is a miracle, the decaying rat is a miracle, the dew drop on the tip of a blade of grass is a universe of microscopic miracles...* or,

2. *Shazam!* A sudden, unexpected, mind-blowing occurrence that changes the course of everything! Hallelujah! It's a *miracle*!

Look at Diagram 10: The Planes of Miracle-Work.

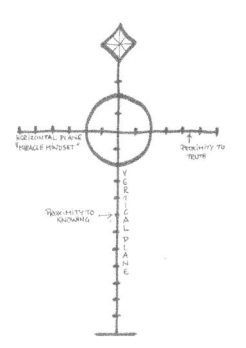

Let's pretend there are these two dimensions to consider for a miracle-maker keen on sharpening their craft:

Horizontal: *Where is my mind currently set, who am I being in relation to what-is? What is the quality standard of my vibrational reality? How am I moving, what am I doing?* Your discipleship here is in maintaining a log of consciousness that is in harmony with miracle-mindedness (500+ on the scale). You are in Love, you expect the universe to continue forming, and you experience the proof of this everywhere as you tend to your devotion and serve the ones in front of you.

Vertical: *The God-drop, formation of quantum potentiality.* All possibilities are ever-present, so your mastery in relation to this axis is your ability to surrender/allow/accept the perfect gift of grace. You intend for complete transcendence of all and any subconscious resistance to the formation of God's will, and you just let it be. *Let there be Light.*

Devotion is always a convergence of horizontal works and vertical faith, therefore Devotion is the mastery that authorizes conscious miracle-making.

The Vertical Plane of Miracle-Work

While miracle-mindedness is indeed the natural culmination of your excellent mastery on the Sovereign Way, a transcendent experience of miraculous phenomena is available no matter who you are or what you believe. There is, after all, nothing but Christ—He is love and He loves Us—every one. This is the part of miracle-work that is completely inexplicable. No mastery can master it. This is the mind-blowing, out of this world miracle that happens just because He loves us: the addiction dissolved and the lost recovered, the relationship saved, the debt forgiven, the wound healed, the body at peace, the child coming home, the self accepted, sovereignty restored, the business flourishing. Just because.

You can be at the throne of your life, or in the heaviest, darkest valleys, right now, in this moment, the Love that you are made of is pouring endlessly into your life and can restore everything it touches. Glorifying the Father through the Son. Turning the substance back into its True form. Redeeming creation as creation becomes.

If we agree that all of creation is quantum entangled in one singularity, then all possibilities exist right where you are. Every last inch of you is in the same place and time as every last inch of everything that ever was and ever will be. **This is the Love of God**. Anything could be actualized in the great sand dunes in the Mind of God, and the only limitation is the amount of control you keep over what may be created here and now. Utter, unexpected, mind-blowing happenings, gifts from God that change the course of everything, forgiving the unforgivable, healing the sick, releasing the debt, raising the dead—these can be allowed by you.

My cousin Dorothy is an example. In 1912 in Tulse Hill, South London, as war was imminent in Europe, Dorothy Kerin, a young girl of 23, lay on her death bed after eight years of being bedridden from chronic tuberculosis. Sixteen relatives and friends, clergy and doctors, were all gathered around her to say their goodbyes. She died.

As the priest approached by my bedside with the chalice, I saw a wonderful golden light, which enveloped the chalice and the priest ... the Divine Presence was a reality, who spoke to me, "Dorothy, will you go back and do something for me: heal the sick, comfort the sorrowful, give faith to the faithless?" ... "Yes," I answered, and I knew it was Jesus Christ ... then the miracle took place. My emaciated body became covered with normal flesh, and I was even plump again. Then I was commanded to get up and walk ... "Mother," I said, throwing back the bedclothes, "I am well again, I must get up and walk."

St Dorothy Kerin

Eight minutes after she died, she got up again. Three days later she began a healing ministry just as Jesus had commanded in her vision. She helped thousands of wounded soldiers, adopted nine children, and was known for facilitating spontaneous remissions—all around the world they attributed their miracle healings to Dorothy's intercession. Witnesses, family members, scientists and mystics alike wrote books about her all trying to "figure out" what could possibly have happened.

Resurrection is the sort of miracle that's available even when you're not in a high-vibe, high-resolution mindset. The rock bottom surrender releases all creative control and opens you up wide for anything God designs. When you're thoroughly broken, at a brick wall, and your only prayer is a groan of desperation, this type of miracle is quick to manifest! Miracles are quantum and all they require is that your creative gears are in neutral and a strong *I Need, What Is It?* The reason it sometimes takes extreme hardship for miracles to show up is merely down to control. How far can you push yourself before you let God work through you?

The risk factor here is that we mentally submit to the idea that God is a deity somewhere out there who either grants or denies wishes. We can get complacent or dejected, and begin to make new creative declarations about what's really happening. I often wondered why God didn't manifest a miracle for my best friend Anna who died many hours after being hit by a drunk driver, even with her mother by her hospital bedside no miracle came. Or why my childhood friend Camilla's desperation wasn't met with the same unconditional love before she committed suicide. I saw death dozens of times growing up, and I have lived with a survivor guilt that created all sorts of hardships to justify me being alive. I have found peace in accepting that the mystery is far holier than the mastery, and that for all our worthiness some realities are not to be.

We also risk associating the size of a miracle with the size of our worth. "*Oh man, I asked for financial deliverance but he only sent me $20.*" God will of course perform outrageous, spectacular miracles, but only to get your attention. Never to take away from the sacred miracle of your everyday Life. When Jesus says *"if you have faith **in me** any miracle can come true"*, it's because he knows you don't have perfect faith in yourself and you don't know enough about divine will, cosmic energetics and quantum mechanics to have perfect faith in God, so being inside this energy field of Mercy delegates the authority of command to the universal intercessor. Miracle is quantum, so it is the *possibility* for miracle that makes it available to you. So if miracles are *possible* for you, then *miracles* are possible for you. I did not consciously manifest our debt forgiveness miracle that finally brought us Home—I could never have visualized what happened. It was an act of God, a deliverance from the heart of pure Love, and we allowed it to be. Yet I can certainly testify that the energy field I held was one of both absolute faith and an awful desperation for what had not yet come. *And suddenly it was done.*

Look at Diagram 9, Expansion By Surrender, and remember that in Christ the awareness that *"We Need"* combined with the command *"What Is It?"* is enough to allow his power and authority move Substance. What happens next is an unfolding that requires your agreement and engagement.

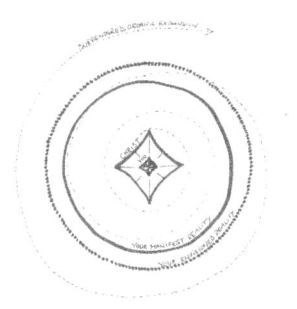

The Horizontal Plane of Miracle-Work

To what extent is your consciousness, energy and form aligned with your true design and with the source of all life-giving energy? Who do you Know yourself to be, and how far out is that from the way God sees you, His Beloved child? An identity separated by *x* degrees from its authentic nature, like the little diamond in **Diagram 5, Walking With Christ,** will distort and disfigure God's will, becoming impotent as a miracle-maker and must resort to forceful control in order to create fleeting impressions of success in creation. So, before facilitating a sorely needed miracle, pay attention to whether you Know yourself as being *One with* the miraculous life. Are you tending to your life's health and mastery, mercifully forgiving all things for being what they are, opening your heart and mind, upholding your sovereign poise, filling the universe with rich droplets of God, and trusting every invitation forward? You know that miracles are easy and wonderful, so you stay in ease and wonder. **I Already Always AM Good Light Becoming, and so is everything else around me.** This is the only mindset that empowers you to take the action that delivers a miracle on behalf of someone else.

It is in your faith that you are healed, and by your works that healing manifests. This is also true for the people and communities you are missioning in. So your end of the bargain, your mental and vibrational mastery as a miracle-worker is to be the space in which the miracle forms for others, to maintain your poise in the devoted convergence between the horizontal and vertical planes of miracle. You do your energy hygiene so the horizontal environment is welcoming for the miracle, and you hold a surrendered gnosis of miracle—I KNOW it. This is how you facilitate that space for others—it spreads by engagement. You don't have to wake everyone up, hustle to empower everyone into their divine sovereignty so they can quickly catch up with you. There is no rush for a time-bender like you, you are allowed to intercede for them *now*, to Know the space in quantum potentiality in which their miracle can incubate and manifest.

Synchronicities are a part of the miracle process and acting on them is paramount. It is the Adventurer's gift of trust that lets you fearlessly leap when opportunities arise, which they do millions of times a day for everyone, regardless of your circumstance. It's a case of spotting the synchronicities, submitting to them as signs of forming miracles, and allowing yourself to act baby step by baby step to bring them into reality. If you want a lucky penny, you need to pick it up. If you want to pick it up, you need to spot it first. Don't go looking for it, you'll never find it. You have to let the glint catch your eye, the reflection of the Son bouncing off its surface. Once you've Recognized it, you will have the strength to do everything it takes to pick up the lucky penny. The power that urged Veronica to fight through the throngs of people so she might just touch the hem of his robe—that power is Love in motion and the True Courage that animates your movements no matter what your method is or what miracle you're asking for.

"Lord, I need help before I lose my House! I need $100,000 in the next two weeks! Where is it?" I pleaded. He didn't send me any money. He sent a letter from a third-party housing initiative who had secured a grant to help families recover from financial disaster. Which is just his sense of humor, because he knew I had an irrational resistance to bureaucracy and an awfully destructive habit of avoiding paperwork, which is what had gotten us into the situation in the first place. The phone number on the paper happened to include the numerological sequence *333-888* for divine abundance, so I Recognized the glint of my Savior's signature in the divine order of elements dancing on the surface! We called the magic number. There followed a thorough review, in which suit-beclad underwriters examined every crevice of our smelly life through the medium of teetering piles of paperwork. There were impossible challenges, like the

instruction to make $6,000 for two months straight, when for two years we had only made an average of $450 a month, living mostly off Duck Eggonomics. But somehow we did it, by just doing the next thing in front of us. We qualified for the program, the debt was forgiven and our house was saved—but not only that, we had also overcome the root cause of the problem, and reconciled with "system", because his method is not just to save, but also to redeem. Recognizing the difference between essence and structure, faith and works, the elixir of life and the philosopher's stone, we understand there is always an action to be done. A miracle is an invasion of reality, the Holy Spirit is movement, *love in action*, and God consciousness isn't just a static **I AM**, it is also **We Become**. Therefore action, method, practice, ritual, *doing the thing*, this is a necessary part of miracle-work, as Veronica, Jesus and I all discovered in our own Sovereign Way.

Then Jesus called the Twelve to him and began to send them out two by two, giving them authority over negative energy. He instructed them to take nothing but a staff for the journey—no bread, no bag, no money in their belts—and to wear sandals, but not a second tunic. And he told them, "When you enter a house, stay there until you leave that area. If anyone will not welcome you or listen to you, shake the dust off your feet when you leave that place, as a testimony against them." So they set out and preached that it was time for people to transform. They cleared energy fields and healed many of the sick, anointing them with oil.

Mark 6:7-12

This week, someone may ask you for help. Listen to them. You won't know the answer, you won't have the resources, you will not be able to resolve the problem. But you will say yes anyway. *Yes, I will help.* The YES you give comes from your heart's sacred intelligence, your tender Knowing that this is God asking for help, and God in you responds. The YES you give comes from your maturity to know that in Love all is provided and flourishes from infinite diverse sources that you do not need to predict. The YES you give comes from the deepest wisdom that everything will work out alright in the end. The YES you give comes from the authority you have as one who represents Jesus Christ, the King of Miracles. He won't let you down.

What to do in the mean time?

What happens next depends entirely on the situation Holy Spirit is designing with you on your Sovereign Way. Whatever the method, prepare:

The Hero's Protocol allows you to quickly and easily take stock of the energetic landscape as it changes so you can confidently act on each step as it materializes—from the tiny things like *change your mascara color* to the ginormous things like *pack up and go*, you can move swiftly to weave the circumstances together as synchronicities occur. Unexpected things are going to start happening and the Hero's Protocol helps you keep surfing the expansion wave.

Don't just say yes, stay yes. You've created a shared space in consciousness, an agreement reality in the quantum potential, and you want to keep that active and alive. Doubt will find all kinds of ways to wiggle in, but you have the faith to stay true to your YES. Make 100% agreement that under the Grace of God, everything is possible. Strengthen your sovereign poise and resolve to remain in the faith. YES. **I do Know God in this situation.**

Help keep the miracle alive for the one you said YES to. Perhaps you'll send them a scripture in the morning, or a photo of something that reminds you of the solution, an affirmation, a quick tally of the resources you're collecting, a case study with a success similar to what you're facilitating, a joke or a story... Whatever your method, to nurture the consciousness of your shared agreement with perfect resolution. *This will work out alright in the end, it is already done and we are just allowing the Substance to reform and manifest the true image of God's will.* Help them stay buoyant in their faith. Remember, all elements are alive and respond to your Love so bring them in to enrich and enliven the energy.

Expect but do not fear counterforce. In quantum the miracle is instantaneous, but in our linear process reality of space and time, every action has an equal and opposite reaction. The perceived force of the opposite reaction depends on the log of consciousness and electromagnetism of the energy field that you're experiencing through. As you begin to see the miracle unfolding, there might also be something that seems like pushback. A spanner in the works, stick in the wheel, sudden sense of failure, or a tension that seems to push the compass needle off course. Call it counterforce or even spiritual warfare if you're the more dramatic type—it's ok, it's harmless, it cannot defeat this masterpiece, this miracle you've called into existence.

You could choose to let it derail you, but you will not, because you are a Sovereign Master in Christ.

> ***Behold, I have given you authority to tread on snakes and scorpions, and over all the power of the enemy. Nothing will harm you. Nevertheless, do not rejoice that the spirits submit to you, but rejoice that your names are written in heaven.***
>
> *Luke 10:19*

Every spiritual tradition has methods to clear these counter frequencies swiftly, precisely and with grace even as they manifest. This hygiene keeps the channels and the space clear for the formation of the miracle. Worry about nothing and pray constantly. Be a fountain of life force. There are of course many facets and dimensions to dealing with evil, but when it comes to the miracle-worker's focus and craft, just clear it. This is not the time to dance creatively with the shadows—this is the time to let the Holy Spirit move.

Ground in the new reality by giving thanks that it is already done. My friend is a humanitarian in Uganda facilitating miracles every day, creating clean water sources for thousands, taking down crime syndicates, saving the lives of hundreds of babies every year. No matter the size of the intervention required, his advice is always the same: "*Give thanks*," he says, "*that it is already done.*" A few years ago I wondered what is gratitude actually made of. How do I know if I'm grateful? I could of course write a thousand pages of things I appreciate, but so could any miserable old miser. I remember being in church listening to the congregation droning in monotony like a sombre snore, "*we sing to the lord with grateful praise, hosanna in the highest forever and ever...*" That didn't seem like grateful praise. If I look at how my children are grateful, it just looks like sunshine! They don't write gratitude lists or formulate elaborate prayers of thanksgiving. They just light up! They beam with joy! Joy is gratitude experienced, joy feeds and nourishes the seedlings unfolding. Give thanks to the Lord that it is done, worship his holy name within and among us, and watch with awe as he moves through the fields of your stewardship. Impossible miracles every day will unfold in your local area and the areas beyond as a whole region rises up under the sovereign faith of just one miracle-worker. That's what happens when you give thanks that it is already done.

***Delight thyself also in the Lord: and he shall give thee the desires of thine heart.
Commit thy way unto the Lord; trust also in him; and he shall bring it to pass.***

Psalm 37:4-5

Jesus sent us out two by two to save the world, to be the holy presence that can gaze upon something that seems unholy and remember it back into the vine of life. Baptizing. He sent us out to transform the darkness, to engage with enemies and challenges—and turn them into allies and quantum leap blessings. He sent us out to heal each other.

The commission always involves connecting hearts and elevating multiple attractor fields at once. There was the terrified single mom with two little boys who was facing eviction and had five days to find an impossible sum. We called for the miracle—a community suddenly rallied round her and she had the money on the time *and* found a better place to live. Only weeks later, a friend discovered an old lady, skin and bones, bleeding on the floor of a filthy apartment. That was the day she had decided to die, for she had drowned under the weight of the lonely deep. We interceded for a miracle, and soon she was swimming in the turquoise waters of the Gulf of Mexico with new friends. A local spa gave her a treatment to nourish her innate beauty, others washed her and cleaned her home, someone else brought her new clothes and food, and now she is planning her future. Emmanuel—**God With Us**—is a community.

Of course, the ability to manifest or allow miracles into our lives doesn't give us a free ticket to a lifetime without adversity. That's not what Devotion is for. Life is rich, and it is in the diversity of our experiences that we really get to Know the dimensionality of our Love Story with God. But miracles do give us the freedom to embrace that richness and to know, when we're standing knee-deep in a terrible mess, that our Loving Father who created all things also knows how to fix this sticky situation. For this reason alone, rest assured: **It'll all be alright in the end.**

Is it true that you can only get to God through Jesus?

Jesus is with his disciples, and he is preparing them for what is about to happen: Betrayal, humiliation, death, resurrection, ascension and the subsequent pentecostal activation of Spirit in the collective consciousness. He is giving the last great teaching:

Let not your hearts be troubled. Believe in God; believe also in me. In my Father's house are many rooms. If it were not so, would I have told you that I go to prepare a place for you? And if I go and prepare a place for you, I will come again and will take you to myself, that where I AM you may be also. And you Know the Way to where I AM going."

Thomas said to him, *"Lord, we don't know where you're going. How can we know the way?"*

Jesus said to him, *"**I AM the Way, and the Truth, and the Life. No one comes to the Father except through me.** If you had known me, you would have known my Father also. **From now on you do Know him and have seen him**."*

Philip said to him, *"Lord, show us the Father, and we'll be satisfied."*

Jesus said to him, *"Have I been with you so long, and you still do not know me, Philip? Whoever has seen me has seen the Father. How can you say, 'Show us the Father'? Do you not believe that **I AM in the Father and the Father is in me**? The words that I say to you I do not speak on my own authority, but the Father who dwells in me does his works. Believe me that I AM in the Father and the Father is in me, or else **believe on account of the works themselves**. Truly, truly, I say to you, whoever believes in me **will also do the works that I do; and greater works than these will he do**, because I am going to the Father. Whatever you ask **in my name**, this I will do, that the Father may be glorified in the Son. If you **ask me anything in my name, I will do it.** If you love me, you will keep my commandments. And I will ask the Father, and he will give you another guide to be with you forever: **the Spirit of Truth**, whom the world cannot receive, because it neither sees Him nor Knows Him. **You*

Know Him, for He dwells with you and will be in you.

Examine Diagram 11: I Am the Way, and the Truth, and the Life.

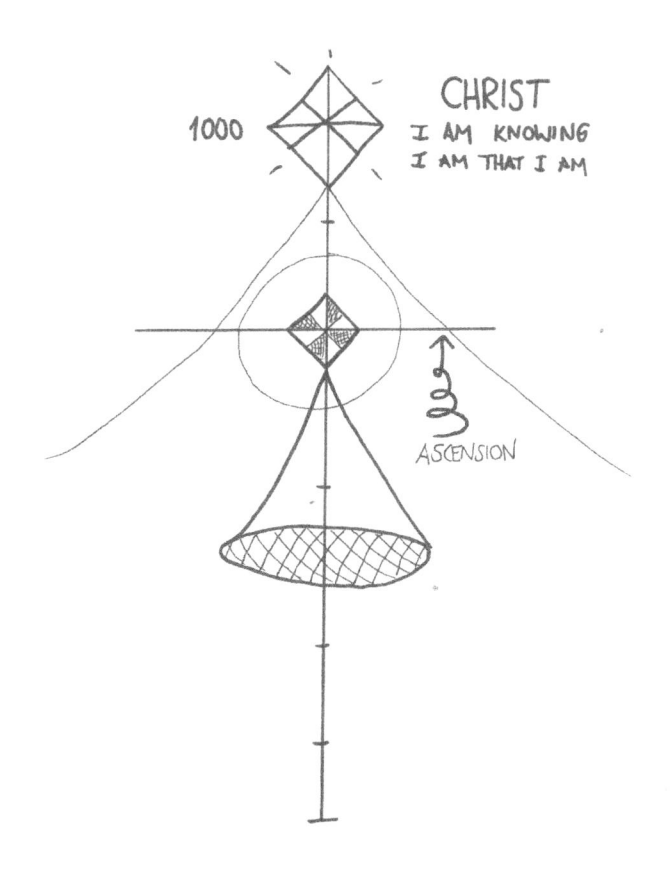

Let's have one final examination of ascension:

We remember that Source, Spirit and Substance are the three elements of the universe, and that embodying the knowing of this is a state of dynamic enlightenment. Increasing the embodiment and integration of this Knowing *is what ascension is*. Your consciousness increases its capacity for knowing Love. Your authority to influence the matrix, or fabric of experience, increases as your consciousness matures and you Know less evil. We have also seen that our electromagnetism increases as we embody more Love so the path of Truth becomes narrower and our expansion is met by an equal and opposite reaction. The collective consciousness of humanity is created of the sum total of our vibrational agreement and realities, and ***everything is enhancing.***

We've discovered that our vibrational reality can be influenced by other energy fields and our attention is easily seduced back into all that stuff that makes us beautifully broken humans. And we also know that despite oppressive counterforce, we still all feel the yearning, the longing into God. We want to continue our ascension. We want more of Him.

Worldwide there is an increasing number of sovereign people, irrespective of religious or political concepts, serving our fellow beings in devotion to planetary welfare. We have established the channels for a guaranteed return of Christ, an implementing of great alignment creating a clear pathway of return as a magnetic power between the will of God and the will of humanity.

Pure Love. 100% divine and 100% human, Emmanuel, **God Is With Us** and every eye shall see Him.

But Jesus doesn't call you "a Christian". He calls you by **Your Name**. In the linear, particularized and manifest Story of Life it is not necessary to convert from one path to another, learn about the life of Yeshua Ben Joseph, perform a baptism ritual to announce your allegiance to a specific religious team, or ever hear the word "*Jesus*"—because his Love is universal.

> *For God so loved the world, that he gave his only begotten Son, that whosoever believeth in him should not perish, but have everlasting life.*
>
> *John 3:16*

The word *believe* was originally written in the Greek *pistevo,* which is more accurately translated as to *have faith in* or *entrusted surrender*—which isn't the same as a mental adherence to an outlined idea. The surrender in Christ is bigger than religious identity and indoctrination. Christ is bigger than any cultural belief system and his Spirit is at work in all places everywhere. Christ is not just the historical man from Nazareth, but—as the apostle John wrote—he is the cosmic Logos that the whole universe is expressed through, and who gives Light and Life to all humanity.

> *In the beginning was the Word, and the Word was* with *God, and the Word* was *God. ... And the Word was made flesh, and dwelt among us, (and we beheld his glory, the glory as of the only begotten of the Father, full of Grace and Truth.*
>
> *John 1:1, 14*

Christ is our Father's first and eternally generated thought. He is the incarnate breath of God, infusing the way and will of God into the world. Christ is the reason our Universe unfolded towards Sovereign beings with a yearning for self-actualization and God's personal intimacy. Christ is the reason our inner agency is urging us to remember meaning and Truth. Christ is enlightening everyone of us, all along on our own individual, Sovereign Ways. Some will recognize in this lifetime that Jesus *is* this Spirit that they have been seeking to follow all along, and some will not. But those who Love are children of God, and those who manifest the fruit of the Spirit are following Jesus whether they know it or not. A little fishing woman sitting peacefully on a boat on a lake in the mountains of Nepal may never have heard the word Jesus, yet she sits in the heart of Christ as she gazes with joyful eyes at the sheer beauty of the shimmering water, even as her arthritis aches when she pulls in the nets to feed her people.

Of course, those who confess "belief" in Jesus, proudly wearing their name badges at the Sunday coffee hour at church but hate their enemies and hold the world in contempt, are not surrendered in the Spirit of Jesus. Their doctrinal ownership is anchored in pride, vanity, greed and scorn, creating the very separation and exclusion that Jesus came to alchemize.

As we have discovered, true Devotion has little to do with linear actions and languages. But in a quantum sense, the wholeness within and as God is only experienced in a field of consciousness that is not influenced by anything other than Love. That's who Jesus is. The path into God goes through the perfectly True human mindset and perfectly devoted vibration, **100% Knowing I AM that I AM and So Are We.**

So you will enter through his gateway as your ascension adjusts your psycho-pneuma-somatic coordinates and you become more True. Everyone will eventually surrender to the Love at the heart of the universe that is Christ. The act of self-sacrificial devotion that actually occurred on the cross 2,000 years ago is bigger than that one event. It the universal truth of who God is. It is what actualizes all of reality, propelling us forward into Home, and one day every mind and heart in creation will Know that this **Relational Love** is the true Sovereign power, to the glory of our eternal Father and loving Source who fills all and is through all.

That being said, there is a big difference between understanding the Christ consciousness portal as a metaphysical collection of data points in the grid of your cosmic energy field—and Knowing him personally as the One who knows you, loves you and has been through it all with you. He is celebrating with you and holding you while you cry, performing the miracles you don't have the strength for, hoisting you out of the mess and cleaning you off, delighting you with his constant sense of humor. Opening and cultivating that personal conversation with him gives you a real, living God companion who relates with you on a human level as your journey within the Kingdom continues and you discover ever more mystery.

He is the Truth, you see—the constant dynamic of wave particle reality, divine mind made utterly real and actually true, of which we are imperfect but beautiful copies.

He is the Life—the endless supply of adamantine particles flying on the breath of renewal, the physical manifestation of God's transcendent power, the bond who holds all Life and being in the universe together by his power and love.

And he is the Way—the path that leads Home, the intercessory field between the vast, eternally creative lifeforce and the little girl who stumbles her Way through the myriad of adventures and Stories here in reality.

In him, all your Love is directed into the Home of your true belonging. The initiation is complete. The endless seeking ends. A dandelion seed—hitherto wafting about on desert winds—lands, settles and grounds in. The seed casing opens and what used to be the extrinsic form of "self" is revealed as nothing more than the temporary House that brought you Home. Your roots stretch and deepen, your stem lengthens, your leaves come alive and start dancing in the free breeze, your crown of glory opens and glints in the sunlight that shines on everything equally and endlessly. The Dragonfly sitting on the yellow crown of the dandelion takes flight, soaring over the pond where a Little Frog rests on a lily pad in the shade of his own sovereignty.

Nothing but your Sovereign reason and magical devotion can authorize your decisions and actions in the world, because you abide inside a framework of Truth and an energy field of immediate and never-ending Grace.

You are like a tree planted by streams of water that yields its fruit in its season, and its leaf does not wither. In all that you do, you prosper.

Psalm 1:3

The storms that once raged in the desert are suspended and still. The unknown expanse of glistening particles beyond beckons to you, and you are there.

You remember.

You Know your Love is the breath of Spirit that carries the sand dunes of becoming.

You have reclaimed your dominion over your Life, and you've surrendered every state of mind to the Sovereign dominance that will forever command the sand dunes.

You recognize Truth and Falsehood, discerning the difference between structure and essence, ascension and entropy, good and evil, and you have forgiven it all, releasing all attachment in a flush of mercy, a true forgiveness through the deepest layers of your cellular consciousness, holy waters flowing through your mind, biofield, body, and the parched lands in which you travel.

And so you've become free for buoyancy and expansion as you rise up in vibration, always balanced and free. The balance radiates and restores equilibrium in your region.

You've empowered the mind, opening to greater realities still and building upon those with the mind of Christ. New languages and innovations become creative solutions all around you.

You've learned the alchemy of changing nothing into something—and something into something better. Even in the most distant desert lands you will make apricots appear.

You've transcended all systems of being, forever *whoomphed* by Grace through every system you must participate in on your future your missions in the desert, and you can never again be enslaved.

You are free now to live and love in a peaceful devotion. You are coordinating with a flourishing family of other miracle-makers on our planet in this time, creating and connecting oases all over the desert.

It's time to go on your Sovereign Way, and *Know God* (**I AM**) and *Be With God* (**we are**). Now look out before you into a universe of Light particles. As you gaze, you see them drawing to one another, becoming the shapes of your life, your friends, your family, the flowers in your garden, your favorite songs, your beautiful body, and the world we are creating together. You see that your Life *is* the Light, and you see that It Is Good.

Amen

I Am Sovereign

Made in the USA
Middletown, DE
14 May 2024